BUDDHIST AND HINDU ARCHITECTURE IN INDIA

BUDDHIST AND HINDU ARCHITECTURE IN INDIA

Suraj Vashishth

CYBER TECH PUBLICATIONS
4264/3, Ansari Road, Daryaganj, New Delhi-110002 (India)
Ph.: 011-23244078, 011-43559448 Fax: 011-23280028
E-Mail: cyberpublicationsdelhi@yahoo.com
Website: www.cybertechpublications.com

BUDDHIST AND HINDU ARCHITECTURE IN INDIA

Suraj Vashishth

First Edition 2010

Asian Offset Printers

Published by :

G.S. Rawat for **Cyber Tech Publications**
4264/3, Ansari Road, Daryaganj, New Delhi-110002 (India)
Ph.: 011-23244078, 011-43559448 Fax: 011-23280028
E-Mail: cyberpublicationsdelhi@yahoo.com
Website: www.cybertechpublications.com

Preface

The Buddhist is one of the important religions of world. Albeit Lord Buddha was not born in Andhra Desa, but the contribution of Andhra Desa to Buddhism is not small. Famous Buddhist Stupas and Viharas as seen at Amaravati, Nagarjunakonda, Bhattiprolu, Guntupalli, Chandavaram are only a few to name in Andhra Desa.

The purpose of the seminar is to bring to light the new discoveries and throw further light on the already existing information on Buddhism from Andhra Desa in particular and India in general. Research is a never ending process and results of research will always be either finding out something new or updating the existing information with the new discoveries. With the passing time, new discoveries on Buddhism are pouring in from different corners. Desa to Buddhism" organized by Birla Archaeological and Cultural Research Institute, Hyderabad a few years ago.

This publication contains papers submitted by both seasoned and budding scholars covering almost all the aspects of Buddhism like art, architecture, philosophy, survey reports, excavation findings etc. As mentioned above, there are papers altogether with new discoveries and papers highlighting new points on the already existing information.

—Author

CONTENTS

1

Introduction of the Buddhism

According to Buddhism, the inequalities which exist are due, to some extent, to environment-which is itself shaped by cause and effect-and to a greater extent to causes, that is kamma, which are in the present, the immediate past, and the remote past. Man himself is responsible for his own happiness and misery. Thus kamma is not fate nor destiny nor blind determinism. Man has a certain amount of free will; he can modify his actions and affect his future. Each act, whether mental or physical, tends to produce its like. If a man does a good deed or thinks a good thought, the effect upon him is to increase the tendencies to goodness in him. In the world around us there are many inequalities in the lot of man-some are rich, others are poor, some live full lives, others die young, etc.

There is only one school of Buddhism and that one school is no other than the Buddhism they have learned from the Buddhist books written or compiled or translated by Western Orientalists--Orientalists who are in many respects prejudiced against the doctrine which they propose to study most impartially. Owing to these unhappy circumstances, the outsiders are either generally ignorant or altogether misinformed of the true character of Buddhism.

For what is understood by the Western people as Buddhism is no more than-one of its main divisions, which only partially expresses the spirit of its founder. I said here "divisions," but it may be more proper to say "stages of development." For Buddhism, like so many other religions, has gone through several stages of development before it has attained the present state of perfection among the Oriental nations. And it will be evident to you that if we catch only a glimpse of an object and try to judge the whole from this transient impression, we place ourselves in a most awkward position, and shall be at a loss how to extricate ourselves from it.

Therefore, let me try in the beginning to take a comprehensive view of the subject we here propose to expound. It seems to be very appropriate and even necessary at the outset to draw a well-defined line of demarcation between what is understood as Hinayana Buddhism and what is known as Mahayana Buddhism. Properly speaking, Hinayana Buddhism is a phase of Mahayana Buddhism. The former is preparatory for the latter. It is not final, but merely a stepping stone which leads the walker to the hall of perfect truth. Hinayanism is therefore more or less pessimistic, ascetic, ethical (to be distinguished from religious), and monastical. It fails to give a complete satisfaction to a man's religious yearnings. It does not fully interpret the spirit of Buddha.

The Buddhist now, prevailing in Ceylon, Burma, and Siam may be considered to be betraying in a certain way a Hinayana tendency. The Buddhism of present Japan, on the other hand, is Mahayanistic. It is more comprehensive, more religious, more humanistic, and more satisfying to the innermost needs of the religious consciousness. It cannot be said to be absolutely free from superstition, error, prejudice, etc., for it is a constantly growing, ever-living faith which knows no ossification or fossilization. Some pious people are apt to consider their religious belief to be absolutely fixed and unchanging since the dawn of human consciousness; but they have forgotten, in my opinion, the fact that the human mind is still keeping on unfolding itself, that it has not yet exhausted all its possibilities, that it is constantly coming to a clearer consciousness as to its own nature, origin, and destiny. But what I firmly believe is that in the Buddhism of Japan today are epitomized all the essential results reached through the unfolding of the religious consciousness during the past twenty or thirty centuries of Oriental culture.

Gotama was born the son of an Indian king on the border of modern Nepal 623 years before Christ. The wise men of the kingdom foresaw that he would become either an emperor or a Buddha, and his father, wanting him to be an emperor, kept him utterly secluded from all unpleasant things, so that he might not become wise by seeing life. But the gods knew that Gotama must become the Buddha, and so they visited earth in various forms to let him see them. On three successive days, while on his way to the royal park, Gotama saw an old man, a sick man, and a corpse, and thus he learned that men-all men-must suffer and die. On the fourth day he saw a monk; from this he understood that to learn the way of overcoming man's universal sorrow lie must give up worldly pleasures. Accordingly, in his twenty-ninth year, he renounced his kingdom and became an ascetic.

Gotama wandered about the countryside, a seeker after truth and peace. He approached many a distinguished teacher of his day, but none could give him what he sought. He strenuously practiced all the severe austerities of monkish life, hoping to attain Nirvana. Eventually his delicate body was reduced almost to a skeleton. But the more he tormented his body the further away he was from his goal. Realizing the futility of self-mortification, he finally decided to follow a different course, avoiding the extremes of pain and indulgence.

The new path which he discovered was the Middle Way, the Eightfold Path, which subsequently became part of his teaching. By following this path his wisdom grew into its fullest power, and he became the Buddha.

In a word, what has been known in the West as the teaching of Buddha does not represent it in its true, unadulterated colour, for it is Hinayanistic in tendency; that is, it is exclusive and not comprehensive, narrow and limited, and not all absorbing and assimilating. What I propose to expound in this lecture tonight is the Mahayana Buddhism, so called by Buddhist scholars of the East.

As a man Prince Gotama, by his own will, love, and wisdom, attained Buddhahood-the highest possible state of perfection-

and he taught his followers to believe that they might do the same. Any man, within himself, possesses the power to make himself good, wise, and happy.

All the teachings of the Buddha can be summed up in one word: Dhamma. It means truth, that which really is. It also means law, the law which exists in a man's own heart and mind. It is the principle of righteousness. Therefore the Buddha appeals to man to be noble, pure, and charitable not in order to please any Supreme Deity, but in order to be true to the highest in himself.

Dhamma, this law of righteousness, exists not only in a man's heart and mind, it exists in the universe also. All the universe is an embodiment and revelation of Dhamma. When the moon rises and sets, the rains come, the crops grow, the seasons change, it, is because of Dhamma, for Dhamma is the law of the universe which makes matter act in the ways revealed by our studies of natural science.

If a man will live by Dhamma, he will escape misery and come to Nirvana, the final release from all suffering. It is not by any kind of prayer, nor by any ceremonies, nor by any appeal to a God, that a man will discover the Dhamma which will lead him to his goal. He will discover it in only one way-by developing his own character. This development comes only through control of the mind and purification of the emotions. Until a man stills the storm in his heart, until he extends his loving-kindness to all beings, he will not be able to take even the first step toward his goal.

Thus Buddhism is not a religion at all, in the sense in which the word is commonly understood. It is not a system of faith or worship. In Buddhism, there is no such thing as belief in a body of dogma which must be taken on faith, such as belief in a Supreme Being, a creator of the universe, the reality of an immortal soul, a personal savior, or archangels who are supposed to carry out the will of the Supreme Deity. Buddhism begins as a search for truth. The Buddha taught that we should believe only that which is true in the light of our own experience, that which conforms to reason and is conducive to the highest good and welfare of all beings. Men must rely on themselves. Even though he may "take refuge in Buddha," the expression used when a man pledges himself to live a righteous life, he must not fall victim to a blind faith that the Buddha can save him. The Buddha can point out the path, but he cannot walk it for us.

The truth which the Buddhist sees when he looks around him is the truth of cause and effect. Every action, no matter how insignificant, produces an effect; every effect in its turn becomes a, cause and produces still further effects. It is meaningless to inquire for a First Cause. A First Cause is inconceivable; rather, cause and effect are cyclical, and this universe when it dies and falls apart will give rise to another universe, just as this one was formed from the dispersed matter of a previous universe. The origin of the universe, like that of every individual person or thing in it, is dependent on the chain of previous causes, which goes on and on in an endless cycle of birth, death, and rebirth. This is the principle of dependent origination.

What of the soul? The Buddha taught that there is no soul or self, and he used the metaphor of the cart. If you take away the wheels and axles, the floorboards and sides, the shafts, and all the other parts of the cart, what remains? Nothing but the conception of a cart, which will be the same when a new cart is built. So the uninterrupted process of psychophysical phenomena moves from life to life. Each life passes instantaneously in death to a new life, and the new life is the effect of the causes in the old life. A candle flame at this instant is different from the flame that burned an instant ago, yet the flame is continuous.

Thus in the chain of interdependent causation all phenomenal existence is constantly changing. The elements combine and recombine with no underlying substance, or soul, to give them permanence. This is the Wheel of Life. The main cause of the restlessness, the suffering, which is the lot of beings turning on the Wheel of Life, is craving or selfish desire for existence, and it is this desire which sets the life force in motion. Desire is manifested in action. This action is in reality volition or will power, which is responsible for the creation of being. It is called karma in Sanskrit, but in the Pali language, which the Buddha spoke and in which all the Buddhist scriptures were written, it is softened to kamma.

In this universe in which nothing is permanent all change is governed by kamma or the kammic force. Kamma means action. In its general sense, kamma means all good and bad actions. Kamma refers to all kinds of intentional actions whether mental, verbal, or physical, that is, all thoughts, words, and deeds. In its ultimate sense kamma means all moral and immoral volition.

Kamma, though it activates the chain of cause and effect, is not determinism, nor is it an excuse for fatalism. The past influences the present, but does not dominate it. The past is the background against which life goes on from moment to moment; the past and the present influence the future. Only the present moment exists, and the responsibility for using the present moment for good or ill lies with each individual.

Every action produces an effect; it is cause first and effect afterward. We therefore speak of kamma as "the law of cause and effect." If you throw a stone into a pond, the ripples spread out to the shore, but that is not all, for the ripples return inward until they touch the stone again. The effects of our actions come back to us, and as long as our actions are done with evil intent, the waves of effect will come back to us as evil. But if we are kind and keep ourselves peaceful, the returning waves of trouble will grow weaker until they die down and our good kamma will come back to us in blessing.

Let me point out in this connection what is most characteristic of Buddhism as distinguished from any other religion. I refer to a predominant tendency of Buddhism toward intellectuality, and it seems to me that the reason why Buddhism is always ready to stand before the tribunal of science and let her pass a judgment upon its merits or demerits is due to this intellectual tenor. It goes without saying that the intellect does not constitute the most essential element of religion, but we must not forget that a religious system too much given up to sentimentalism (understanding it in its purely psychological sense) is generally prone to accede to unwarranted mysticism, ignoring altogether the legitimate claim of the intellect. Buddhism is fortunately saved from this grievous blunder, and always endeavours not to give a free rein to the wantonness of imagination and the irrationality of affection. Love without enlightenment excludes, discriminates, and contradicts itself. Love is not love unless it is purified in the mill of spiritual insight and intellectual discrimination.

What are, then, the fundamental teachings of Buddhism? I deem it best to consider it from two standpoints, ethical and philosophical, or practical and speculative, or affective and intellectual. The philosophical or speculative is preparative for the ethical or practical, for religion is not a system of metaphysics which plays with verbalism and delights in sophistry, but its aim is pre-eminently practical and spiritual. It must bear fruit in this our everyday life.

To begin with the metaphysical side of Buddhism:

(1) We Buddhists believe that as far as phenomenality goes, things that exist are all separate and discrete, they are subject to the law of individuation and therefore to that of limitation also. All particular things exist in time and space and move according to the law of cause and effect, not only physically but morally. Buddhism does not, though sometimes understood by Western people to do so, advocate the doctrine of emptiness or annihilation. It most assuredly recognizes the multitudinousness and reality of phenomena. This world as it is, is real, not void. This life as we live it, is true, and not a dream.

(2) We Buddhists believe that all these particular things surrounding us come from one ultimate source which is all-powerful, all-knowing, and all-loving. The world is the expression or manifestation of this reason or

spirit or life, whatever you may designate it. However diverse, therefore, things are, they all partake of the nature of the ultimate being. Not only sentient beings, but non-sentient beings, reflect the glory of the Original Reason. Not only man but even the lower animals and inorganic substances manifest the divinity of their source. To use the Christian term, God, it 1 is visible and audible not only in one of its highest manifestations, whom Christians call Jesus Christ, but also in the meanest and most insignificant piece of stone lying in a deserted field. God's splendour is seen not only in the Biblical lilies, but also in the mud and mire from which they grow. The melody of divine reason is heard not only in the singing of a bird or in the composition of an inspired musician, but also in the "slums of life" as Emerson phrases it.

(3) This recognition of the oneness of things naturally leads to our third belief, that the one is the many and the many is the one. God does not dwell in the heavens. It does not direct its affairs in a closed office situated somewhere outside this world. It did not create heaven and earth out of nothingness. According to Buddhism, it is a serious error to seek God outside this life, outside this universe. It is living right among ourselves and directing the course of things according to its innate destiny. Though Buddhists refuse to have God walk out of us, they do not identify it with the totality of existence, they are not willing to cast their lot with pantheists so called. God is immanent, surely enough, but it is greater than the totality of things. For the world may pass away, the universe may be shaken out of its foundation, but God will remain and will create a new system out of the former ruins. The ashes of existence will never be scattered to the winds, but they will gather themselves in the ever designing hand of God and build themselves up to a new order of things, in which it is ever shining with its serene radiance.

To sum up the first part of this discourse, what may be called the metaphysical phase of Buddhism is to recognize (1) the reality of the phenomenal world, (2) the existence of one ultimate reason, and (3) the immanence of this reason in the universe.

Now to come to the practical side of Buddhism: The aim of Buddhism, to state it briefly, is to dispel the clouds of ignorance and to make shine the sun of enlightenment. We are selfish because we are ignorant as to the nature of self. We are addicted to the gratification of the passions, because we are ignorant as to the destiny of humanity. We are quarrelsome and want to make ourselves powerful and predominant at the expense of our fellow-beings, because we are ignorant of the ultimate reason of the universe.

Buddhists do not recognize any original sin, but acknowledge the existence of ignorance, and insist on its total removal as the surest means of salvation. Let us, therefore, all be enlightened as to the statement made before. Let us know that we are all one in the reason of the universe, that the phenomenal world is real only to the extent it manifests reason, that egoism has no absolute sway in this life, for it destroys itself when it tries to preserve itself through its arrogant assertion, and that perfect peace is only attained when I recognize myself in you and you in me. Let us all be enlightened as to these things, and our ignorance and egoism are forever departed; the wall that divides is destroyed, and there is nothing which prevents us from loving Our enemies; and the source of divine love is open in our hearts, the eternal current of sympathy has now found its unobstructed path. This is the reason why Buddhism is called the religion of enlightenment.

Now that we stand on this eminence of religious sanctity, we know what Buddhist practical faith is. It is threefold: W to cease from wrong-doing, (2) to promote goodness, and (3) to enlighten the ignorant. Buddhist ethics is the simplest thing to Practise in the world. It has nothing mysterious, nothing superstitious, nothing idolatrous, nothing supernatural. Stop doing anything wrong, which is against the reason of things;

do whatever is good, which advances the course of reason in this life; and finally help those who are still behind and weary of life to realize enlightenment: and here is Buddhism in a nutshell. It has nothing to do with prayer and worship and singing and what not. Our simple everyday life of love and sympathy is all that is needed to be a good Buddhist. I was once asked whether there was such a thing as religious life particularly. To which my answer was simple enough: "Attend to Your daily business, do all you can for the promotion of goodness in this world, and out of fullness of heart help your fellow-beings to gain the path of enlightenment. Outside of this there cannot be anything to be specially called a religious life."

In the latter part of the T'ang Dynasty in China, there was a famous poet-statesman who is known in Japanese as Hak-Rak-Ten. He learned that there resided in his district a Buddhist monk greatly noted for his saintly life and scholarly learning. The governor went to see him, intending to discuss some deeply religious topics. As soon as he was ushered into the pretence of the monk, he inquired what was thought by the saint to be the most fundamental teaching of Buddhism. The monk immediately replied that it is the teaching of all enlightened ones to cease doing anything evil, to promote goodness, and to purify one's own heart.

Hak-Rak-Ten was nonplused to receive such a commonplace instruction from the mouth of such a scholarly personage professing the faith of Buddha; for he secretly expected to have something highly metaphysical and profoundly speculative, which would naturally lead them to further philosophizing and contentless abstraction. The poet-statesman therefore retorted: "This is what every child of three summers is familiar with. I desire on the other hand what is most abstruse, most essential, most vital in Buddhism." The monk, however, coldly replied: "Every child of three summers may know what I said now, but even a silvery-haired man of eighty winters finds it difficult to put the Buddhist instruction into the practice of everyday life."

And it is said that thereupon the Governor reverentially bowed and went home wiser.

What is philosophical in Buddhism is no more than a preliminary step toward what is practical in it. Every religion, if it deserves the name, must be essentially practical and conducive to the promotion of the general welfare and to the realization of Reason. Though intellectualism is one of the most characteristic features of Buddhism, making it so distinct from any other religious system, it never forgets the fact that our religious consciousness ever demands something concrete, that which is visible to our senses, that which is observable in our everyday life. Religion does not necessarily consist in talking on such subjects as the continuation after death of individual personality, original sin committed by some mythical personages, the last judgment to be given by an unknown quantity, a special historical revelation which takes place in a congested brain, and what not. At least, practical Buddhism does not trouble itself with solving these problems through speculation or imagination or sophistry. Let those theologians who delight in abstraction and supernaturalism discuss them to their hearts' content, for that is their profession. We, plain ordinary Buddhists, will keep on removing selfishness, seeking the light that is everywhere, practising lovingkindness that does not contradict or discriminate. Says an ancient sage, "The Way is near, and thou seekest it afar." Why, then, shall we ever attempt to walk away from the path which extends right in front of us, so wide and well paved?

The teaching founded by the Buddha is known, in English, as Buddhism. It may be asked, who is the Buddha? A Buddha is one who has attained Bodhi; and by Bodhi is meant wisdom, an ideal state of intellectual and ethical perfection which can be achieved by man through purely human means. The term Buddha literally means enlightened one, a knower. Buddhists believe that a Buddha is born in each aeon of time, and our Buddha-the sage Gotama who attained enlightenment under the bo tree at Buddh Gaya in India-was the seventh in the succession.

The understanding of kamma gives us power. The more we make the doctrine of kamma a part of our lives, the more power we gain, not only to direct our future, but also to help our fellow beings more effectively. The practice of good kamma, when fully developed, will enable us to overcome evil and even to overcome kamma itself, thus bringing us to our goal, Nirvana.

The principle of dependent origination and the law of kamma provide the background for understanding the nature of rebirth. According to Buddhism, death is "the temporary end of a temporary phenomenon." It is not the complete annihilation of the being, for although the organic life has ceased, the kammic force which hitherto actuated it is not destroyed. Our physical forms are only the outward manifestations of the invisible kammic force. When the present form perishes, another form takes its place according to a good or bad volitional impulse-the kamma that was the most powerful-at the moment before death.

At death the kammic force remains entirely undisturbed by the disintegration of the physical body, and the passing away of the present consciousness creates the conditions for the coming into being of a fresh body in another birth. The stream of consciousness flows on like a river which is built up by its tributaries and dispenses its water to the countryside through which it passes. The continuity of flux at death is unbroken in point of time; there is no breach in the stream of consciousness, and therefore there is no room whatever for an intermediate stage between this life and the next. Rebirth takes place immediately.

The present being, present existence, is conditioned by the way one faced circumstances in the last and in all past existences. One's present character and circumstances are the result of all that one has been up to the present, but what one will be in the future depends on what one does now in the present. The true Buddhist regards death as a momentary incident between one life and its successor and views its approach with calmness. His only concern is that his future should be such that the condition of that life may provide him with better opportunities for perfecting himself.

Buddhism teaches that with the practice of meditation and concentration the memory can be trained. By meditation and mind culture one can acquire the power to see one's rebirth as a link, or a succession of links, in a chain of births; one can also acquire the power of looking back into one's previous lives. Not only this, but Buddhism also teaches that with the attainment of Nirvana in this life itself, through enlightenment and true wisdom, one can reach the end of this chain of rebirths.

Nirvana, the state to which all Buddhists aspire, is the cessation of desire and hence the end of suffering. Nirvana in Sanskrit means "the blowing out." It is understood as the extinguishment of the flame of personal desire, the quenching of the fire of life. Among Westerners Nirvana is often thought of as a negative state, a kind of "nothingness." But in the Buddhist scriptures it is always described in positive terms; the highest refuge, safety, emancipation, peace, and the like. Nirvana is freedom, but not freedom from circumstance; it is freedom from the bonds with which we have bound ourselves to circumstance. That man is free who is strong enough to say, "Whatever comes I accept as best."

Nirvana is the dying of the kammic force. The Buddhist ascends to Nirvana through many stages of the Middle Way, the path of wisdom, morality, and control. There is not space enough here even to mention these phases or the various aspects of the regimen recommended by the Buddha in his vast scriptures; but it may be taken for granted that the life of the conscientious Buddhist is full and rich. Through the cycle of rebirths he ascends, he perfects himself, he conquers his cravings through wisdom and love. Slowly the kammic force ebbs away, the flame dies down.

At the root of man's trouble is his primal state of ignorance. From ignorance comes desire, which sets the kammic force in motion. Hence the way to Nirvana lies through knowledge, and we come again full circle to Dhamma, the Buddha's teachings. For in Dhamma, as truth, lies release from ignorance and desire and perpetual change, and the Buddha has shown us the way to truth.

What, then, is the meaning of Buddhism? Ultimately Buddhism, although not strictly speaking a religion, is a systematic exercise in spirituality, certainly one of the greatest ever conceived. It offers the individual a means by which he may fulfill himself through understanding, reaching eventually the plane of the supraperson on which both the self and self-knowledge are no longer useful. Meister Eckhart, the great Christian mystic, said: "The kingdom of God is for none but the thoroughly dead." The Buddhist would agree, though he would probably prefer a less grim way of saying it. Nirvana in life, the peace which "passeth all understanding," is the conquest of life, the discovery of the permanent in its flux of psychophysical accidents and circumstances. The Buddhist believes that through meditation and good hard thought he can follow the Buddha through the successive stages of enlightenment and achieve at last the perfect wisdom which surmounts all need.

But by no means all Buddhists are monks or adepts. What does Buddhism mean for the ordinary person going about his work in the world? All through the Buddha's teaching, repeated stress is laid on self-reliance and resolution. Buddhism makes man stand on his own feet, it arouses his self-confidence and energy. The Buddha again and again reminded his followers that there is no one, either in heaven or on earth, who can help them or free them from the results of their past evil deeds. The Buddhist knows that the powers of his own mind and spirit are enough to guide him in the present and shape his future and bring him eventually to the truth. He knows that he possesses a strength which is ultimately unsurpassable.

Moreover, Buddhism points unequivocally to the moral aspect of everyday life. Though Nirvana is amoral, in the sense that final peace transcends the conflict of good and evil, the path to wisdom is definitely a moral path. This follows logically from the doctrine of kamma. Every action must produce an effect, and one's own actions produce an effect in one's own life. Thus the kammic force which carries us inevitably onward can only be a force for good, that is, for our ultimate wisdom, if each action is a good action.

This doctrine finds its highest expression in metta, the Buddhist goal of universal and all-embracing love. Metta means much more than brotherly feeling or kindheartedness, though these are part of it. It is active benevolence, a love which is expressed and fulfilled in active ministry for the uplifting of fellow beings. Metta goes hand in hand with helpfulness and a willingness to forego self-interest in order to promote the welfare and happiness of mankind.

It is metta which in Buddhism is the basis for social progress. Metta is, finally, the broadest and intensest conceivable degree of sympathy, expressed in the throes of suffering and change. The true Buddhist does his best to exercise metta toward every living being and identifies himself with all, making no distinctions whatsoever with regard to caste, color, class, or sex.

In addition, of course, the teachings of the Buddha are a prime cultural force in Oriental life, just as the Bible is the ultimate source of much Western art and thought. The Buddhist scriptures are larger and more detailed than the Christian Bible, however, and in translation would fill a dozen volumes. In Pali, the language of the scriptures, the Buddha's teachings are called Tripitaka, which means "The Three Baskets."

Vinaya Pitaka, "The Basket of Discipline," consists of five books which expound the rules of monastic life. Sutta Pitaka, "The Basket of Discourses," is a collection of discussions, stories, poems, and proverbs, written in simple language, imparting all the precepts of practical Buddhism. The third basket, Abhidhamma Pitaka, or "Basket of Ultimate Things," deals with epistemological, metaphysical, and psychological matters and is of interest mainly to trained philosophers.

THE NAMES OF THE BUDDHA

Accounts of the life of the Buddha, meaning "the enlightened one," contain historical and legendary materials, which are difficult to distinguish clearly. He was named at birth Siddhartha, meaning "he who will succeed," belonged to the Gautama clan, and was called Shakyamuni, "sage of the Shakya people."

BIRTH AND YOUTH OF THE SIDDHARTHA (563-547)

According to traditional accounts, Siddhartha was born in 563BC. His father was Shuddhodana, a leader of the Shakya peoples, who ruled from Kapilavastu, near the border between India and Nepal. At his conception, his mother, Maya, dreamt that a great white king elephant touched her with a lotus blossom. As the time of his birth neared, she set out for her native village of Devadaha, but when she reached a grove at Lumbini, she gave birth, Siddhartha appearing from her side. She died only seven days after his birth. The Mauryan Emperor Ashoka (r. 273-36] erected a pillar to mark the place, which was rediscovered in 1898.

The circumstances of his conception and manner of his birth made it evident that he was no ordinary child. This was confirmed when a sage named Asita came down from the Himalayas to see the child, and, after inspecting his features, declared that he would either be a world conqueror or become the enlightened one (Buddha).

To those who are lost in the desert tracks of Samsara, he shall proclaim a way which shall lead to liberations;...creatures scorched by the fire go greed fueled by sense objects, he will refresh with the rain of the Law (dharma).

Lamenting that he would not live to hear his teachings, he directed his disciple Nalaka to follow the new teacher.

The King, naturally pleased that his son might become a world-conqueror and equally alarmed at the prospect he might become a religious teacher, resolved that his son would know only the pleasures of the princely life and never encounter anything which might tempt him toward religion.

Prince Siddhartha accordingly grew up amid the luxury and pleasures of the palace, became adept at archery, and excelled in other princely accomplishments. A princely education included the Vedas, together with phonetics, ritual, grammar, etymology, metrics, and astronomy, which made it possible to better understand their meaning. Yet even though kept away from the sorrows of the world, the boy evinced an unusual sensitivity that presaged his future.

Once when his father was performing a ritual plowing ceremony, the boy, effortlessly and without any training, became absorbed in a deep meditative concentration, which would later be called the First Meditation (dhyana). On another occasion, he observed birds pulling worms from the earth, and reflected on how every living thing harms other things as a consequence merely of living.

MARRIAGE, AWAKENING, AND THE GREAT RENUNCIATION (547-533)

Despite these awakenings of his meditative nature, at 16 he married Yasodhara and continues to live a life of ease and luxury, having three palaces-one for the hot season, one for the cold, and one for the rainy season. Later he is said to have recalled: I was delicate, excessively delicate. In my father's house were three lotus ponds made expressly for me, one with blue lotuses, one with red and another with white. I used no sandalwood except that of Kashi and my turban, tunic, dress, and cloak were all from Kashi. A white umbrella was held over me night and day so that I would be untouched by heat or cold, dust, leaves or dew.

But when he ventured out of the palace, he encountered human misery. Four episodes are counted as his awakening. When he saw an old man, Prince Siddhartha reflected that though old age is unwelcomed it is inevitable. Later he saw a cripple and reflected that though people try to avoid contact with sick people, illness is unavoidable. And when he saw a corpse, he realized that though people hate death it is the inevitable end of all. Finally when he saw an ascetic, he reflected that it was possible to renounce worldly things and be free of the entanglements of things and he came to realize that the pleasures of the palace were a hindrance to his development.

A life in a household is cramped and confined, a den of dust, but the life of the homeless wanderer is as the open air of heaven! About this time his son was born and named Rahula because his father said "an impediment (rahu) has been born; a fetter has been created." Against his parents' wishes, and in the middle of the night on his birthday at 29, he awoke to see the dancing girls from the party sleeping:

Some with their bodies wet with trickling phlegm and spittle; some grinding their teeth, and muttering and talking in their sleep; some with their mouth agape; some with their clothing dishelved displaying their nakedness.

The scene awakened in the Prince an aversion to sensual pleasures, showing him such pleasures concealed loathsomeness of material things. So Siddhartha secretly left the palace on his favourite horse with his charioteer to seek the good (kusala). When he reached the Anoma river, he shaved his head, put on the robes of an ascetic, giving his charioteer his princely clothes to return to the palace. He then continued southward toward Rajagriha, the capital of Magadha.

The Intellectual Milieu

In India there was an ancient tradition of meditation and asceticism, dating to the Indus Valley civilization about 2500BC. A great body of literature, called the Upanishads, had developed which summarized the teachings of ascetics. There were two patterns of asceticism: that of the brahmans (priests) and that of the wandering ascetics, called sramanas, "those who strive." The Brahmans followed the Four Stages of life: studying under a teacher when young; returning home to marry and raise a family; turning over daily affairs to a son and taking up meditative practices; and, finally, leaving home to live in the forest, there to die.

The Sramanas take up the life of wandering as youths, discipline themselves through austerities, and practice a "discipline" or yoga. The goal of all their efforts was Liberation, which was defined differently by different thinkers. But a common thread was disdain for the gods and practices of the Vedas and a ferment of ideas, ranging from atheism to personal devotion to a personal god (bhakti). We know from Buddhist and Jain texts that more than twenty different sects, today mostly known only by name, flourished at that time.

The Six Teachers

- At the time Siddhartha began his life as a wandering ascetic, there were in northern India six famous ascetics who led groups of disciplines: Purana Kassapa who argued that the person is unaffected by the goodness or badness of his actions. Morality did not exist; murder and theft were acceptable as those acts did not harm those who performed them.
- Makkhali Gosala who contended that a person's success or failure was due to fate and that an individual's actions could not influence the course of his life. His followers were knows as the Ajivakas, which probably refers to their practice of extreme austerities, love of solitude, and disdain for any kind of comfort. So difficult a practice never had many followers, yet the school continued to exist until the 14th century AD.
- Ajita Keshakambala, who was materialist, held that everything was composed of four elements (earth, water, fire, and wind), and that moral acts were meaningless. This position was later maintained by the Lokayata or Charvaka tradition.
- Pakudha Kacchayana who held that there were seven elements, the four recognized by Ajita plus pain, pleasure, and life. The elements are unchanging and are the only reality. Thus if a person is stabbed with a knife, the knife does nothing but pass through the spaces between the elements, thus is of no consequence, even if the person dies. This position is later represented in the Vaisesika school.
- Sanjaya Bellatthiputta who refused to answer any question directly, being a skeptic because of doubts about the nature of knowledge and investigations of logic, and who, through his students, exercised a significant influence on Buddhism.

- Mahavira, one of the founding figures of Jainism. Mahavira belonged to the nirgrantha ascetics, those who freed themselves from all fetters through the practice of austerities until they conquered (jain) ignorance. Jainism belongs with Buddhism as one of the great heterodox schools of Indian thought.

The Wandering Ascetic (533-528)

Siddharta as Student of Meditation: When Siddhartha reached Magadha, an important kingdom in Central India, he studied first under Alara Kalama from whom he learned the technique of meditation that enabled the adept to attain a state of nothingness. But Siddhartha found this teaching lacking, so he left. On his way to another teacher, King Bimbisara offered to make him a minister, but Siddhartha declined. He then sent a retainer to persuade Siddhartha to abandon his meditation, but to no avail. Siddhartha then sought out Uddaka Ramaputta who taught the technique of meditation of neither perception nor non-perception, a meditation which removed the mind from all contact with the world of sensation. Though more profound than the meditation of nothingness, when the meditation was over, the problems of the world returned, thus quieting the mind was an inadequate technique for attaining true wisdom.

Siddharta as a Forest Ascetic

In the company of Kondanna, Bhaddiya, Vappa, Mahanama, and Assaji, Siddharta entered the forests to practice the greatest austerities of self-mortification in order to gain wisdom and freedom. He would clench his teeth and press his tongue against his palate continually, learning to ignore the pain. He once tried to stop all breathing, closing his nose and mouth, only to have his ears begin to breath which he stopped for a while only with the greatest effort.

He experienced pain as strong as if a "man were to bore one's skull with a sharp drill" or to "bind one's head tightly with a hard leather thong" or to "rip up the belly with a sharp butcher's knife" or to "seize a man by his arms and scorch and thoroughly burn him in a pit of charcoal." Finally he began a great fast, gradually reducing the amount of food he ate until he no longer required food. He became progressively more emaciated, his hair fell out, his skin hung loose in folds, the skin of his stomach clinging to his backbone, and his body was in constant pain.

To such a pitch of asceticism have I gone that naked was I, flouting life's decencies, licking my hands after meals....I have visited only one house a day ... or one every seven days, or only once a fortnight ... and there taken only one morsel of food. ...I have plucked out the hair of my head and the hair of my beard, ... have couched on thorns, have gone down to the water punctually thrice before night fall to wash away the evil within. In such a fashion have I lived to torment and torture my body, to such a length in asceticism have I gone.

In this state he discovered a fundamental truth about austerity and self-mortification: the pain such practices create produces in turn delusions, fears, and doubts magnified by deprivation and by clinging to life. It will not, cannot, lead to wisdom. He was closer to wisdom as a small child when he fell into the First Meditation. For six years he had practiced austerities and self-mortifications so extreme that they amazed his companions, but now he resolved to abandon them, to their disappointment and disgust at his apparent weakness. "The ascetic Gautama has fallen into luxurious ways and abandoned his spiritual efforts," they decided and abandoned him. Later legend says that he performed these austerities near Mount Dandaka in Gandhara.

The Attainment of Enlightenment (April/May 528)

Having rejected the luxury of the princely life with his "great renunciation" and now having abandoned its opposite, the way of austerity and self-mortification, Siddhartha returned to his first intuitions, meditation without austerity, but disciplined with the yoga he has learned from Alara Kalama and Uddaka Ramaputta. He took enough food to gain some strength, accepting rice and milk from Sujata, and sat under a ficus tree, later called the bodhi or enlightenment tree at

Bodhgaya. What was needed was to move beyond all that could be experienced, until it came to an end, which did not reveal ultimate reality as was usually assumed, but was a state of non-cognition.

According to the Therevada tradition the enlightenment occurred on the night of the full moon, in the month of Visakha, corresponding to April/May of the Western calendar. Later legend explains that as Siddhartha sat under the tree, the demon Mara came terrorizing him with the fear of death, in the form of a huge army with soldiers holding every imaginable weapon, windstorms, whirlwinds, showers of hot rocks, sandstorms, but none could come close to the meditating Prince. Mara then tried darkness, but the light of his meditation defeated it. Clubs, spears, axes, arrows, and other weapons hurled at him turned into fragrant flowers that fell harmlessly at his feet. No one can escape the desire for life, and the food and sleep that sustain it, and the fear of death is the most difficult thing to over come. But Siddhartha overcame all the challenges of Mara, at the most desperate moment touching the earth for security. The earth responded with a deafening roar that scattered the frightened hosts of Mara. When Mara was vanquished, Siddhartha attained enlightenment and became the Buddha.

The legendary account of Mara's temptation is to seen as a parable of Siddhartha's struggles to understand what binds us to existence. Having returned to a disciplined meditation, Pali tradition says that in the first part of the crucial night he acquired a supernatural ability to remember all his previous lives and he began to reflect on his past and how his lives had been directed by certain factors. Then in the middle of the night, he saw how similar factors directed the lives of others, understanding how one's own actions contribute to the course of life and how things beyond one's total control also influence it. He saw that greed and hatred produced evil consequences which destroyed both the person who had them and what they exercised that greed and hatred on, that one's own dispositions and lusts urged on one courses of action which needed to be curbed, and that confusion, our inability to understand what our actions entail and how our lives are shaped, bedevils us longest. We must eliminate them, one by one, and as we do so our freedom and wisdom increase. At the end of the night, he discovered the Four Noble Truths, became the Buddha, and called himself the Tathagata, "he who has arrived," meaning he had attained the truth.

What, then, was the content of his insight and how did it occur? Was it only the Four Noble Truths, or these and the Chain of Dependent Origination, or another of his first teachings? Was it a matter of a disciplined control over our desires and dispositions or knowledge that overcame the ignorance which kept us from wisdom? Was it attained by series of progressively more profound insights into the nature of existence or of deeper meditative states? Was it a sudden leap of understanding that transfigures the mind and its grasp of the world? Did it consist in a discipline of meditation or action which could be mastered, or in a body of wisdom which could be taught, or in intuition which were beyond language and thought and could be attained but not directly taught? None of these questions can, or could be answered, and important differences among Buddhist philosophers hinge on the different answers to these questions. The meaning of the words which Siddhartha, now the Buddha, did use-moksa "freedom" or "release" (vimoksa, vimukti) and nirvana "cessation"-do not resolve any uncertainty.

2

Buddhists Effort and Order

INTRODUCTION

Within three months, the Buddhist had converted sixty monks to his cause, from every class, brahmans to outcastes. He travelled between the capitals of the main states of north India--Magadha, the Licchavi Confederacy, Kosala, and Kashi. During the twenty years of travel when he never had a home, he converted many to his teachings. Buddha accepted people from every part of society, men and women, whoever sought enlightenment. At first his mendicant followers stayed in caves and forests, begging for food and dressing in rags, and were called bhikkhu or "beggars." To prevent excesses of indulgence or mortification, the Buddha developed a simple rule for the monks. They were permitted to live in monasteries, accept food and clothing from the faithful, and take medicines from physicians.

At the urging of his step-mother who cut off her hair and wore the yellow robes of the Order, the Buddha accepted women into the Order, but provided special rules for nunneries. At the beginning Buddha himself accepted lay persons as monks with the simple proclamation: "Come, Oh Monk." Those accepted into the order shaved their heads, removed their moustaches, dressed in yellow robes, and studied under a teacher. Monks took their refuge in the Buddha, his teachings (the law or Dharma), and the Order (Sangha), the Three Jewels of Buddhism.

The monastic movement began to take shape after Buddha's conversion of King Bimbisara when Kalanda donated a bamboo grove and the King built a monastery, known as the Bodhimandala, for the Buddha and his thousand followers. Two disciples of the ascetic Sanjaya, Sariputta noted for his wisdom and Moggallana noted for his psychic powers, converted to Buddhism and became among his most important disciples. A third disciple of importance was Mahakassapa who was noted for his asceticism. The Buddha enjoined his disciples to convert others saying:

Go forth, O Monks, on your journey, for the profit of the many, for the bliss of the many, out of compassion for the world, for the welfare, the profit, the bliss of the gods and mankind. Go not any two together. Proclaim, O Monks, the Law (dharma), good in its beginning, in its middle, and in its ending. ...Make known the perfect, pure, and righteous life.

In addition, they were expected to abstain from eating after midday, attending music or dance performances, and using perfumes and garlands on six days each month. Observance was an injunction, but it was not compulsary and there was no penalty for violations. For monks and nuns the Rule was compulsary and there were penalties the most severe of which might involve suspension from the Order or, in extreme cases, expulsion. Expulsion might result from sexual misconduct, stealing, taking human life, or lying about spiritual attainments. Monks wandered for most of the year, but during the rainy season, they congregated at retreats where they undertook concentrated study of the Law and Rule.

The character of the Buddha's teaching is well illustrated by a Burmese account of two princes who were quarrelling about where to place a dam. They were about to fight over the matter when the Buddha suddenly appeared, asked about the conflict, was told the reasons, and then asked:

Tell me, O Kings, is earth of any intrinsic value?

"Of no value whatever," they replied.

"Is water of any intrinsic value?"

"Of no value whatever."

"And the blood of kings, is that of any intrinsic value?"

"Its value is priceless"

"Is it then reasonable," asked the Tathagata, "that what is priceless should be risked over what has no value whatever?"

The angry kings saw the wisdom of this reasoning and abandoned their dispute.

Return to Kapilavastu, 516BC

Seven years after he had left the palace, the Buddha returned to see his father, wife and child. During the visit, at the urging of his mother, Rahula asked to be made the next king, but the Buddha replied "What you want to inherit is impermanent and will make you suffer," and turning to his disciple Sariputta, said "receive him into the Order."

While staying there the Buddha converted his father, many members of his family, including Devadatta who would later oppose him, and many of the Shakya people. On his return, a wealthy merchant offered him land and buildings in Kosala which became the second important monastery, the Jetavanna Grove, where he spent the last twenty years of his life.

The Death or Parinirvana of Buddha 483 BC

After a lifetime of missionary efforts, called retreats, the Buddha saw dissent among his followers. His cousin Devadatta and Prince Ajatasatru, who had killed his father King Bimbisara, plotted to take control of the order and the kingdom of Magadha. Devadatta asked to lead the order, but the Buddha refused, saying that the monks follow his teachings not his person, leading Devadatta to attempt to kill him. First he released a mad elephant which charged the Buddha, thundering "like the black clouds at the end of the world," but was stopped by the Buddha raising his hand, evoking in the elephant a loving kindness and causing it to kneel down in homage. Devadatta then pushed a boulder which broke apart merely scratching the

Buddha's foot and proposed new austerities for monks in the attracting new recruits. All his efforts failed. Prince Ajatasatru, now King, regretted the murder of his father and became a Buddhist. Devadatta created a schism, but the Buddha sent Moggallana and Sariputta to win them back, and they returned to the Order. Devadatta regretted his error and was received back into the Order as well.

The Buddha, now about 80, left for a visit to Vaisali where he converted the courtesan Amrapali who gave her garden to the Order. He continued his journey and was given some food by a blacksmith which poisoned him, causing violent diarrhea and hemorrhaging. Weakened by this, he continued on to Kusinagara where he died in a grove of sala trees.

He refused to name a successor, saying "What does the Order expect of me? I have preached without distinguishing between secret and public doctrines. In the teachings of the Buddha there is no closed fist in which the teacher hides things from his disciples." The Buddhist Order was to be a community held together by a common understanding of the truth which was not something secret which some might know and others not know. "If some other person thinks that he should lead the Order or that the Order depends on him, let that person lay down instructions concerning the Order. But the Thatagata has no such thought, so why should he leave instructions?" Then he urged his disciples not to think that his words died with him and that they no longer had a teacher, for the "teachings (dharma) and the rules (vinaya) I have set forth should be your teacher after I die." He reminded them that each monk should "Be a lamp unto yourselves. Be refuges unto yourselves. Let the Law be your lamp. Let that be your refuge." His last words were "All composite things must decay; be diligent in striving for freedom"

His body was cremated, as was the custom of the time, and his remains were divided among the peoples of northern India who constructed stupas to enshrine them. The account of the division (the Mahaparinibbana-sutta) of his relics gives us a detailed view of the extent of the Buddhist community, the number of adherents in particular places, and a synopsis of his teachings. In 1898, Peppe excavated an old stupa at Piprahwa and found an urn with an inscription from the time of King Asoka or before which stated that the contents were the remains of the Buddha. In 1958 another urn was discovered in Vaisali and, though without an inscription, has been identified as containing his remains on the basis of its similarity to the one found by Peppe.

The Conversion of Sariputta and Moggallana

Now at that time, Sanjaya, the wandering ascetic, was dwelling at Rajagriha in company with a large following of wandering ascetics, two hundred and fifty in number; and at that time Sariputta and Moggallana were leading the religious life under Sanjaya, the wandering ascetic. And they had made this compact: "That one of us who shall first attain to the deathless is to tell it to the other." Then the venerable Assaji, having put on his tunic in the morning and taken his bowl and his robes, entered Rajagriha for alms, winning the minds of men with his advancing and his retiring, with his looking and his gazing, with his drawing in his arms and his stretching out his arms, and having his eyes cast down, and perfect in his deportment. And Sariputta, the wandering ascetic, saw the venerable Assaji going the rounds of Rajagriha for alms, winning the minds of men with his advancing and his retiring, with his looking and his gazing, with his drawing in arms and his stretching out his arms, and having his eyes cast down, and perfect in his deportment. And when he had seen him, it occurred to him as follows:-

"This must be a monk who is either an arhat already, or has entered the path which conducts to becoming an arhat. What if now I draw near to this monk, and ask him, 'To follow whom, brother, did you retire from the world? Who is your teacher? and whose doctrine do you approve?'" Then it occurred to Sariputta, the wandering ascetic, as follows: "It is not a fit time to ask this monk questions while he is inside the city, and going the rounds for alms. What if now I follow in the wake of this monk in the manner approved of for those who have requests to prefer?"

Then the venerable Assaji, after he had gone the rounds of Rajagriha and obtained alms, issued from the city; and Sariputta, the wandering ascetic, drew near to where the venerable Assaji was; and having drawn near, he exchanged greetings with the venerable Assaji; and having passed with him the greetings of friendship and civility, he stood respectfully at one side. And standing respectfully at one side, Sariputta, the wandering ascetic, spoke to the venerable Assaji as follows: "Placid, brother, are all your organs of sense; clear and bright is the colour of your skin. To follow whom, brother, did you retire from the world? Who is your teacher? and whose doctrine do you approve?"

"Brother, there is a great Shakyaputta monk, one who has retired from the world out of the Shakya clan. To follow this Blessed One have I retired from the world, and this Blessed One is my teacher, and the Doctrine of this Blessed One do I approve."

"But what, venerable sir, is your teacher's doctrine? and what does he proclaim?"

"Brother, I am a novice and a new-comer, and the time is but short since I retired from the world under this Doctrine and Discipline. I am not able to expound to you the Doctrine at any great length, but I can tell you the substance of it in brief."

Then Sariputta, the wandering ascetic, spoke to the venerable Assaji as follows: "So be it, brother. Whether little or much, tell it me. Tell me only the substance; it is the substance I want. Why should you make a long matter of it?"

Then the venerable Assaji recited to Sariputta, the wandering ascetic, the following exposition of the Doctrine:-

The Tathagata has explained the causes

Of all things springing from a cause,

And also how things cease to be-

This the great Adept has proclaimed.

On hearing this exposition of the Doctrine, there arose in the mind of Sariputta, the wandering ascetic, a clear and distinct perception of the Doctrine that whatever is subject to origination is subject also to cessation. "If this is the Doctrine," said he, "then, indeed, have you reached the sorrowless state lost sight of and neglected for many myriads of world-cycles."

Then Sariputta, the wandering ascetic, drew near to where Moggallana, the wandering ascetic, was. And Moggallana, the wandering ascetic, saw Sariputta, the wandering ascetic, approaching from afar; and when he had seen him, he spoke to Sariputta, the wandering ascetic, as follows:-

"Placid, brother, are all your organs of sense; clear and bright is the colour of your skin. Brother, have you attained to the deathless?"

"Yes, brother, I have attained to the deathless."

"But how, brother, did you attain to the deathless?"

"Brother, just now I saw Assaji the monk going the rounds of Rajagriha for alms, winning the minds of men with his advancing and his retiring, with his looking and his gazing, with his drawing in his arms and his stretching out his arms, and having his eyes cast down, and perfect in his deportment; and when I had seen him, it occurred to me as follows:-

"This must be a monk who is either an arhat already, or has entered the path which conducts to becoming an arhat. What if now I were to draw near to this monk, and ask him, 'To follow whom, brother, did you retire from the world? Who is your teacher? and whose doctrine do you approve?' Then, brother, it occurred to me as follows: 'It is not a fit time to ask this monk questions while he is inside the city and going the round for alms. What if now I follow in the wake of this monk in the manner approved of for those who have requests to prefer?' Then, brother, Assaji the monk, after he had gone the rounds of Rajagriha and obtained alms, left the city; and I, brother, drew near to where Assaji the monk was; and having drawn near, I exchanged greetings with the venerable Assaji;

and having passed with him the greetings of friendship and civility, I stood respectfully at one side. And standing respectfully at one side, I spoke, brother, to the venerable Assaji as follows: 'Placid, brother, are all your organs of sense; clear and bright is the colour of your skin.

To follow whom, brother, did you retire from the world? Who is your teacher? and whose doctrine do you approve?' 'Brother, there is a great Shakyaputta monk, one who has retired from the world out of the Shakya clan. To follow this Blessed One have I retired from the world, and this Blessed One is my teacher, and the Doctrine of this Blessed One do I approve.'

'But what, venerable sir, is your teacher's doctrine? and what does he proclaim?' 'Brother, I am a novice and a newcomer, and the time is but short since I retired from the world under the Doctrine and Discipline. I am not able to expound to you the Doctrine at any great length, but I can tell you the substance of it in brief.' 'So be it, brother. Whether little or much, tell it me. Tell me only the substance; it is the substance I want. Why should you make a long matter of it? ' Then, brother, Assail the monk recited to me the following exposition of the Doctrine:-

The Tathagata has explained the causes

Of all things springing from a cause,

And also how things cease to be-

This the great Adept has proclaimed."

On hearing this exposition of the Doctrine, there arose in the mind of Moggallana, the wandering ascetic, a clear and distinct perception of the Doctrine that whatever is subject to origination is subject also to cessation. "If this is the Doctrine," said he, "then, indeed, have you reached the sorrowless state, lost sight of and neglected for many myriads of world-cycles."

The Fire Sermon

Then The Blessed One, having dwelt in Uruvela as long as he wished, proceeded on his wanderings in the direction of

Gaya Head, accompanied by a great congregation of priests, a thousand in number, who had all of them aforetime been monks with matted hair. And there in Gaya, on Gaya Head, the Blessed One dwelt, together with the thousand priests. And there The Blessed One addressed the priests:-

"All things, O priests, are on fire. And what, O priests, are all these things which are on fire?

"The eye, O priests, is on fire; forms are on fire; eye-consciousness is on fire; impressions received by the eye are on fire; and whatever sensation, pleasant, unpleasant, or indifferent, originates in dependence on impressions received by the eye, that also is on fire.

"And with what are these on fire?

"With the fire of passion, say I, with the fire of hatred, with the fire of infatuation; with birth, old age, death, sorrow, lamentation, misery, grief, and despair are they on fire.

"The ear is on fire; sounds are on fire;... the nose is on fire; odors are on fire;... the tongue is on fire; tastes are on fire;... the body is on fire; things tangible are on fire;... the mind is on fire; ideas are on fire;... mind-consciousness is on fire; impressions received by the mind are on fire; and whatever sensation, pleasant, unpleasant, or indifferent, originates in dependence on impressions received by the mind, that also is on fire.

"And with what are these on fire?

"With the fire of passion, say I, with the fire of hatred, with the fire of infatuation; with birth, old age, death, sorrow, lamentation, misery, grief, and despair are they on fire.

"Perceiving this, O priests, the learned and noble disciple conceives an aversion for the eye, conceives an aversion for forms, conceives an aversion for eye-consciousness, conceives an aversion for the impressions received by the eye; and whatever sensation, pleasant, unpleasant, or indifferent, originates in dependence on impressions received by the eye, for that also he conceives an aversion. Conceives an aversion for the ear, conceives an aversion for sounds,... conceives an aversion for the nose, conceives an aversion for odors,... conceives an aversion for the tongue, conceives an aversion for tastes,... conceives an aversion for the body, conceives an aversion for things tangible,... conceives an aversion for the mind, conceives an aversion for ideas, conceives an aversion for mind-consciousness, conceives an aversion for the impressions received by the mind; and whatever sensation, pleasant, unpleasant, or indifferent, originates in dependence on impressions received by the mind, for this also he conceives an aversion. And in conceiving this aversion, he becomes divested of passion, and by the absence of passion he becomes free, and when he is free he becomes aware that he is free; and he knows that rebirth is exhausted, that he has lived the holy life, that he has done what it behooved him to do, and that he is no more for this world."

Now while this exposition was being delivered, the minds of the thousand priests became free from attachment and delivered from the depravities.

The Synopsis of the Truth

Thus have I heard. Once when the Lord was staying at Benares in the Isipatana deer park, he addressed the monks as follows: It was here in this very deer park at Benares that the Truth-finder, Arhat, all-enlightened, set in motion the supreme Wheel of the Doctrine-which shall not be turned back from its onward course by ascetic or Brahmin, god or Mara or Brahma or by anyone in the universe,-the announcement of the Four Noble Truths, the teaching, declaration, and establishment of those Four Truths, with their unfolding, exposition, and manifestation.

What are these four?-The announcement, teaching... and manifestation of the Noble Truth of sufferings [dukkha]-of the origin of suffering-of the cessation of suffering-of the path that leads to the cessation of suffering.

Follow, monks, Sariputta and Moggallana and be guided by them; they are wise helpers unto their fellows in the higher life.... Sariputta is able to announce, teach... and manifest the Four Noble Truths in all their details.

Having thus spoken, the Blessed One arose and went into his own cell.

The Lord had not been gone long when the reverent Sariputta proceeded to the exposition of the Truth-finder's Four Noble Truths, as follows:

What, reverend sirs, is the Noble Truth of suffering?-Birth is a suffering; decay is a suffering; death is a suffering; grief and lamentation, pain, misery and tribulation are sufferings; it is a suffering not to get what is desired;-in brief all the factors of the fivefold grip on existence are suffering.

Birth is, for living creatures of each several class, the being born or produced, the issue, the arising or the re-arising, the appearance of the psychic constructions, the growth of faculties.

Decay, for living creatures of each several class, is the decay and decaying, loss of teeth, gray hair, wrinkles, a dwindling term of life, sere faculties.

Death, for living creatures of each several class, is the passage and passing hence, the dissolution, disappearance, dying, death, decease, the dissolution of the impressions, the discarding of the dead body.

Grief is the grief, grieving, and grievousness, the inward grief and inward anguish of anyone who suffers under some misfortune or is in the grip of some type of suffering.

Lamentation is the lament and lamentation, the wailing and the lamenting of anyone who suffers under some misfortune or is in the grip of some type of suffering. Pain is any bodily suffering or bodily evil, and suffering bred of bodily contact, any evil feeling. Misery is mental suffering and evil, any evil feeling of the mind. Tribulation is the tribulation of heart and mind, the state to which tribulation brings them, in anyone who suffers under some misfortune or is in the grip of some type of suffering. There remains not to get what is desired. In creatures subject to birth-or decay-or death-or grief and lamentation, pain, misery, and tribulation-the desire arises not to be subject thereto but to escape them. But escape is not to be won merely by desiring it; and failure to win it is another suffering.

What are in brief all the factors of the fivefold grip on existence which are sufferings?-They are: the factors of form, sensation, perception, psychic dispositions, and consciousness. The foregoing, sirs, constitutes the Noble Truth of suffering.

What now is the Noble Truth of the origin of suffering? It is any craving that makes for re-birth and is tied up with passion's delights and culls satisfaction now here now there-such as the craving for sensual pleasure, the craving for continuing existence, and the craving for annihilation

Next, what is the Noble Truth of the cessation of suffering?-It is the utter and passionless cessation of this same craving,-the abandonment and rejection of craving, deliverance from craving, and aversion from craving.

Lastly, what is the Noble Truth of the Path that leads to the cessation of suffering?-It is just the Noble Eightfold Path, consisting of right outlook, right resolves, right speech, right acts, right livelihood, right endeavour, right mindfulness and right rapture of concentration.

Right outlook is to know suffering, the origin of suffering, the cessation of suffering, and the path that leads to the cessation of suffering. Right resolve is the resolve to renounce the world and to do no hurt or harm.

Right speech is to abstain from lies and slander, from reviling, and from tattle. Right acts are to abstain from taking life, from stealing, and from lechery.

Right livelihood is that by which the disciple of the Noble One supports himself, to the exclusion of wrong modes of livelihood.

Right endeavour is when a monk brings his will to bear, puts forth endeavour and energy, struggles and strives with all his heart, to stop bad and wrong qualities which have not yet arisen from ever arising, to renounce those which have already arisen, to foster good qualities which have not yet arisen, and, finally, to establish, clarify, multiply, enlarge, develop, and perfect those good qualities which are there already.

Right mindfulness is when realizing what the body is-what feelings are-what the heart is-and what the mental states are-a monk dwells ardent, alert, and mindful, in freedom from the wants and discontents attendant on any of these things.``

DEATH OF THE BUDDHA

...Then the Blessed One addressed the monks.-

" Where, O monks, is Ananda? "

"Reverend Sir, the venerable Ananda has entered the monastery, and leaning against the bolt of the door, he weeps, saying, 'Behold, I am but a learner, and not yet perfect, and my Teacher is on the point of passing into Nirvana, he who was so compassionate to me.'"

Then the Blessed One addressed a certain monk, saying,-

"Go, O monk, and say to the venerable Ananda from me, 'The Teacher calls you, brother Ananda.'"

...Ananda ... drew near to where The Blessed One was; and having drawn near and greeted The Blessed One, he sat down respectfully at one side. And the venerable Ananda being seated respectfully at one side, The Blessed One spoke to him as follows:-

"Enough, Ananda, do not grieve, nor weep. Have I not already told you, Ananda, that it is in the very nature of all things near and dear unto us that we must divide ourselves from them, leave them, sever ourselves from them? How is it possible, Ananda, that whatever has been born, has come into being, is organized and perishable, should not perish? That condition is not possible.

For a long time, Ananda, have you waited on the Tathagata with a kind, devoted, cheerful, single-hearted, unstinted service of body, with a kind, devoted, cheerful, single-hearted, unstinted service of voice, with a kind, devoted, cheerful, single-hearted, unstinted service of mind. You have acquired much merit, Ananda; exert yourself, and soon will you be free from all depravity."

'Go thou, Ananda, and enter the city Kusinara, and announce to the Kusinara-Mallas:-

"Tonight, O you Vasetthas, in the last watch, the Tathagata will pass into Nirvana. Be favourable, be favorable, O you Vasetthas, and suffer not that afterwards you feel remorse, saying, 'The Tathagata passed into Nirvana while in our borders, but we did not avail ourselves of the opportunity of being present at the last moments of the Tathagata.'"

...The Mallas, on hearing the speech of the venerable Ananda, and their children and their daughters-in-law and their wives were grieved and sorrowful and overwhelmed with anguish of mind, and some let fly their hair and cried aloud, and stretched out their arms and cried aloud, and fell headlong to the ground and rolled to and fro, saying, "All too soon will The Blessed One pass into Nirvana; all too soon will The Happy One pass into Nirvana; all too soon will The Light of the World vanish from sight." Then the Mallas and their children and their daughters-in-law and their wives, being grieved and sorrowful and overwhelmed with anguish of mind, drew near to the sala-tree grove Upavattana of the Mallas, and to where the venerable Ananda was.

Now at that time Subhadda, a wandering ascetic, was dwelling at Kusinara. And Subhadda, the wandering ascetic, heard the report:-

"Tonight, in the last watch, the monk Gautama will pass into Nirvana."

Then it occurred to Subhadda, the wandering ascetic, as follows:-

"I have heard wandering ascetics, that were old men, advanced in years, teaches, and teachers' teachers, declare, 'But seldom, and on rare occasions, does a Tathagata, a saint, and Supreme Buddha arise in the world.' And tonight, in the last watch, the monk Gautama will pass into Nirvana. And a certain question has arisen in my mind, and I am persuaded of the monk Gautama that he can so teach me the Doctrine that I shall be relieved of this my doubt."

Then Subhadda, the wandering ascetic, drew near to the sala-tree grove Upavattana of the Dallas, and to where the venerable Ananda was, and having drawn near, he spoke to the venerable Ananda as follows:- "Ananda, I have heard wandering ascetics, that were old men, advanced in years, teaches, and teachers' teachers, declare, 'But seldom, and on rare occasions, does a Tathagata, a saint, and Supreme Buddha arise in the world.' And tonight, in the last watch, the monk Gautama will pass into Nirvana. And a certain doubt has arisen in my mind, and I am persuaded of the monk Gautama that he can so teach me the Doctrine that I shall be relieved of this my doubt. Let me, then, Ananda, have an opportunity of seeing the monk Gautama."

When Subhadda, the wandering ascetic, had so spoken, the venerable Ananda spoke to him as follows:-

"Enough of that, brother Subhadda; trouble not the Tathagata. The Blessed One is weary."

[Subhadda persisted a second and a third time, and was refused by Ananda each time.] ... Now the Blessed One chanced to hear the conversation between the venerable Ananda and the wandering ascetic Subhadda. And The Blessed One called to the venerable Ananda:-

" Enough, Ananda; hinder not Subhadda. Let Subhadda, Ananda, have an opportunity of beholding the Tathagata. Whatever Subhadda shall ask of me, he will ask for the sake of information, and not for the sake of troubling me, and he will quickly understand my answers to his questions."

Then the venerable Ananda spoke to Subhadda, the wandering ascetic, as follows:-

"You may come, brother Subhadda; The Blessed One grants you an audience."

Then Subhadda, the wandering ascetic, drew near to where The Blessed One was; and having drawn near, he exchanged greetings with The Blessed One; and having passed with him the greetings of friendship and civility, he sat down respectfully at one side. And seated respectfully at one side, Subhadda, the wandering ascetic, spoke to The Blessed One as follows:-

"Gautama, all those monks and Brahmans who possess a large following and crowds of hearers and disciples, and who are distinguished, renowned leaders of sects, and highly esteemed by the multitudes,-to writ, Purana Kassapa, Makkhali Gosala, Ajita Kesakambali, Pakudha Kaccayana, Sanjaya Belatthiputta, Nigantha Nathaputta,-have they all done as they maintain, discovered the truth, or have they not? or have some of them done so, and others not? "

"Enough, O Subhadda! let us leave the question, 'Have they all done as they maintain, discovered the truth, or have they not? or have some of them done so, and others not?' The Doctrine will I teach you, Subhadda. Listen to me, and pay strict attention, and I will speak."

" Yes, Reverend Sir," said Subhadda, the wandering ascetic, to The Blessed One in assent. And The Blessed One spoke as follows:-

"Subhadda, in whatever doctrine and discipline the noble eightfold path is not found, therein also is not found the monk of the first degree, nor the monk of the second degree, nor the monk of the third degree, nor the monk of the fourth degree; and in whatever doctrine and discipline, O Subhadda, the noble eightfold path is found, therein also are found the monk of the first degree, and the monk of the second degree, and the monk of the third degree, and the monk of the fourth degree.

Now in this Doctrine and Discipline, O Subhadda, the noble eightfold path is found: and therein alone, O Subhadda, are found the monk of the first degree, and the monk of the second degree, and the monk of the third degree, and the monk of the fourth degree.

Destitute of true monks are all other creeds. But let these my monks, O Subhadda, live rightly, and the world will not be destitute of saints.

What time my age was twenty-nine,

Subhadda, I left the world to seek the highest good.

Now fifty years and more have passed, Subhadda,

Since I renounced the world and lived ascetic

Within the Doctrine's pale, that rule of conduct

Outside of which no genuine monk exists, nor the monk of the second degree, nor the monk of the third degree, nor the monk of the fourth degree. Destitute of monks are all other creeds. But let these my monks, O Subhadda, live rightly, and the world will not be destitute of saints."

When The Blessed One had thus spoken, Subhadda, the wandering ascetic, spoke to him as follows:-

"O wonderful is it, Reverend Sir! O wonderful is it, Reverend Sir! It is as if, Reverend Sir, one were to set up that which was overturned, or were to disclose that which was hidden, or were to point out the way to a lost traveller, or were to carry a lamp into a dark place that they who had eyes might see forms. Even so has The Blessed One expounded the Doctrine in many different ways. Reverend Sir, I betake myself to The Blessed One for refuge, to the Doctrine, and to the Congregation of the monks. Suffer me to retire from the world under The Blessed One; suffer me to receive ordination."

"Subhadda, any one who aforetime has been an adherent of another sect and afterwards desires to retire from the world and receive ordination under this Doctrine and Discipline, must first spend four months on probation; and after the lapse of four months, strenuous-minded monks receive him into the Order and confer on him the monkly ordination. Nevertheless, in this matter of probation I recognize a difference in persons."

"Reverend Sir, if all they who aforetime have been adherents of other sects and afterwards desire to retire from the world and receive ordination under this Doctrine and Discipline, must first spend four months on probation, and after the lapse of four months strenuous-minded monks receive them into the Order, and confer on them the monkly ordination, then am I ready to spend four years on probation, and after the lapse of four years, let strenuous-minded monks receive me into the Order and confer on me the monkly ordination."

Then The Blessed One said to the venerable Ananda,

"Well, then, Ananda, receive Subhadda into the Order."

Then The Blessed One addressed the venerable Ananda:-

"It may be, Ananda, that some of you will think, ' The word of The Teacher is a thing of the past; we have now no Teacher.' But that, Ananda, is not the correct view. The Doctrine and Discipline, Ananda, which I have taught and enjoined upon you is to be your teacher when I am gone. But whereas now, Ananda, all the monks address each other with the title of 'brother,' not so must they address each other after I am gone. A senior monk, Ananda, is to address a junior monk either by his given name, or by his family name, or by the title of 'brother;' a junior monk is to address a senior monk with the title 'reverend sir,' or 'venerable.' If the Order, Ananda, wish to do so, after I am gone they may abrogate all the lesser and minor precepts. On Channa, Ananda, after I am gone, the higher penalty is to be inflicted."

"Reverend Sir, what is this higher penalty?"

"Let Channa, Ananda, say what he likes, he is not to be spoken to nor admonished nor instructed by the monks."

Then The Blessed One addressed the monks:-

"It may be, O monks, that some monk has a doubt or perplexity respecting either The Buddha or the Doctrine or the Order or the Path or the course of conduct. Ask any questions, O monks, and suffer not that afterwards you feel remorse, saying, 'Our Teacher was present with us, but we failed to ask him all our questions.'"

When he had so spoken, the monks remained silent.

And a second time The Blessed One, and a third time The Blessed One addressed the monks:-...

And a third time the monks remained silent.

Then The Blessed One addressed the monks:-

"It may be, O monks, that it is out of respect to The Teacher that you ask no questions. Then let each one speak to his friend." And when he had thus spoken, the monks remained silent. Then the venerable Ananda spoke to The Blessed One as follows:-

"It is wonderful, Reverend Sir! It is marvelous, Reverend Sir! Reverend Sir, I have faith to believe that in this congregation of monks not a single monk has a doubt or perplexity respecting either The Buddha or the Doctrine or the Order or the Path or the course of conduct."

"With you, Ananda, it is a matter of faith, when you say that; but with the Tathagata, Ananda, it is a matter of knowledge that in this congregation of monks not a single monk has a doubt or perplexity respecting either The Buddha or the Doctrine or the Order or the Path or the course of conduct. For of all these five hundred monks, Ananda, the most backward one has become converted, and is not liable to pass into a lower state of existence, but is destined necessarily to attain supreme wisdom."

Then The Blessed One addressed the monks:-

"And now, O monks, I take my leave of you; all composite things are transitory; strive onward diligently."

And this was the last word of the Tathagata.

Thereupon The Blessed One entered the first stage of meditation, and rising from the first stage of meditation, he entered the second stage of meditation; and rising from the second stage of meditation, he entered the third stage of meditation; and rising from the third stage of meditation, he entered the fourth stage of meditation, and rising from the fourth stage of meditation, he entered the realm of the infinity of space; and rising from the realm of the infinity of space, he entered the realm of the infinity of consciousness; and rising from the realm of the infinity of consciousness, he entered the realm of nothingness; and rising from the realm of nothingness, he entered the realm of neither perception nor yet non-perception; and rising from the realm of neither perception nor yet non-perception, he arrived at the cessation of perception and sensation.

Thereupon the venerable Ananda spoke to the venerable Anuruddha as follows:-

"Reverend Anuruddha, The Blessed One has passed into Nirvana."

"Nay, brother Ananda, The Blessed One has not passed into Nirvana; he has arrived at the cessation of perception and sensation."

Thereupon The Blessed One rising from the cessation of his perception and sensation, entered the realm of neither perception nor yet non-perception; and rising from the realm of neither perception nor yet non-perception, he entered the realm of nothingness; and rising from the realm of nothingness, he entered the realm of the infinity of consciousness; and rising from the realm of the infinity of consciousness, he entered the realm of the infinity of space; and rising from the realm of the infinity of space, he entered the fourth stage of meditation; and rising from the fourth stage of meditation, he entered the third stage of meditation; and rising from the third stage of meditation, he entered the second stage of meditation; and rising from the second stage of meditation, he entered the first stage of meditation; and rising from the first stage of meditation, he entered the second stage of meditation; and rising from the second stage of meditation, he entered the third stage of meditation; and rising from the third stage of meditation, he entered the fourth stage of meditation; and rising from the fourth stage of meditation, immediately The Blessed One passed into Nirvana.

THE CHARACTERISTIC OF BUDDIST

Religion is a social phenomenon and studying it with a view to understanding its historical development has special significance today. We can see similar trends in other countries where the rapid developments of science and technology do not in any significant way lessen the people's sense of, nor interests in, religion. Even the people of China, for some reason or other, show similar interests in the development of religion. This phenomenon is enough to raise several theoretical questions concerning the need for a better understanding of religion: what is the nature of religion? Does the human psyche require a religious faith? Is religion synonymous with religious belief? Is religious belief beneficial to social life? Is science complementary to, or inconsistent with, religious belief? Can religion be a modernizing agent? and so forth. This paper does not pretend to deal specifically with these questions, But, why do we study the history of religions? Should an ideal history of religions be time-conscious? Can such an history help people think seriously about the problems of religion that exist in the world today? All historians of religions need to address themselves to these kinds of problems.

The religions which had been popular in Chinese history include Buddhism, Buddhism, Islam, Christianity and animism. However, of all these religious traditions, only Buddhism is indigenous to China. To be sure, Buddhism is a Chinese religion; it has characteristics peculiar to the Chinese. Besides, it has exercised considerable influence on the development of Chinese culture and psychology, customs and habits, science and technology, philosophy and thought, medicine and hygiene, and even political life. Can our investigation into one of the more influential religions--the origin of Buddhism, its development and characteristics--help us deepen our understanding of Chinese culture, personality and way of thinking? Can it indirectly help us understand, more intimately, the theoretical and practical problems of religion in the world today? I think it can and toward this end the present discussion is an attempt to analyze and discuss the following issues.

GENERAL BACKGROUND

The development of Buddhism was an attempt to orientate the Han Chinese to their social, political, economic, moral and psychological lives at the end of the Eastern Han.

Why did Buddhism develop only at the end of the Eastern Han period? Historically, such Daoist ideas, as `immortality' and `sanctification of the bodies' had already existed during the time of the Warring States (Zhanguo). They became even more popular during the Qin and Han dynasties--why? We know that not just any kind of superstition can be called religion, although religion often embodies a good deal of superstitious elements. Neither can we say that any theistic discourse can become a religion, even if it is capable of extending its influence over a sizeable cross-section of the population. Its growth and development were directly related to the social life of the people, their history, and other objective facts. The development of Buddhism during the Eastern Han may be attributed to the following factors.

First, the reality of social life at the end of the Eastern Han had laid fertile grounds for the growth of Buddhism. The social and political conditions, since Shundi of the Eastern Han, had begun to deteriorate. There was outside interference in the day-to-day administration and the administrative machinery was in the hands of a bureaucracy. Debauchery, unruly behavior and social strife, both from within and without, were the order of the day. Finally there were crop failures due to severe drought, and large numbers of people died in ditches (Chong Zhangdong, Changyuan). Undue economic exploitations and political pressure at that time had made it impossible for the populace to lead a decent life; bankruptcy and emigration were common.

The conflict between the ruling class and the ruled was intense and acute. According to historical records, from Shundi's time, peasant uprisings were rampant. At that time, apart from the common class-interest that united them in social movements, their leaders resorted to magic and superstitions as organizing agents. That is why, in history books, the rebels after Shundi's time were often called yaozei, or `the goblin thieves'.

Two conclusions may be drawn from the above discussion. First, a period of economic and political unrest, as well as spiritual and moral decay, provided an objective vantage for the development of religion. Second, as the leaders of the peasantry had used magic and superstitions to rally support in their movements, they knew that these could be used as tools for mobilizing the people, thus paving the way for the widespread development of religion. As is always the case, social turbulence often caused great hardship and suffering to the lower class. Thus, when people became desperate they tended to hinge their hopes upon some kind of spiritual power, or shenling. This was one of the most common avenues through which people, in antiquity, reconciled themselves with their social reality. This also explains why a majority of the early Daoist believers were members of the lower social strata.

Second, the social conditions at the end of the Eastern Han had provided useful material for the founding of Buddhism. Since the time of Han Wudi, when Dong Zhongshu pointed out that "of the hundred schools, only Confucianism is the most revered," Confucian thought had adapted itself to the needs of building a unified feudal society and serving as an ideology for the ruling class. From then on the development of Confucianism depended primarily on the teaching of a reciprocal relationship between heaven and man, followed by an increased interest in the development of theology and metaphysics. Though ideally a religion is theistic, not any form of theism is adequate or sufficiently meaningful to become a religion. This is because such a religion (namely, the religion of the masses) must include not only the worship of spiritual beings, but also possess a body of canon together with an endurable form of church organization, doctrines and dogmas, and an historical medium for the dissemination of religious knowledge. Generally, religion must see the world in two forms: the real and the supernatural. Based on this premise, human beings feel that they can only disengage themselves from the problems of social life in a supernatural world--believing that an ideal life can manifest itself only in the yonder shore of the supernatural world.

Despite the fact that Confucianism acknowledged the existence of Shen or God, especially during the Han dynasty, it had never thought it necessary that its ideals be fulfilled outside the world, but required rather that the ideals of "governing the state and pacifying the world" (zhi guo ping tianxia) be actualized in the real world, even though this were merely an illusion. Although religion had played a very important role in feudal China, it had never become a force to reckon with. Instead it had, many a time, occupied a secondary position, which state of affairs clearly bespoke as well the dominance of Confucian ideology.

From the developmental point of view, after the Eastern Han Confucianism could very well have become a religion, because its metaphysics together with the conception of the sacred could be easily converted into religion. However, Confucianism did not become a religion during the Han dynasty for the simple reason that it attempted to materialize the ideals of "governing the state and pacifying the world" in the real world. Thus, following the decay of the Han dynasty, Confucian ideology not only fell short of becoming a religion but its position as an ideology of the ruling class continued to decline. Because of this decline, Confucian thought had given way to the growth of Buddhism. History shows that, whenever the dominant ideology of the ruling class lost its power, it often signalled the growth and dominance of a countervailing religion.

Even though Confucianism had declined at the end of the Eastern Han, certain facets of its ideology could still be absorbed and put to good use by an ongoing religion. The fact that Confucian ideas are found in Buddhism is clear proof that such assimilation did take place. For example, the idea of "the ultimate peace in the unity of the three (heaven, earth and man) in one" (tian-di-ren san heyi zhi taiping) shows that the Confucianists were concerned about political reality and the notion of sancai (three endowments) mentioned in Yi Zhuan2. The idea that the sky and the universe were formed by breath (qi) could have derived from the knowledge of world creation as well as the yin-yang principles and the five elements mentioned in the apocryphal texts. All these ideas were closely connected to Han Confucian thought. That most of the scholars who studied the development of Buddhism focused their attention on its relationship with Daoist sources and overlooked the nexus between Daoist and Confucianist ideas is a bias.

Buddhism could have another source in its gradual mingling with the tradition of the saints. Although there was a connection between the Daoists and the saints of the early Qin, both seem to belong to quite different schools of thought. Until the beginning of the Western Han, the popular Huang-Lao learning was essentially Daoist. It frequently emphasized the exemplary qualities of the sage and was thus deemed capable of exercising its power over the state and the cosmos. That is why Sima Qian, in his preface, commented that the importance of the Huang-Lao learning lies in the doctrine of "self-actualization through non-action, and self-correction through expiation" (wuwei zihua, qingjing zizheng).

The Huang-Lao Daoist learning underwent a change during the Eastern Han: part of its adherents sought the help of the gods installed in shrines, thus becoming unified with the saints. Huandi, for example, made sacrifices to Laozi (Lao Tzu) at the latter's shrine with the aim to "preserve shen for the uplift of character and the ultimate ascent to heaven," thus signalling the initial transformation of Huang-Lao's Daoist teaching. Also, as early as the end of the Western Han, there was already in existence what was known as "Huang-lao's Dao" (the Way of Huang-Lao) and, later on, the "Fangxian's Dao" (the Way of the Saints), all of which actually belonged to the immortalist sects. Further, the saints' underlying objective was to attain `eternal life' (changsheng busi) and to cause the bodies to be sanctified (routi chengxian). Thus, once it merged with the Daoist ideas of "attaining peace through inaction, and remaining in peace through abstinence" (qingjing wuwei, tiandan guayu), it increasingly began to attract the masses and became a powerful social force. Lastly, the basic tenets of Buddhism, such as "immortality" and "the sanctification of the bodies," although derived from the Way of the Saints, became part of the Daoist system. Hence, its transformation also represents an important factor contributing to the growth of Buddhism.

From the above viewpoints, Buddhism as a religion may be said to have deviated from the Confucianists' and Daoist' schools of thought. However, its source of ideas was inseparable from both. Hence, from the beginning, it had distinguished itself as a religious system in which Confucian and Daoist ideas supplemented each other. This system represents some of the characteristics typical of Chinese culture, psychology and way of thinking.

Third, the introduction of Buddhism into China had greatly stimulated the development of Chinese religion. From the time Buddhism spread to China during the Western Han till after the middle of the Eastern Han, it maintained a steady level of propagation. Buddhism, acting like a catalyst, escalated the development of Buddhism. Actually, the school of the saints was already popular during the Western Han, and disciples frequently had given tributes to Huang-Lao. This was evidenced in the existing learnings of "Huang-Lao's Dao" and "Fangxian's Dao." The former sanctified Huangdi and worshipped him in shrines dedicated to him; the latter talked about "non-death and everlasting life" (zhongshen busi). Shiji3 records that the teacher of the river elder, Le Jigong, learned about Huangdi.

The book of Fengchan records that Huangdi became an immortal because of Fengchan. Yujie (more appropriately, Ganjie), who compiled the Daoist scripture Taiping Jing, suggested that the book was originally by Laozi (Lao Tzu). During Han Mingdi, Chu Wangying had already worshipped Huangdi and Foutu. Chu Wangying recited Huang-Lao's words and honored Foutu's shrine. Huandi erected Huang-Lao's and Foutu's shrines in his palace. The fact that Huang-Lao and Foutu were worshiped manifestly shows that Huangdi was at that time regarded as a deity or a Buddha. Sainthood was in fact a form of sagehood. Living the life of an immortal is but a human discipline. There was no formal, nor endurable form of organization to be used as a base for the interaction of the religious community. But after the spread of Buddhism to China, it became an organized form of religion, possessing not only a set of teaching which differed from that of traditional China, but also an organized church, with a religious canon and a spiritual community, all of which served as a blueprint for the founding of Buddhism.

It is true that Buddhism had served as a model for the establishment of Buddhism. Of even greater importance is that Buddhism was alien to Chinese culture, and its propagation in China was greeted with protests by the bearers of Xia's cultural tradition. This defensive attitude acted as a stimulus spurring the Chinese to strive even harder towards establishing an indigenous religion. When an ethnic culture encountered an alien culture it often gave rise to mutual absorption or rejection.

This situation was particularly marked in the case of the Chinese response to Indian Buddhism. We can provide evidence to show how it was actually reflected in the earliest Daoist scripture, Taiping Jing. In this scripture, we see how some Buddhist ideas, like benqi (the primal beginning) and sanjie (the three worlds), had their origins in the Buddhist canon. On the other hand, there were criticisms about Buddhism, for example, the talks that "the conduct of the four destructions collectively denigrates the spiritual way of heaven" (Shihui zhi xing, gong wuru huangtian zhi shendao).

Moreover, upon the establishment of Buddhism, its adherents circulated the story about Laozi (Lao Tzu)'s role in bringing about a renaissance among the northern Chinese (Laozi [Lao Tzu] huahu). This was designed not only as a blow to Buddhism but also as an attempt to boost the image of Buddhism. All this suggests a kind of antagonistic reaction against the entry of the alien culture.

Therefore, it is not at all surprising that the end of the Eastern Han period saw the need for the development of an indigenous religion. The founding of this religion could be traced to the existing tradition of the saints. The fact that it adopted Confucian and Daoist ideas as a basis for the development of Buddhism is even less surprising. Once it emerged, it immediately became charged with an intense ethnic fervor and came into direct conflict with the alien Buddhist religion. The outcome is, precisely, a manifestation of an indigenously endowed Chinese culture.

As a form of religious philosophy Buddhism has special characteristics which can be illuminated only through comparison with other religions.

An established religion has characteristics which are distinctively different from those of other religions. Besides such external forms, as church organization, religious doctrines and canon, as well as its conception of the sacred, its characteristics should be reflected in the theoretical system which forms the core of the religion. This theoretical system usually contains a body of basic ideals and conceptual schema. For instance, the ultimate reality of the Buddhist belief, as embodied in the concepts of self-denial, transcendentalism and nirvana, is the insignia which distinguishes it from other religions. The three doctrines of the medieval Christianity--namely, "the existence of God," "the resurrection of the soul" and "free will"--form its religious philosophy and conceptual schema.

If that be the case, does Daoist philosophy contain any doctrines and tenets which differ from those of other religions? I think it does, especially in the earlier form of Buddhism. Whilst almost all religions ask the question, "what happens after the demise of a person?" Buddhism wanted to know "why humans don't die?" This basic question serves as the key to the theoretical system of Buddhism. All this shows that it has characteristics different from those of other religions.

The early form of Buddhism held that its body of belief was made up of the tenet of "the ascent of the three in one," that is, "the unity of heaven, earth, and man for the attainment of the Great Peace" (tian-di-ren, sanzhe heyi yi zhi taiping); "the blending of the essence, breath, and shen to become a saint" (jing-qi-shen, sanzhe hunyi er cheng shenxian). From this it evolves into "non-death and eternal life" (zhongshen busi), "resurrection of the bodies" (routi feisheng), and "transformation of the breath into the three pure ones" (qihua sanqing), thus forming the basis of Buddhism.

To understand the tenets of the Buddhist philosophy, one must know the meaning of nirvana. Hence, a Russian Buddhist scholar wrote a book analyzing the meaning of nirvana. In Mou zhongsan's book, he analyzed the concept of nirvana from the Chinese Buddhist viewpoint. In studying Christianity, one should analyze the concept of "God." Thus, Aurelius Augustinus (354-430) in his The City of God, formulated his thesis regarding the `godliness' of the `Almighty'. In his Shenxue Dazhuan, Thomas Aquinas (1225-1274) put forward five parameters to prove that "God exists." In Daoist philosophy, the basic concept is breath (qi), the existence of which may be proved by the following.

First, the unity of the three in one refers to the unity of heaven, earth and man, and the reason why "heaven, earth and man" can be unified is due to the fact that the breaths of Tian-di-ren are the same. The three Jing-qi-shen (essence, breath, and god) blend to become one, and the reason why Jingqishen can be fused in one is due to the fact that the breaths of the Jingqishen are the same.

Second, the so-called one breath giving birth to the three pure ones means the three most respected worthies of Buddhism were the manifestations of the breath, or the three layers of the most sacred heaven were manifested by breath, or qi. This also shows how the basic concept of Buddhism came to be formed.

Third, although dao (the way) is the highest form of Daoist doctrine. its early period identified three circumstances under which the relationship between dao and qi was highlighted. The first circumstance was that dao is more basic than qi, but dao cannot be isolated from qi. Another circumstance showed that qi is more basic than dao, because Buddhism used qi as its prime mover--for example, Liu Xie in his Mie Huo Lun (On the Extinction of Illusion), while citing Sampolun (The Three Breakthroughs), said "qi is the prime mover of dao." The third circumstance was the synthesis that dao is qi--for example, Tao

Hongjing in his Yangsheng Yanminglu cited Fuqijing (Breathtaking Scripture) that "dao is qi." In studying the philosophical basis of the Daoist canon, if one could analyze the meaning of qi and the conceptual base upon which it is built, one would be able to gain further insight into the various salient features of Buddhism.

Hegel in his Lectures on the History of Philosophy said, "the difference in cultures is due to the difference in the systems of ideas." If we compare Buddhism with other religious systems, the doctrines formulated by Daoist ideas, and the school of thought which formed the basis of these doctrines, we would be able to understand more clearly the characteristics of Buddhism. Although Buddhism is indigenous to the Chinese, it actually owes its development to the inspiration of Buddhism when the latter spread to China. Thus, we are able to identify the rival relationship between Buddhism and Buddhism as one of its special characteristics.

The earliest Daoist scripture, Taiping Jing, on the one hand, shows that it was influenced by Buddhism. For example, it relates to the question of conformity, a concept which was already in use in traditional Chinese thought. But in Taiping Jing this was discussed in such a detailed and outstanding manner that it became obvious that it was influenced by the Hinayanist Zen Buddhist concept of "mind control" or "control of desire." On the other hand, the scripture also shows that it was antagonistic to Buddhism. For example, Taiping Jing's satirical expression, "the way of the four destructions" (sihui zhi xing), was clearly aimed at Buddhism. It also put forward the argument that "one's burden is one's responsibility" (chengfu) as a direct confrontation to the Buddhist concept of "reincarnation" (laishi baoying). After the Eastern Jin, Buddhism gradually developed into a full-fledged religion. It had a theoretical system of its own, and consequently its differentiation from Buddhism became more and more pronounced. At that time, the differences between Buddhism and Buddhism might be related to the following problems: (i) life and death and the form of god; (ii) the cause and effect of one's deeds and misdeeds (yinguo baoying); and (iii) this-worldly and other-worldly orientations. By analyzing of all these issues, we would be able to appreciate the special characteristics of Buddhism as a religion.

In comparing Buddhism and Buddhism, we may encounter yet another question: why does not Buddhism become a world religion as did Buddhism rather than remaining merely a Chinese religion? From the historical point of view, it is possible that Buddhism could have spread to Korea at the end of the Northern and the Southern dynasties.

Sanguo Shiji (The History of the Three Kingdoms) recorded how Buddhism spread to Korea at the beginning of the Tang dynasty but, shortly afterwards, Buddhism became popular in Korea and very soon it outran Buddhism, which thence forward ceased to retain its foothold there. During the same period, Buddhism passed through Korea to Japan, where it might have exercised some influence on Japan's Shinto, though this does not mean that the development of Shinto was due to the Daoist influence. Unlike Buddhism, however, Buddhism also failed to spread its wing over Japan. In history Buddhism had even less influence on other countries (notwithstanding its continuing impact on Chinese devotees who made their homes outside China).

In my opinion, the main reason why Buddhism could not become a world religion is that it not only contains defects in its system of beliefs and practices, but also carries a heavy load of sentiments which are peculiarly Chinese. The goal Buddhism seeks to achieve is "non-death and eternal life" and "the sanctification of bodies." All this differs from the monotheistic doctrine that "the soul does not die." On the one hand, its theoretical arguments, such as "the sanctification of bodies" and "non-death and eternal life" are too crude and difficult to be absorbed. Consequently, Buddhism had no alternative but to take in some Buddhist ideas, such as "when the form ceases, its spirit remains" (xingjin shen bu mie) and "the three kalpas' wheel of karma" (somshi lunhui).

Thus, the spread of Buddhism has been seriously restricted, whereas wherever it goes Buddhism has been able to take the place of Buddhism wherever the latter goes. On the other hand, Buddhism is too closely related to science. For the sake of preserving life, ensuring "non-death and eternal life" and sanctifying the dead it emphasizes a great deal of physical conditioning for lifting the breath (qi) of material reality to the highest level.

Consequently, China's science and technology, especially medicine, came to be developed alongside Buddhism. Buddhism's use of science was bound to curtail its dynamism as a religion.

Thus, the "non-science" and "anti-science" components, in conjunction with the basic qualities of science, began to contradict each other. Religion usually emphasizes "other-worldly orientations," but Buddhism seems to insist instead on "this-worldly orientations" instead. Its adherents believe that they could blend "the three (jing, qi, shen) to become saints" (sanzhe heyi er cheng xian). But as a religious system Buddhism also advocates the unity of the three (tian, di, ren) in one to ensure the Great Peace (sanzhe heyi er zhi taiping) and for this reason can be a potent disruptive force in the political process. In thus fabricating the supernatural world of the saints, Buddhism hopes to translate the real world into an ideal one--this undeniably is a conflict of ideas.

The study of the characteristics of Buddhism is of great importance for it enables us to understand the difference between Buddhism and other religions. By analyzing its characteristics we are able to illuminate the salient features of Chinese culture, psychology and philosophy, as well as the direction of developments in science and technology, medicine and hygiene, and the ensuing shortcomings hidden therein. For a people to succeed in development, they must know not only the present and the future, but also the past.

They must come to grips not only with the reality of political life and economic exigencies, but also with their traditional culture, religious belief and pattern of thought. Herein lies the reason why serious research must be conducted on Buddhism so as to enable us to understand its role as a Chinese religion.

THE DEVELOPMENT OF BUDDHISM

The Process through which Buddhism developed into an organized religion also a clear manifestation of how a religious community came into being.

What is the nature of religion? It can be defined in a great number of ways. Even in Marx's writings, religion is conceived differently under different circumstances. He said, "religion is the opiate of the people," which is interpreted in terms of the use of religion as a way of hypnotising the masses. This statement came not from Marx but Feuerbach. It means that the purveyors of religion who claimed that it could bring comfort to humankind were not being honest. Lenin conceived of "religion as the workers' groaning sound," which is interpreted as relating to the agony of the proletariat. Brezhnev said, "Religion has a countless number of definitions. . . . It may be interpreted as a form of relationship that helps to realize the existence of the mystical superhuman power, for humans believe that they can depend on this power." Brezhnev's definition seems to be more relevant and practical, but is there such a mystical power? How do we adjust to the existence of such a power? Why do people find it necessary to believe in such a power? Is belief in a mystical superhuman power superstitious? This raises some philosophical problems, viz., the problems of religion vis-a-vis superstition and belief.

Is religion a superstition? This question can be debated for a long time and no one knows when it will end, but devout believers most certainly will reject the pronouncement that "religion is superstition." Why? It is because believers frequently rely upon certain ideal principles to interpret what often is called the "mystical superhuman power" in the form of ultimate "truth, goodness, and beauty" (zhen, shan, mei), or else they often look upon the ideals of "truth, goodness, and beauty" as a form of "mystical superhuman power." They sincerely believe it to be true and try very hard to apply these ideals in their social life. Probably the belief in, and dependence upon, this ultimate "truth, goodness and beauty" in the guise of a "mystical superhuman power" is a matter of the human psyche's response to specific social conditions. But believers of the "mystical superhuman power" assume superstition and religion to be two different things. To them, `superstition' can only be a trick played upon those who lack scientific knowledge, i.e. a manifestation of spiritual poverty due to a lack of ideals. Devotees who believe that the "mystical superhuman power" is a manifestation of "truth, goodness, and beauty" may perhaps accept the idea that "religion is synonymous with belief" but certainly will not accept that "religion is superstition." According to them people should have faith: even the agnostics believe in agnosticism.

Religion and belief are undoubtedly related. Religion is based on belief, but whether belief is based on religion, in the classical sense, is a different matter. As a matter of illustration we can say that "we believe in the scientific explanation of atheism" or even accept that "we believe in Confucian philosophy." Nonetheless, there is no doubt that atheism is not a religion, but a scientific doctrine. Even Confucianism may be said to have embodied certain religious elements, although it is not a religion. Therefore, we should distinguish not only between `religion' and `belief,' but also between `religion' and `religious thought.' Otherwise, almost any kind of philosophical discourse could be regarded as a religion, and if that be the case, it would be as good as abnegating the existence of religion.

Based on our understanding of the human psyche, we may postulate that human beings really need a certain kind of belief. The question is whether there is the need for a religious belief. If we could divide religion into two categories--one a scientific belief--and another a non-scientific belief - religion may be said, generally, to belong to the latter category. What follows immediately will be questions like whether human spiritual life requires a certain kind of self-satisfaction obtained from a non-scientific discipline, or whether social life looks upon religious belief itself as a psychological need. This is too gigantic a problem to be discussed here. We can only postulate that for a non-scientific belief to become an organized religion, it must offer some kind of theoretical bases or support. Also, these arguments must be able to reflect the spirit of the time.

If there were no religious teachings to be used as a theoretical system, non-scientific beliefs could become an established religion. Besides, as an established religion, especially one that had colored the history of the social masses, there must be a perduring church organization, a religious canon, a community of devotees, and a history of religion.

In Chinese history, there were thousands of the so-called "religious sects," but not all of them could be regarded strictly as "religious organizations." In fact, a number of them could only be looked upon as "superstitious cults." If that be the case, what then may be thought to be an organized religion? We shall analyze the growth of Buddhism first before illuminating the really meaningful form of religious organization.

An organized religion must have a canon with a philosophical base of its own. The religious teachings should not be nonsensical, but must contain a well-organized system of ideas for the advancement of humankind. The reason why Indian Buddhism has become an influential world religion is that it provides an impressive system of thought which is capable of enlightening the human mind. If Buddhism merely confined itself to a haphazard way of thinking, as is represented in the Taiping Jing, it would have been difficult to become an established religion in China.

Thus, from the end of the Han dynasty, through the Three Kingdoms, till after the Western and Eastern Jin, there emerged Daoists like Ge Hong, Lu Xiujing, Kou Qianzhi, Tao Hongjing and others who, in an attempt to fulfill the requirement of the time, not only integrated some of the Daoist and Confucian ideas but also absorbed some of the Buddhist elements to enrich Buddhism.

A really meaningful and influential religious community must have a formal or more serious form of church organization. Even though the ideas of `immortality' and `the sanctification of the bodies' were subsequently incorporated into the Daoist religion, the saints relied heavily on personal devotion without developing a distinctive church, and so they failed to develop a religion. It was not until the end of the Han dynasty that

Buddhism became an established religion with a permanent membership of disciples, together with a body of clergy and church leaders. However, the regimes of the Three Kingdoms and the Western Jin banned this organization, subjecting it to dissolution until the Eastern Jin when Du Zhigong and others revived it and once again set it on course.

An organized religion must also have a more permanent set of religious teaching and canon. Although Buddhism had its own precepts and canon when it was first instituted at the end of the Eastern Han, they were rather simple and impermanent in nature. From the Eastern Han onward, Buddhism gradually became more firmly established under the impact of Buddhism and with the tireless efforts of Lu Xiujing, Kou Qianzhi and others.

An organized religion must have its own canon and scriptures for the guidance of its believers. Although there were a number of Daoist books, like the Laozi (Lao Tzu) and the Zhuangzi, before the Wei and the Jin dynasties, these books came to be accepted as scriptures only after being popularized by the devotees. All these books were written by Daoist philosophers of the early Qin, and they had hardly any connection with Daoist religion. It was due to the believers' attempt to look for historical evidences that they decided to upgrade them as scriptures.

Taiping Jing, for example, was written before the inception of the Daoist religion. Hence, it served only as a groundwork for the development of Buddhism. However, by the time of the Eastern Jin and the Northern and Southern dynasties, when Buddhism was firmly rooted and a church was organized, a large quantity of scriptures expounding the Daoist canon began to appear (Ge Hong's Pao Pozi, This period saw the appearance of three distinctive categories of scriptures: Sanhuangjing (the Three Emperors Scripture), Shangqingjing (the High Pure Scripture), and Lingbaojing, (the Spirit Protected Scripture). All these scriptures subsequently combined to form the `three caves' (sandong) of the Dizhangjing, namely: the cave of the real (dongzhen), the cave of the gods (dongshen), and the cave of the occult (dongxuan).

An established religion must have a spirit being, or shenling, as a specific object of worship and a history of its own. When Buddhism was first instituted it had inherited part of the saints' tradition. The Daoist disciples claimed that it was imparted to them by the immortals, mostly with Laozi (Lao Tzu)'s assistance. Until the Northern and the Southern dynasties, Daoist disciples created the "rank of the real being" based on the conception of the social hierarchy prevailing at the time.

Tao Hongjing's Zhenlin Yueweitu (Real Spirit's Occupational Status Chart) divided the immortals into seven classes, the highest of which was occupied by the first three: the Primal Lord of Heaven (Yuanshi Tianzun), the Daoist Lord on High (Gaoshang Daojun), and the First Divine Daoist Lord (Yuanhuang Daojun). From then on, these three deities became the most honored in the objects of worship in the Daoist temples (daoguan). Since a religion always finds it necessary to undermine the existence of other competing religions, it has to create a history of its own in order to raise its own status. Thus, being an indigenous Chinese religion, Buddhism had to tackle the entry of alien Buddhism. Besides emphasizing the differences between `Chinese' and `non-Chinese' (huayi zhi bian) to undermine Buddhism, Daoists also spread the story of "Laozi (Lao Tzu) huahu" and elevated Laozi (Lao Tzu)'s position to that of Buddha Sakyamuni's teacher. Consequently, both Buddhism and Buddhism remained in conflict for a long time.

However, it was not until the Eastern Jin and the Northern and Southern dynasties that Buddhism finally became an established religion. The various stages of its development may be summarized as follows. First, from the Eastern Jin onward, the Daoists began to revive their religion by reorganizing the Daoist community which had become scattered and unstable. At the same time, in order to overcome the inadequacy of Daoist teaching and theoretical formulations, Ge Hong and others had provided a body of Daoist canon and precepts. Thereafter, as an attempt to consolidate the founding of the Daoist church, a set of religious teaching was formulated; and in order to propagate Daoist teaching the required scriptures were made available. Lastly, so as to set the religion on a proper footing, a compendium of fairy tales and legendary stories was kept alive. The various phases involved in the development of Buddhism may thus be said to be characteristic of the circumstances under which a religious body came into existence. One of our aims of studying the history of religion is to use it as a source for illuminating the various phases of its development so as to enable us to assess, more accurately, the role it played in society.

3

Indian Culture of Buddhism

INTRODUCTION

The question of the importation of an alien ideological culture and its interaction with an existing native ideological culture is a very complicated one, and there is great significance in studying this problem. Our country's philosophical thinking [and, in fact, its entire culture and society] underwent a major transformation in the time of the Wei and Jin dynasties and the North and South dynasties; it can easily be said that the introduction of Buddhism was one of the most significant causes of this transformation. As for China Buddhism was an alien ideological culture, it is very helpful to study the interaction between the two and the process by which this alien ideological culture integrated with China's own pre-existing traditional ideological culture. This would include its development from being formalistically attached to the body of China's traditional ideological culture, to emerging with its own characteristics which clearly conflicted with and were contradictory to China's ideological culture, and finally to becoming an integral part of the Chinese ideological culture.

The formation of an ideological culture is certain to have its roots in social history; thus in the history of the world various ideological cultures have emerged which are separate and different in both type and form. To understand the characteristics of an ideological culture and the level of its development, one must compare it with other ideological cultures. If we were to compare the Buddhism introduced into China during the period of the Wei, Jin, and North and South dynasties with what existed at that time as China's native traditional ideological culture, we would be able to understand more profoundly not only the characteristics and level of development of that traditional Chinese ideological culture, but also the reasons for which an alien ideological culture was able to be assimilated by the Chinese. The method of analytically studying the comparisons between the ideological culture of one nation [or country or region] and that of another is known as comparative philosophy, which is guided by Marxist thought.

Another significant phenomenon which emerged in the period of the Wei, Jin, and North and South dynasties was the Daoist religion. This was formed in the late years of the Eastern Han dynasty and acquired its own theoretical system. Although it can be said that the formation of the Daoist religion was influenced or stimulated by the introduction of Buddhism, it was nonetheless a religion peculiar to the Chinese, particularly to the Han people, and was bound, therefore, to have characteristics which set it apart from Buddhism. Prior to the Wei and the Jin, Buddhism had just been introduced and in the early stages of its introduction had been grafted to the already existing body of the daoshu [Daoist techniques and crafts].

Hence, the contradictions between the two religions, although already real, were not obvious or outstanding. Since the Wei and Jin, however, because the Daoist religion's own system of thought and theory had gradually formed and because Buddhism, as an imported alien ideological culture, needed to shed gradually its own earlier attachment to the pre-existing native ideological culture, the contradictions and conflict between the two religions became daily more acute and intensified. If we were to analyze and draw comparisons [between these two religions] on the issues upon which they debated, it would be easy for us to see more clearly the characteristics of the Daoist religion as well as the mutual influence which their two religions had upon one another in the midst of their contradictions and polemical struggles. This is the task of those who undertake the study of comparative religion. At this time, we ought also to develop and promote this field of investigation, so that we may form a comparative study of religions, guided, also, by Marxist thought.

What were the most notable characteristics in Buddhism after it was introduced into China and as it became popularized and developed in China? What are the ones we should study and what general laws [of development] can we extract from [such a study]? What conclusions can be drawn? In the following discussion we shall suggest three major problem areas for analysis.

Adaptation to Tradition

When Buddhism was introduced into China at first it was grafted upon the body of pre-existing Chinese ideological culture; then it gradually developed on its own and began to exert its own influence on that culture and Chinese society. It should be understood that Buddhism did not have a great deal of influence immediately after its introduction.

After being introduced into China in the Han dynasty, Buddhism at first attached itself to the daoshu. In the Wei and Jin period, because of the popularity and influence of xuanxue [Daoist metaphysics] Buddhism switched and was attached to the latter. During the time of the Han dynasty, thc central tenets of [Chinese] Buddhism were "the imperishability of the soul, or spirit," and "causes and effects." These were ideas that were already originally carried within traditional Chinese thought, or, in some cases, were at least similar in ways to certain ideas which already existed in Chinese philosophical traditions.

Furthermore, the Hinayana methods of chan meditation [dhyana] which were preached at that time also generally were quite similar to the breathing exercises taught by the Huang-Lao School of Daoism (Taoism) and the Immortality [shen xian jia] school. By the time of the Wei and Jin Daoist metaphysical teachings had become popular, and, since Kong zong [the Emptiness sect] of Buddhist prajna teachings was somewhat similar to these Daoist metaphysical teachings, this branch of Buddhism was therefore able to gain popularity by attaching itself to the body of xuanxue. However, it was not until Kumarajiva translated the sutras and commentaries [sastras] such as the Zhong lun that the Chinese understanding of the teachings of the Kong zong of Indian Buddhist prajna philosophy came close to capturing the original intents of those teachings. From the above brief description, we can see that, when Buddhism was first introduced into China, it had first to exist as an attachment, or graft, on the body of some previously existing ideology, and only thus was it able to achieve popularity of its own.

There is one question here which needs to be raised and calls for some discussion. When Zhi-lou-jian translated the Dao Xing Jing [Sutra on the Practice, or Way, of the Truth] in the year 179 A.D., there was in it a pin [segment, or folio] known as the ben wu pin [segment of Original Nothingness]. This appeared long before the [xuanxue] ideas of gui wu [exalting nothingness] and yi wu wei ben [taking nothingness as the origin] which are identified with He Yan [190-249] and Wang Bi [226-249]. Does this then mean that Wang and He's idea of "taking nothingness as the origin" was a product, a result of the influence of Buddhism? We do not believe that this is the answer; it would accord with the facts of the historical record to think that Daoist metaphysical thinking [or, xuanxue] was generated only under the influence of Buddhism.

First of all, the formation of Daoist metaphysical thinking responded to the social needs at the time. Moreover, the emergence of xuanxue should be considered in the light and context of other intellectual developments, either of the period or slightly earlier. These include the development of the teachings of ming li zhi xue [on names and principles] and the distinction between cai [ability] and xing [nature, or character] which appeared during the interim period between the fall of the Han and the rise of Wei, as well as the revival of various schools of Confucianism, Daoism (Taoism), the School of Names [Ming jia] and Legalism, and their mutual intersection and influence. This makes it possible to see that, from the angle of certain inevitable trends in ideological and intellectual development, this emergence of xuanxue was a product of the natural processes of China's indigenous intellectual evolution.

We have not found any convincing evidence that Wang Bi and He Yan were influenced by Buddhism. Even if one or two pieces of evidence were to be discovered indicating that Wang, He, and company may have been in contact with the Buddhism of the day, either directly or indirectly, nonetheless we must still maintain that the ideas of xuanxue were products of the development of preexisting indigenous Chinese ideas themselves. Furthermore, there is a great deal of evidence showing that by and large, during the Han-Wei period, the Chinese officer-scholar gentry did not in the least think highly of Buddhism. For instance, Mouzi in Li huo lun [Treatise on the Disposition of Error] said for the record that "the people of the age, and scholars, mostly sneer at it [i.e., Buddhism] and defame it," and, "we have not heard that, among the rules and teachings accepted by the five talents or among the discussions taken up in the Forest of Confucianist Scholars, the practicing of the ways of Buddha is valued or self-disfigurement is esteemed."

One thing serves to illustrate this point even more clearly and conclusively, namely that, while in the prajna Buddhist teachings of the time the term ben wu [original nothingness] was used, it did not mean the same thing as Wang Bi's idea of yi wu wei ben [taking nothingness to be the origin]. In the various prajna sutras, the idea of ben wu was taken to mean that "all fa [dharma] do not have ontological self-substance" [zhu fa ben wu zi xing]--that is, that all things did not, in and of themselves, have real substance. This, if fact, negated the notion that there was original substance to things. When Wang Bi spoke of ben wu [original nothingness], on the other hand, he meant that "nothingness was the original substance"--that is, ontological reality--of existence [wu shi you di ben ti].

The Buddhist teachings that were imported into China in the Wei-Jin period were for the most part teachings of the Mahayana prajna Kong zong [Emptiness school]. Its fundamental premise was that "all things did not originally have ontological substance, or self-substance" [zi xing]. In this, the term fa [dharma] referred to all things, material but also spiritual. These were known as adharma in the Buddhist sutras. In the Da bo you jing [Great Collection of Prajna Sutras], volume 556, we find the following passage:

> *Take ourselves, for instance; we are, ultimately, not life. We are jia ming [false names or unreal names] [i.e., we are illusions, or falsehoods.] We have no zi xing [self-nature, or nature in and of ourselves]. Likewise, all dharma--they too are nothing but false names, and no nature in and of themselves. What is se [appearance]? It cannot be assumed and cannot be born. What is shou [acceptance, or destiny] or xiang [thought] or xing [action] or shi [perception, or understanding]? They, too, are incapable of being assumed or being born.*

The Kong zong [Emptiness school] of prajna teaching believed that while people have always held to the notion that there was something which could be called you wuo [having oneself, or self-existence], i.e., zi ti [self-substance], they have done so without realizing that "self" was nothing but the combination produced by the five elements [wu yin] of se [appearance], shou [acceptance or destiny], xiang [thought], xing [action], and shi [perception or understanding]. They were indeed wrong to have believed that there was such a thing as "self." How could "self" exist apart from or independent of these five elements? Therefore, it argued, the term "self" was really nothing but a hypothesis, an unreal name [jia ming], and did not contain any self-nature. Not only was this true of people but of all dharma [things] as well. Therefore, the Guan si ti pin [Segment of the Meditation on the Catvariarya satyani, or Four Noble True Statements] in the Zhong lun argued:

> The various causes and effects generate the dharma. The idea of self is but an idea of emptiness, and also a false name. This is the meaning of the Central Way, or the Mean.

The argument here, apparently, was that, since all things were generated by causes and effects, there is in reality no such thing as zi xing [self-nature, or real self-substance] but only kong [non-existence]. The idea of self, therefore, is itself a "non-existence."

However, although things did not contain "self-substance," there are, nonetheless, all sorts of separate phenomena in the world after all. What then are such things? To say that they do not have real existence; still possible, however, are all sorts of unreal existences or phenomena. For purposes of convenience, the argument went, these are given hypothetical, or false, names. The Fangguang banruo jing [Prajnaparamita Sutra Emitting Light] said:

> *Buddha spoke thus to Subhuti [One of the Ten Major Disciples of Buddha, said to have been the best exponent of the Sunya, or Doctrine of the Void--Tr.]: Names are not real; an unreal designation is given and is known as a name, or as the five yin [elements] or as a human being, man or woman.*

The Monk Shao, in Bu zhen kong lun, provided the following explanation:

> *The Fangguang [sutra] said: All dharma have false designations which are not real. For example, Man is the product of the transformation of illusions; this is not to say that there is no man who is the product of the transformation of illusions, but simply that Man who is the product of the transformation of illusions is not really Man [i.e., there is no reality to Man who is produced by the transformation of illusions].*

This raises a secondary question which must be discussed here. Does the idea of kong [emptiness or non-existence] in the saying "self, as it is expressed, is kong, or empty or non-existent" [wuo shuo ji shi kong] signify the position that while things, phenomenologically speaking, did not really exist, there was, nonetheless, an ontologically real "non-existence" [similar to Wang Bi's ontologically real wu, or non-being] which itself was true? This, we shall see, was not the viewpoint of the Kong zong [Emptiness school] of prajna Buddhist teaching. To the adherents of the Kong zong, kong simply referred to the absence "of ontological self-substance in all dharma." This arose because the dictum "dharma is produced or generated by causes and effects; the statement of self is itself non-existent" was proposed for the very purpose of dispelling people's insistence on holding to the idea of real ontological substance in all things. But if people were simply to switch to insist on [the idea of the reality of] non-existence, alluded to in the sentence "the statement of self is itself a non-existence," then the purpose would be defeated, because people would still be insisting on the reality of something-i.e., of "non-existence." That is why, the Kong zong believed, it was necessary to add: "Even this [non-existence itself] is but a false name." Hence the formulation, completed, would be: Not only are the names of things, i.e., phenomena, jia ming [false names] and merely hypothetical; kong [emptiness, or non-existence] itself is a false name also.

Volume 556 of the Da Bo You Jing contained this parable:

At one time, the various sons of heaven asked He Who Appeared in Goodness [a name for Buddha]: Is it possible to be in Nirvana and still revert to the realm of illusion? He Who Appeared in Goodness replied: If there was a thing [dharma] that overcame Nirvana and yet, then, reverted to the state of illusion, what would Nirvana then be?

One must, therefore, not only understand that all dharma do not have real ontological substance; one must at the same time not insist on [the reality of] non-existence. The Da zhi du lun [Treatise on the Ferrying Across by Means of the Great Wisdom] said:

The situation is like the taking of medicine. Medicine can dispel the sickness. When the illness has been dispelled, the medicine should also be expelled. If not, then an illness will be acquired. Kong [non-existence] is something that was used to dispel all our troubles, but we should be wary lest kong itself remain to plague us. Therefore, what we suggest is that we must use kong to shed kong--that is, we must understand the non-existence of non-existence itself.

This means that the assertion of "non-existence" was for the purpose of dispelling the insistence on existence. When and if the notion of existence has been dispelled, the time would come for one to know that "non-existence" is itself an illusion, an unreality, or false name. Yet one cannot say that all is "non-existence" (because there is still, for example, Man who is the product of the transformation of illusions). To understand both of these aspects would be to achieve the Zhong dao guan [True Meditation of the Middle Way, or Mean]. It was, however, not until the late years of the Eastern Jin dynasty, after Kumarajiva had already translated such treatises as the Zhong lun, that this idea of "not existence and yet not non-existence" [fei you fei wu] was truly accepted and understood among Chinese Buddhists and epitomized in the Bu zhen kong lun of the Monk Shao.

Prior to the time of the Monk Shao, the general understanding which the Chinese monks had regarding prajna teaching was on the whole derived from the perspectives of the Daoist metaphysical [xuanxue] thought which was popular at the time. This is something we have already discussed. To further substantiate this argument, let us now analyze again some of the problems raised in connection with Dao An's theory of Original Nothingness. We have, earlier, cited the following passage from Ji Kang (Chi Kang)'s Zhong Lun Shu[Commentary on the Treatise of the Mean]:

When Master An expressed [the doctrine of] Original Nothingness, he meant that all dharma's original nature was emptiness and extinction. That is why he said "Original Nothingness."

Is this not the same idea as that contained in the saying: "All dharma do not originally have any ontological self-substance"? In fact it is not. The sentence here, "all dharma's original nature is emptiness and extinction," meant that emptiness and extinction made up the original nature of all dharma, or, in other words, all things have emptiness and extinction for their original nature or ontological substance. This was an interpretation that could be traced as far back as the Monk Hui Da's Shao lun Shu[Commentary on the Arguments of the Monk Shao]. There he criticized Dao An's theory of Original Nothingness by saying: "[He, Dao An,] was simply unable to realize that originally all dharma was nothing; and therefore he called original non-existence real, but resulting existence vulgar."

The same idea was contained in An Cheng's Zhong Lun Shu[Commentary on the Treatise of the Mean], which said: "The Bie ji [Alternative Record] says" 'The true statement [zhen ti] is the origin of the vulgar statement [shu ti].' That is why we say that Non-existence existed prior to the Original, or Primeval, Transformation." From all the above illustrations, we can see that, in Dao An's understanding of kong [non-existence] or wu [non-being], he still took them to be the ontological substance for you [existence].

Why did such a set of circumstances come about? Because, as Engels pointed out, tradition is an immense force of conservatism. It appears that every ideological cultural tradition is bound to have its conservative aspect which resists imported alien ideological cultural influences. For that reason, an imported ideological culture must first adapt itself to the requirements and demands of the originally existing native ideological culture and be grafted onto its body. Those elements within the imported ideological culture which are relatively close to the original native ideological culture or which resemble it will be easier to be propagated; only then, after the grafting and the initial propagation, will it be possible for the various parts of the imported culture gradually to infiltrate the original culture and exert some of their own influence, until eventually [the imported culture] modifies, or effects transformations in, the original ideological cult

INTENSIFICATION OF TRADITION

When an imported ideological culture is capable of having a relatively great impact on the country [or nation or region] to which it was imported, in addition to the real and practical societal needs, this would often also occur because the imported culture in general approximated a potential or possible product of the evolution--or certain aspects of the evolution--of the original indigenous ideological culture itself.

It is possible to trace a line of development in the ideas of xuanxue [Daoist metaphysics] from Wang Bi and He Yan's ideas of gui wu [valuing nothingness or non-being] which were based on the notion of "taking non-being as the origin" to Guo Xiang's idea of cong you [exalting being] which was based on the notion of "all things generating themselves" [wan wu zi sheng]. Subsequently, the ideas of Zhang Zhan emerged during the time of the Eastern Jin, which were exemplified in the saying, "Things are generated by themselves spontaneously and instantly, and yet they share one common origin in non-being" [fu er er zi sheng, ze ben tong yu wu]. What then followed in this line of development was the notion of "not being and yet not non-being" [fei you fei wu]. This was similar to the doctrine of "not real non-existence" [bu zhen kong] in the Kong zong [Emptiness school] of prajna Buddhist teaching. Why was it possible for Wei-Jin Daoist metaphysics to develop into the idea of "not being and yet not non-being?" One may say that this was a "potential" product of the evolution of Wei-Jin Daoist metaphysics, or, in other words, it can be said that such an evolution was not only not antithetical or contradictory to the essence of Wei-Jin Daoist metaphysics; it was in fact an enrichment of Wei-Jin Daoist metaphysics.

Beginning with Wang Bi and He Yan, and particularly in the case of Wang Bi, Wei-Jin Daoist metaphysical thought carried out rather penetrating examinations and logical reasoning on the question of the relationship between you [being] and wu [non-being]. Wang Bi used the idea of ti [substance] and yong [effect, function, usage, or phenomenon] to illustrate the relationship between being and non-being. He posited that "non-being cannot be without expression, and therefore must have cause in being." Therefore he believed that, while "non-being" was the ontological substance, it was contained in "being" and had expression in "being." Therefore he viewed substance [ti] and use [yong] as essentially one and the same thing. However, since there was an emphasis in Wang

Bi's system of thought on the absoluteness of "non-being," the idea of "exalting the origin and ending the result" [cong ben shi mo] emerged. This brought about an inconsistency in Wang Bi's system of thought. From the perspective of this cong ben shi mo idea, it can be said that there was a notion of negating the being, or, an idea of "not being." Through Xiang Xiu and Pei Wei, Wang Bi's idea of gui wu [valuing the non-being] later made the transition to Guo Xiang's idea of cong you [exalting being].

In Guo's view, being was the only existence, and there was nothing that existed over and beyond wan wu [all things] and that could have served as the ontological substance for wan you [i.e., a Creator substance]. He believed that the existence of all things was based on their respective "self-nature" [zi xing] and that this self-nature was generated spontaneously and instantaneously. For this reason he argued: "Non-being is non-being; that is it. It cannot generate being." In this way he directly challenged and refuted the idea of an ontologically substantial non-being. This idea in itself contained the notion of "not non-being."

In the Eastern Jin dynasty, Zhang Zhan wrote a commentary and annotations to the book Lie Zi, and in it he attempted to bring together in his own way the ideas of Wang Bi and Guo Xiang. On the one hand he argued that "all beings [qun you] have the Ultimate Void [zhi xu] as their ancestor [zong]"--i.e., wu [non-being] or zhi xu [the Ultimate Void] was the basis for the existence of you [being]. This was his idea of wu as ontological substance. To him, Non-being was neither created nor perishable; it does not come together and does not dissipate, whereas all being is created and is perishable, and clusters and dissipates. Moreover, he believed that all species [wan pin] have their ultimate test in their ultimate perishability and, therefore, are "not being." Yet, at the same time, Zhang argued that all things were instantaneously and spontaneously created--their existence was neither purposeful nor conditional. This had the potential or possibility of leading toward the idea of "not non-being."

Nevertheless, in the case of Zhang Zhan, these two ideas were put together mechanistically and were mutually incompatible and contradictory. His system of thought was not one which was tightly woven. And yet, incidentally, it was at this juncture that prajna Buddhist teachings, in particular those of the Kong zong, posited the idea of fei you fei wu [not being and yet not non-being], which itself was far more solid and tightly argued in theory and reasoning methods.

For that reason, one can say that the doctrine of the Bu zhen kong lun [Treatise on the Fallacy of Real Nothingness] proposed by the Monk Shao was a development of the ideas of xuanxue [Daoist metaphysics] after Wang Bi and Guo Xiang. Although the ideas of the Monk Shao came directly from Indian prajna Buddhist teaching, they in fact became an important component of Chinese philosophy itself and helped to make up the following circle in the development of Wei-Jin xuanxue-Wang Bi-Guo Xiang-the Monk Shao.

Why was such a development possible? One may ascribe it to the demands or requirements of the heritage or continuity of ideological cultures [as they came into contact with one another]. As long as the development of an ideological culture is not drastically interrupted, what follows must be the product of a continuous evolution from what preceded it.

The development of preceding ideas often would contain several possibilities, and the idea(s) which would continue to be developed, representing the subsequent parts of the development, would be bound to take the shape of one or another of these possibilities.

If an imported alien ideological culture can, on the whole, adapt or conform to a certain aspect of a potential or possible development of the original indigenous culture and ideology [or fit into a trend or tendency of one of the possible developments], not only will it be itself developed and thus exert relatively great influence in itself, but it may even become directly a component part of the original indigenous ideological culture and perhaps even to some extent alter the course of the development of that original ideological culture.

REAL CONTRIBUTION

If an imported alien ideological culture affects the original indigenous ideological culture, and if this is not a temporary influence but a long lasting one, in some aspects or even in all aspects in general it would have to achieve a higher level of development than that of the indigenous culture. Only in this way can the imported ideological culture serve as a stimulus to the native culture and affect the development of the native culture itself.

Whether or not the level of development and sophistication in reasoning achieved by the Kong zong [Emptiness school] of Indian prajna Buddhist teaching was generally higher than that of China's own native and traditional ideological culture which existed at that time is a question which may not be realistically and honestly resolved until very careful and meticulous analysis has been made.

This is not a problem which we may attempt to discuss here. However, in one specific aspect of its ways of reasoning and philosophizing, namely, its analysis of the questions of being and non-being [you wu], the Kong zong of prajna Buddhism, in postulating the dialectical thesis of "not being and yet not non-being" [fei you fei wu], clearly demonstrated a superior level of theory and reasoning in comparison with the ideas of Wang Bi and Guo Xiang, although its own ideas, like those of Wang and Guo, were drawn from the general source of idealism. In terms of development, although it appeared to have been derived out of Wang Bi and Guo Xiang's xuanxue thought, the Monk Shao's doctrine of bu zhen kong [not real emptiness] was closer to the original intents of the Kong zong's teachings and should be acknowledged as having made certain advances beyond Wang and Guo's ideas.

As I see it, it was after the baptism of the introduction and assimilation of prajna philosophy introduced from India that the idealist philosophies of the Chinese tradition became themselves a truly influential and meaningful system of thought. In them, the doctrine of the Creator [a spiritual ontological substance which created Heaven and Earth and all things] no longer occupied a central position.

In its stead, abstract concepts such as li [principle] or dao [Way], which determined, rather than personally created, the existence of Heaven, Earth, and all things, were put into the position of first or primal importance. In another case, it was the mind that was put into that position, as in ideas which posited that "mind equals principle" [xin ji li] or "the principle is possessed in the mind" [li ju yu xin]; i.e., the notions that the principles of Heaven, Earth, and all things were all present in the mind. It was only after such idealistic concepts were developed that the fundamental forms of China's traditional idealist philosophy were set. This itself set the stage for the emergence of the li xue [neo-Confucianist philosophy of Principle] in the Song and Ming dynasties, whether it be the Cheng and Zhu [Cheng Hao, Cheng Yi, and Zhu Xi] school or the Lu-Wang [Lu Xiangshan, Wang Yangming] school.

However, for an imported alien ideological culture, even one with a relatively higher level of development in reasoning, to have a great and long-lasting impact on the country [nation or region] to which it is introduced, it not only would have to subject itself, nonetheless, to the limitations of the political and socioeconomic conditions of the host country, nation, or region, but it must also be in possession of the first and second sets of conditions described in the afore-discussed sections. This is particularly true of ideological cultures, especially if the original, indigenous ideological culture did not experience an abrupt and radical interruption, or if such an interruption was not to be caused by the introduction of the alien culture. Only in such a way could the new culture affect the original culture in a profound and long-lasting way. Without these conditions, no matter how advanced or superior the imported ideological culture may be, it would be difficult for it to strike roots into the soil of the host country and over the long run exert any deep influence.

For example, the Wei shi [Vidjnana, or Consciousness Only school] teachings of Buddhism introduced [later] by the [Tang dynasty] Monk Xuan Zang, and the related teachings of vidjna [yin ming, or hetuvidya, or nyaya teachings] which were introduced at about the same time and in conjunction with the Consciousness Only school, were also superior in the levels of their reasoning and development, and yet, though they gained much ground in establishing a reputation for themselves for a time, they did not eventually have a very long-lasting impact on the development of Chinese thought as a whole. Even though specific categories of thought in the Consciousness Only [Wei shi] school, such as the dual categories of neng [ability or possibility] and suo [identity or proper placement], were individually absorbed into Chinese thought, on the whole the Wei shi school did not become an integrated component of the Chinese traditional ideological culture, and to this day we still have the tendency to think of the Wei shi [vidjnana, or Consciousness Only] teachings as an Indian ideology.

Out of the three points of argumentation outlined above, we may draw out one proposition: that it is meaningful, at least in one aspect, to focus the comparative study of philosophies on the general and historical laws which govern the extent to which an imported alien ideological culture may influence [the ideological culture(s) of] the country, or nation or region to which it was introduced, and on the conditions without which such an influence may not take place. In comparing and analyzing, for example, two ideological cultures which stemmed from different traditions we must understand, first, the characteristics and level of development and reasoning which have been achieved by the original indigenous ideological culture [i.e., that which, of the two, is the host culture] and, second, the differences and similarities between these two cultures, their mutual influences, their assimilation and conflict, the amelioration of their conflict, and so on.

As we study the introduction of Buddhism from India to China in the first century A.D., and its subsequent development we must ask its meaning for the practical way of life today. The tendencies in the development of current world ideological cultures are manifested as patterns conflict and harmony between many different ideological cultures stemming from many different traditions. The instability, contradictions and conflicts in the world today may also be ascribed, in addition to certain other [political and economic] factors, in part to differences in ideological and cultural [i.e., philosophical and religious] traditions. The contradictions between the Arab and Islamic world, on the one hand, and the West, on the other, for example, are themselves fraught with philosophical and religious factors. At the same time, because of the increasing frequency and intimacy in terms of intercultural contacts in today's world, the propensity for mutual interaction and influence and for harmonization and assimilation between various ideological cultures is also very obvious.

In particular, the broad spread of Marxism throughout the world today has provided many new lessons to be learned and emulated in the relations between ideological cultures which stem from different traditions and backgrounds. Marxism itself was generated in Western Europe under historical conditions peculiar to Western Europe and therefore as an ideological culture it was alien to many other parts of the world. Out of this, problems have surfaced in the relationship between Marxism and the various indigenous ideological cultures of the places to which it has been introduced. Even though Marxism is a proletarian philosophy and the cause of the proletariat is not confined by national boundaries--[Marxism] is the ideological weapon with which the proletariat and the revolutionary peoples of all countries carry out their revolutionary struggles--in order for Marxism to take root in any country [or nation or region] in a certain sense it will still have to become integrated with the native ideological culture of that country [nation or region]. Or, shall we say, it must undertake critically to carry on the legacy of that original indigenous ideological cultural tradition. Unless this is achieved, Marxism will not be able to exert any real influence.

Is it possible then for Marxism to be enriched and furthered in its development by, say, the study of the relations between Marxism and China's traditional indigenous ideological culture?

We believe so. In the essay "The Task of the Youth League," Lenin said: "It is only when we have indeed understood fully the culture which is created through the entire developmental process of humanity at large, and are capable of transforming this culture of the past, that we can proceed to construct a truly proletarian culture." Undoubtedly Marxism is a methodology which will guide us in dealing accurately with our various ideological cultural traditions. It is "not a doctrine, but a methodology. It provides, not ready-made dogma, but points of departure for further investigation and a methodology which may be employed in such an investigation" (see The Complete Works of Marx and Engels [Chinese edition], vol. 39, p. 406]).

It should be acknowledged that in the history of human civilization each nation or people had, and has, its own special contribution to make. If we were to study, with the correct method, these contributions, we would be able to render accurate assessments regarding them and turn these assessments into parts of the legacy of the spiritual civilization of humanity, which we are to inherit. It is not the intent of Marxism to reject the spiritual cultures which have made contributions to the human society; rather, it hopes to absorb them, and transform them, and in the process continue to enrich and develop itself.

PHILOSOPHIES AND RELIGIONS

The present age is vastly different from past ages. As the world marches into the 1980s, developments in science and technology and social progress have made the interaction between the various countries and nations of the world immensely different from that of the past when the world was still in a stage of feudalism.

These objective circumstances compel us to absorb imported alien ideological cultures more quickly. What methods can we use to turn those parts of alien ideas which are of use and value to us more speedily into integrated parts of our own ideological culture? One important method would be to engage in the comparative study of philosophies. In the past, the absorption of alien ideological cultures as a natural and spontaneous process was often slow and sluggish, and incidental and accidental factors tended to have a great deal of influence on the process. If we were to carry out such work today in a conscious and deliberate fashion, we are bound to be able to absorb the valuable and refined portions of an alien ideological culture more speedily. This problem applies to Marxism as well.

If we are able to deal correctly with the relationship between Marxism and our own ideological cultural tradition, so that Marxism may become even more compatible with the circumstances and sentiments of the people in our country, if we may create a Sinicized Marxism, then it not only would take deeper and stronger roots in China, but would also more effectively absorb and retain the good and valuable parts of Chinese ideological cultural tradition and expel those which are valueless or corrupted so that our country's fine spiritual culture may be further developed. Therefore, the establishment of comparative philosophical studies under the guidance of Marxism is a most important task for us. The question is, how we should undertake the study of comparative philosophy?

THE SEARCH FOR COMMON LAWS

In comparatively studying two ideological cultures from different traditions we should attend to the discovery of certain common laws which govern the evolution of human ideological culture.

The study of comparative philosophy, like the comparative study of religions and literature, has a specific meaning of its own. The study of comparative philosophy does not mean simply the comparison between two, any two, philosophers (taking, for instance, Zhu Xi and Wang Shouren [Wang Yangming]), any more than the study of comparative religion means the simple comparison of any two Buddhist monks [say, Zhi Dun and Dao An].

Comparative philosophy or comparative religion refers to comparing two systems of philosophical thought which stem from different traditions, or two religious systems that come from different sources and origins. Therefore, such comparative studies must be comparative analyses of two different countries [such as China and India] or regions [such as East and West] or nations [such as the Chinese people and some other nationality].

Philosophy is the most general science in the study of Nature, society, and human reasoning, and the laws which govern the development of human thought are, fundamentally speaking, similar or for the most part identical. Thus, when we have understood the laws which governed and sustained the evolution of the philosophical thought of a certain ideological cultural tradition, analyze the philosophical thoughts of another ideological cultural tradition promises to be of great help. In "On the Problems of the Dialectical Method," Lenin said:

[These are] the circles which describe the history of philosophy: The Ancient World: Dialectics from Democritus through Plato to Heraclitus; The Modern Age: Feuerbach to Hegel [through Berkeley, Hume, and Kant]; Hegel to Feuerbach to Marx.

In his "Outline to Hegel's 'Notes on the History of Philosophy'" Lenin also said:

> *It is possible to see the history of philosophy in terms of circles . . . Each type of philosophical thinking equals a smaller circle on the big circle (spiral) of the evolution of human thought.*

Hegel's idea of "the history of Philosophy as a circle," which Lenin cited in the above-mentioned essays, is not only a law which summarizes the development of Western thought, but also a profound reflection of the general law of the history of the development of philosophy and of thought in the universal sense. If we took this idea to be a compass to guide us in studying the laws which governed the development of traditional Chinese philosophy, we could see that, in general, traditional Chinese philosophy was also made up of three major spirals? The first would be the philosophy of the pre-Qin period: From Confucius to Mencius to Xunzi [through the philosophies of other schools of the time]: the second would be Wei-Jin xuanxue

[Daoist metaphysics]: Wang Bi to Guo Xiang to the Monk Shao; the third would be Song-Ming neo-Confucianism: Zhang Zai to Zhu Xi to Wang Fuzhi.

Between these three circles, which are to be seen as being put together as spirals, there would be the connecting tissues of development--the Han Classical scholarship [jingxue] which made up the transition from the first circle to the second one, and the development of Sui-Tang Buddhism, which made up the transition from the second circle to the third. Together these three ascending circles would make up a vast circle which would express the whole of Chinese philosophical tradition: from the pre-Qin and Han philosophy, whose primary substance was Confucianism; to the Wei-Jin and Sui-Tang philosophy, whose primary substance was xuanxue [metaphysics] built on the foundation and framework of the ideas of Laozi (Lao Tzu) and Zhuangzi as well as a gradually Sinicized Buddhism; to the neo-Confucianism [Song-Ming Confucianism], which absorbed the thought of both Daoism (Taoism) and Buddhism, and on that basis developed [Confucianism] to a higher stage of evolution.

In the book Comparative Religion F. B. Jevons cited one example which quite clearly demonstrated the general significance of the study of comparative religion. He said that it was difficult to understand, or explain, the demotion of the Thunder God in the religion of ancient Babylon from his original status to the rank of a demon. The answer seemed to lie, he also said, in the study of comparative religion and its methodology, because in the history of the development of various religions we often encounter in the history of the development of various religions, the phenomenon of deities of an earlier religion being demoted to another rank in a new religion when the older, earlier religion is overcome and replaced. In this case, the method of the study of comparative religion provides us with a rational explanation for such a phenomenon as the demotion of the Thunder God of Babylon to the rank of a demon. At the present time, the methods of comparative studies generally fall into two categories: namely, "parallel studies" and "influence studies." The former refers to conducting comparative studies between two different ideological cultures which do not have direct or indirect influences upon one another, and yet between whom there obviously are comparable points. In this case, the task would be to discover the similar as well as the dissimilar phenomena between the two and to demonstrate common laws and dissimilar, individual qualities. The latter is to conduct comparative studies where there are direct or indirect mutual influences, or, in some cases, unilateral influence, in order to discover the shared phenomena as well as points of dissimilarity so as to demonstrate the contradictions, conflicts, assimilations and compromises that exist between them.

No matter to which category it may belong, when a comparison is made it should not simply draw one or two elements from the ideological culture of a country, nation, or region and study them in comparison with a few sayings or one or two isolated phenomena from the ideological culture of another country, nation, or region. This would be what is known as piecemeal comparison which, strictly speaking, has hardly anything to do with the study of comparative philosophy or comparative religion. The comparative study of two different ideological cultural traditions ought to be conducted on the basis of a rather comprehensive and exhaustive comparison of a problem or problems found in both traditions. Only in this way can we discover the phenomena [within each] which reflect the presence of laws, and only then can we be led from knowledge or its absence to knowledge regarding this particular law of the development of human ideological culture, and from the understanding of the individual to an understanding of the general.

THE SPECIFIC CHARACTERISTICS OF A CULTURE

In undertaking to study comparatively the ideological cultures of two different traditions, we should base conclusions on the special characteristics and features of both of these cultures. Only when a certain ideological culture is compared and analyzed in the light of a different ideological cultural tradition that its own special characteristics and features can become clarified. It is impossible to express the special characteristics of an ideological culture when it is studied only by itself or internally.

In the first and second part of this essay we discussed the fact that, although there were apparent similarities between metaphysics [xuanxue] in China during the Wei-Jin period and the prajna teachings of Indian Buddhism, they ultimately were separate and not the same, each having its own special characteristics. We were able to draw such a conclusion because we had made a comparative study of these two ideological cultures which stemmed from separate traditions.

For example, we came to know that the analysis which Wei-Jin xuanxue made of "being" and "non-being" was made from the angle or perspective of "existence," that is, from the perspective of the relationship between "ontological substance" and "phenomenon," with the latter being seen as the various expressions of ontological substance. Indian prajna Buddhist teaching, on the other hand, often analyzed wu [or kong, or non-existence] and you [being] as a pair of abstract concepts.

Therefore, although both may have appeared to be speaking of ben wu [nothingness or origin], when Wang Bi employed the term he was referring to the idea of yi wu wei ben [taking nothingness to be the origin]--i.e., non-being [wu] being the substance behind being [you]--whereas when prajna teaching used the same term it referred to the idea that "all dharma did not have original self-nature" [zhu fa ben wu zi xing]. In this latter formulation, wu [or kong, or non-existence] did not refer to substance, but rather [to the idea] that all things did not have real self-substance [zi ti] and therefore that the existence of all things was merely illusory. Furthermore, the method of reasoning behind Wei-Jin metaphysics and that behind Indian Buddhist prajna teaching were also different. The tendency for the Indian Buddhist prajna teachers was to employ an analytical method to reason out their viewpoints whereas the Wei-Jin xuanxue metaphysicists would reason by way of the philosophical methods represented by such sayings as: de yi wang yan [Once the meaning, or intent, is attained, the words may be forgotten] and ji yu chu yan [The meaning resides outside of the words, which are only its temporary abode].

For example, in the Kong zong [Emptiness school] of prajna Buddhism, the postulate "all dharma did not originally have self-nature" [zhu fa ben wu zi xing] would often be analyzed in the following logical manner:

(1) When things are analyzed at the utmost level of minutiae, further analysis would, presumably, bring the object of analysis to the realm of lin xu [the neighborhood of Void or Nothingness]. That is, further analysis would bring about the logical conclusion that the object of analysis does not really have substance or a self--thus the saying: "Observe and contemplate the minutiae of things; when the final minutiae is reached, there would be found no substance."

(2) When one analyzes things from the angle of the relationship between time and object, one will understand that neither wu xiang [material or physical phenomenon or appearance] nor xin xiang [mental or psychological phenomenon] is real. First, all things are generated instantaneously and also perish equally instantaneously, that is, all things are no sooner generated than they perish. Second, nothing lasts at all, that is, not things are first generated and then perish, but that they are generated and perish all at once: generation and perishing happen at one and the same time. For these two reasons therefore things cannot be said to have any real self-substance.

(3) The analysis of the object itself leads inevitably to the conclusion that it is made up of the combination of causes and effects and therefore it does not have any real ontological substance of its own. Since all dharma does not have real self-substance, all things or phenomena are therefore without original existence--

thus the saying: "not that appearances (phenomena) perish, but that they are non-existent."

The method which the Wei-Jin xuanxue [Daoist metaphysics] scholars, such as Wang Bi, used to argue for their idea of "having origin in non-being" [yi wu wei ben] was very different from that of the prajna Buddhists. In the Laozi (Lao Tzu) Zhi Lue [An Outline of the Intentions of Laozi (Lao Tzu)], Wang Bi said:

The cause for the generation of a thing and the fulfilling of its achievement is this: It must be born of the Form-less [wu xing] and have origin in the Name-less [wu ming]. The Form-less and the Name-less is the origin of all things. It is neither warm nor cold, neither gong nor shang [Gong and shang are sounds of special characters--Tr.]; its sound cannot be heard; one cannot see its expression if one were to look at it, nor know it by feeling, nor taste it. This is made of a primal combination of forces; as a phenomenon it does not have a form, as a noise it has but a little sound, and in terms of taste it does not have any presentation. It is for this reason that it can be the origin of all species and objects. It exists as an embryo, in which all Heaven and Earth is contained and all parts of Heaven and Earth are connected. There is nowhere it cannot go, and yet it will not be directed.

If something is warm, it cannot be cool; if something is gong, it cannot be shang. Once things take form, they are inevitably divided; sounds, too, naturally belong to separate divisions. Therefore, if something that is a phenomenon has form, it cannot be the Great Phenomenon; the sound that has noise cannot be the Great Sound. Nevertheless, if the Four Phenomena did not have form, the Great Phenomenon cannot be free. If the Five Sounds did not have noise, the Great Sound cannot arrive. If the Four Phenomena do take form, and yet objects are not made to submit to a master, the Great Phenomenon will be free; if the Five Sounds have noise but the mind does not follow them, the Great Sound will arrive.

In Wang Bi's view, Heaven and Earth and all things have many forms and appearances. What is one thing therefore cannot be any other thing at the same time; if something has a specific form, it cannot take another form. Thus, it is only the Form-less that can accomplish any form, only the Sound-less that can become any sound, only the Non-being [that which is not any specific being] that can accomplish being [can become anything]. It is because Non-being can become, or accomplish all being that it can be the foundation of the existence of all existence. Therefore:

All things under heaven are born of "being." The beginning of being is in having non-being as its origin. If one desired to accomplish "being" one must first revert to "non-being" (see Laozi (Lao Tzu) Zhu [Annotations on Laozi (Lao Tzu)]).

All things under heaven are specific and concrete existences with forms and phenomena. That these things with forms and phenomena can come into being, or be generated, is be ause they have "non-being" as their ont

logical substance; only then can this

ubstance be expressed as many specific things with many orms and appearances. For example, it was argued, the wat r of the sea is manifested in waves and billows of many diff rent colors and shapes. That it can be manifested in these many phenomena is preci

ely because it has its origins in water. Therefore, in orde to preserve all things of various forms and phenomena, one must grasp the "non-being" which is their ontological substance.

However, the "non-being" which is the ontological substance is not a "thing" which exists outside of "all things." Although one can say that "a phenomenon which has form is not the Great Phenomenon," unless "the Four Phenomena have form the Great Phenomenon cannot be free." Therefore, it is only when one can understand things through specific forms and phenomena, and yet not be confined by the specific forms and phenomena, that one can grasp "the phenomenon which is without phenomenon" [wu xiang zhi xiang], or, "the scenery outside of the picture" [hua wai zhi jing]. It is only when one can understand through specific sounds and yet not be insistent on, or confined by, specific sounds that one can grasp "the sound that has no noise" [wu sheng zhi yin] or, "the sounds outside the chords" [xuan wai zhi yin], and it is only through the understanding of language [words] and yet not insisting on language that one can attain the "meaning without words" [wu yan zhi yi] or, the "meaning outside the words" [yan wai zhi yi].

From the above we can see quite clearly that the method with which the argument "taking non-being as the origin" [yi wu wei ben] was made by Wang Bi was very different from the analytical approach adopted by the Kong zong of prajna Buddhist teaching. The approach taken by Wang Bi was the method of de yi wang yan [attain the meaning and lose, or forget, the words] which is a peculiarly metaphysical method of the xuanxue scholars.

When we have compared and studied the various aspects of the gui wu [valuing non-being] school of Wei-Jin xuanxue, as exemplified by Wang Bi, and the Kong zong [Emptiness school] of Indian prajna teaching, we shall be able to see more clearly each school's characteristics and its level of development. Only on such a basis can we clarify the relationship between Buddhism and Wei-Jin Daoist metaphysics during the period immediately or shortly after the introduction of Buddhism into China.

In issue no. 1, 1980 of Zhexue Yanjiu [Philosophical Studies], an article was published on "A Brief Discussion on the Theories of Early Daoist Religion on the Questions of Life and Death and Form and Spirit." In that essay, comparisons were made of the Daoist religion and Buddhism during the period of the Wei, Jin, and North and South dynasties, focusing on their respective views regarding life and death, and the question of jietuo [emancipation, or, in the Buddhist case, more commonly known as deliverance; in Sanskrit, mukti, or moksa]. The article pointed out that on these questions between these two religions, both of which were popular at the time, there were three major differences:

(1) On the question of life and death, the Daoist religion advocated adopting the notion of "everlasting life" [i.e.,

non-perishing] as the goal, whereas Buddhism advocated taking "eternal extinction" [i.e., non-life] as the goal. Daoism (Taoism)'s idea of emancipation advocated the transformation of mortal flesh into immortality by way of an integration of the body and the spirit such that this integrated substance may live on in non-perishable eternal life and in so doing be separated from the trouble-laden world of the present and enter the spiritual world of fantasy and illusion. Buddhism, on the other hand, believed that the source of the pains of human life was the "life of being," which was the state in which the spirit was connected to the body. Within this state of "life of being," until the spirit achieves Nirvana it must always return in the cycles of incarnation. Only by transcending these cycles of incarnation becoming separated from the body and returning to everlasting extinction, can the spirit be delivered from the sea of bitterness that is human life.

(2) On the question of form and spirit, Daoism (Taoism) advocated the achievement of immortality by having the spirit and form become one. Buddhism advocated having the form and spirit separated from one another and thereby achieving Buddhahood. Buddhism believed that, unless the spirit became separated from the form, it would not be able to escape the cycles of incarnation and could not be delivered: to be delivered the spirit must be separated from the form, and, in response to its own completed destiny, enter extinction and perish. Daoism (Taoism) believed that the path of transcending life and death and becoming liberated did not lie in this sort of completed destiny or extinction but in the immortalization of the flesh and for the flesh to become immortal it cannot, and must not, be separated from the spirit.

(3) As to the methods of achieving liberation or deliverance Daoism (Taoism) advocated the tempering of the form, whereas Buddhism advocated the nurturing of the spirit. As Buddhism believed that the achievement of

Buddhahood depended on enlightenment and realization, the chief means of achieving Nirvana was to cultivate the inner mind and enhance one's own realization or awareness. As Daoism (Taoism) believed that the achievement of immortality depended on the accumulation of successes and attainments, its chief means of achieving liberation was to temper body and mind, nurture life, and be assisted by external matter [foreign substances].

From these three points of comparison, we generally can know the characteristics of the Daoist and the Buddhist religions in China during the period of the Wei, Jin, and North and South dynasties. Daoism (Taoism)'s goal was the achievement of immortality. Though this was an impossibility, because of this people's attention was directed toward the tempering and nurturing of the functions of their own bodies and spirits [e.g., the qi gong, or breathing exercises] and to the study of external matter such as the manufacturing of pills and elixirs (foreign substances) whose assistance they counted upon for the achievement of the goal of immortality. The goal of Buddhism was to achieve Buddhahood. Though this, too, was obviously an unattainable goal, nevertheless it directed people's attentions toward the analysis of psychological activities and to the study of the cognitive processes.

Therefore, we have been able to discover that in Daoism (Taoism) there was, and is, much material related to understanding of "the way of materials" and to knowledge concerning the human body that is worthy of our own efforts of analysis and investigation. For example, the book Dao Zang [The Treasury of the Way] comprised of 5,000 to 6,000 volumes all of which, unfortunately, have yet to be systematically organized and studied, contains a wealth of information on such things as breathing exercises, medicines and herbacology (pharmacology), chemistry, hygiene, and physical education.

On the other hand, there are also over 10,000 volumes of Buddhist sutras [including sastras, annotations, and other exegetical treatises] in Chinese. In many areas, such as the analysis of psychological and psychic activity, of the processes of knowledge and cognition, the analysis of the relationship between subject and object, the analysis of concepts, perception and conceptualization, and the logical process known as vidjnana, or sometimes hetu-vidya-these Buddhist canons have much to add to our enlightenment. If we could but purge from these Daoist and Buddhist materials those parts which are unscientific, fabulous, fantastic or superstitious and analyze the remaining parts which are of positive value, it would be a most meaningful endeavor.

One of the purposes of studying comparative philosophy or comparative religion is to discover, through comparison and analysis, the characteristics of individual ideological cultures of various traditions, to identify and establish their peculiarities so that people may correctly understand and assess the status and role of these particular ideological cultures in the development of world history, and to ascertain the contributions they have made.

The great treasure trove of human ideological and intellectual culture inevitably is made up of the good and superior parts of many individual ideological cultures, each with its own tradition and characteristics. If an ideological culture did not contain any special characteristic of its own, it would be difficult for it to make any contribution to human intellectual civilization.

On the other hand, a culture which becomes the ideological culture of a nation, or a part thereof, is bound to have its own special characteristics and therefore is bound to make some contribution to the ideological culture of the human race as a whole.

OLD TOPICS AND NEW ISSUES

Finally, in the comparative study of two ideological cultures of different traditions we should attend to the discovery and re-discovery of problems to be mulled over and solved, and to proposing new topics or lessons for investigation and study.

Jin Kemu, in his article "Shi lun fan yu zhong di 'you yi chuanzai'" [A Tentative Discussion of the Terms, or Expressions, for 'Being, Unity and Existence' in Sanskrit] pointed out that there are several roots, or radicals, for the expressions in Sanskrit that stand for the notions of being, unity, or existence. The more common ones, he tells us--and there are two of them--are as and bhu. These are both translated in the Chinese language as you [being]. For example, in the translation of the Zhong bian fen bie lun [The Treatise on the Differences between the Mean and the Extremes] [written by Vasubandhu] made by Chen Zhenti, and in the translation of the Bian zhong bian lun [The Treatise on the Debate Between the Doctrines of the Mean and the Extremes] made by Xuan Zang, the term "sattvau." was consistently translated as you [being]. However, bhava [having, or possession], one of the dvadasanga pratityasamutpada, or Twelve yinyuan [nidanas, or combinations of causes], was also translated as you [being]. As refers to existence or being in the simple, abstract sense, or, if you will, the static, absolute sense, whereas bhu refers to existence in the transforming or specific sense, or in the moving, relative sense.

We also know that in ancient Greek philosophy, particularly in the Aristotelian system of thought, "substance" was also divided into two categories: primary substance and secondary substance. The two possessed different meanings. The former does not refer to simple and pure matter, nor to the general form common to the various matters, but to the individual units of matter and their forms. The second meaning of substance [or, secondary substance] referred, on the other hand, to the general form, or concept or category of matter, which becomes individualized in each separate matter.

Does this fact--that, while in Sanskrit, corresponding to various linguistic radicals, the terms for "being, unity, and existence" have different meanings, and that the term "substance" in the Aristotelian system of thought also has various meanings--enlighten us in any way? In the Chinese translations of the Buddhist canons the term for existence and being, which had different meanings in the original, all were translated as you. In Chinese traditional philosophy, then, did the concept conveyed by the term you also have various meanings? When Pei Wei, in his Cong you lun [Treatise on the Exaltation of Being] spoke of "self-generating and inevitably existent in substance" [zi sheng er bie ti you] did the term you there refer to specifically existent matters or to the general existence of matter? Again, in the usage of Guo Xiang's Zhuangzi Zhu [Annotations on Zhuangzi] did the term you sometimes refer to the specifically existent matters and sometimes to the general existence of matter? These are all questions which call for further investigation and require deeper analyses of the meaning(s) contained in the term you in traditional Chinese philosophy.

In his book Ti yong lun [On Substance and Use], Xiong Shili proposed that the essential and fundamental difference between traditional Chinese philosophy and Indian Buddhism was that where traditional Chinese philosophy talked about the "oneness of substance and use" [ti yong ru yi] Indian Buddhism separated substance from use, rending the two asunder. Whether or not Xiong's conclusion was correct is not something we wish to make a point of in our discussion here, but certainly it can be said that the problem which he raised in his study of these two ideological cultures stemming from different traditions is most likely to have considerable significance for the study of the characteristics of the Chinese philosophical tradition itself.

From the perspective of the general trends in the development of traditional Chinese philosophy, it can be seen that the notions of tian dao [Heaven's Way] and ren dao [the way of humanity] generally are considered to be consistent and integrated one with the other--in other words, it was assumed that the ideal should and could be realized in present reality. Even in the xuanxue metaphysics of the Wei-Jin period, although this system of thought took the ideas of Lao Zi and Zhuangzi to be its framework, the ultimate pursuit of the metaphysicians was still to achieve the "way of the inner sage and the outward monarch combined" [nei sheng wai wang zhi dao] which was contained in the "paradise which is naturally possessed by the Great Teaching" [ming jiao zhong zi you le di], i.e., in

Confucianism. When the Song-Ming neo-Confucianists opposed Buddhism and Daoism (Taoism), they did so chiefly on the grounds that Buddhists and Daoists, according to the neo-Confucianists, "pursued the illusory transcendental periphery of the universe of that which was real."

The neo-Confucianists claimed to believe fundamentally that "the ethics of the norm" [gang chang] and the great teaching [ming jiao] equaled "the principle of heaven" [tian li]. On the other hand, in Chinese Buddhism, too, and particularly in the Chan School, the teaching was that "achieving Buddhahood" did not require leaping out of, or being separated from a life of reality. The Chan Buddhists said, "Carrying water, cutting firewood, all these contained the most wonderful way and truth"--that is, it was possible for one to become enlightened to the wonderful way of achieving Buddhahood even in the mundane routines of everyday life.

When we compare China's traditional philosophy with the transcendentalist "going outside of the world" notion in Indian Buddhism, can we say that Chinese philosophy, after all, remained indeed faithful to the idea of "one-ness of substance and use" and that it was for this reason that the notions of complete transcendentalism were never able to become part of the mainstream of traditional Chinese thought? As I see it, this, too, is a question which merits further and more penetrating investigation. If we were to apply the comparative method to the study of the philosophical ideas and religious doctrines of various ideological cultures which stemmed from different traditions, such as the ideological culture of China and that of India, or that of the Western world, we will, I believe, discover even more lessons to be learned and topics to be discussed.

Over a hundred years ago that Marx and Engels pointed out: "Because the bourgeoisie opened up a world market, the production and consumption of the various countries have become universalized. . . . This is true not only of material production, but of the products of the mind and spirit as well. The spiritual products of the nations have become their common property, and the partialism and parochialism of the individual nations have become daily increasingly impossible. Therefore, out of the literature of the many nations and places of the world a world literature has been formed."

According to the editor-annotator, the term "literature" here referred to writing in many areas, including science, art and philosophy. We have now reached the 1980s; our age is much more advanced than that of 1848 when Marx and Engels wrote the Communist Manifesto. The interflow of ideas and culture and the interaction between peoples and civilizations have become even more widespread and profound. The comparative study of philosophy and religion is bound to promote the study of the history of Chinese philosophy. In the comparative study of ideological cultures of different traditions we can discover the common laws which govern the development of things; we can expose and demonstrate the characteristics and levels of development of various ideological cultures and expand the contents and scope of our study. Will this also play a part in the enrichment and enhancement of the development of Marxism? I am sure that it will.

INDIANISM AND HINDI

From early in the century, in the Madras Presidency as in other parts of the subcontinent, there were many who were concerned with the problem of developing a national language so as to overcome the dependence on English for interregional communication. Hindi was an early favorite candidate among many Tamil speakers, as it was in its own "home" in northern India (Dasgupta 1970). In 1906, in an article he published in *Intiyâ,* Bharati endorsed the view that since Hindi was already spoken by eighty out of India's three hundred million, Tamil speakers, too, should embrace it. Yet, he lamented, no steps had been taken to promote it in the South (C. S. Subramaniam 1986: 443-44). Soon after, in a 1908 letter to the nationalist Tilak, Bharati wrote that he and his friends had started a small Hindi class in Madras city (Padmanabhan 1982: 48-49; see also Nuhman 1984: 55-61). In subsequent decades, other devotees of the Indianist persuasion backed the cause of Hindi and countered Dravidianism's demonization of the language by reminding their fellow speakers that supporting it did not necessarily amount to the "murder" of their mother, Tamil (Kalyanasundaranar 1935: 21; Sivagnanam 1974: 136-41). Convinced that the regional Congress Party was dedicated to the twin causes of promoting Tamil at the regional level and Hindi at the national level, devotees inclined to Indianism supported that party.

Yet the promotion of Hindi as key to national unity and integration posed many dilemmas for Indianism, caught as it was between devotion to "Tamil" and "India." Over the years and especially in the decade following independence, many an Indianist became increasingly suspicious of the Congress Party's aggressive Hindi policy, which was perceived as endangering Tamil, as Dravidianists had long maintained (Sivagnanam 1974: 138-41, 416-18, 505-7). They came to appreciate the realities of functioning in a multilingual polity in which, contrary to their conviction that all languages are equal "children" of Bhârata Mâtâ, one of them would be the privileged "imperial state language." Ramalinga Pillai captured their conflicting sentiments when he wrote that Tamil speakers were famed the world over for inviting other languages into their home and honoring these. However, he asked, to what extent should they let their own language and culture suffer in this process (Thaninayagam 1963: 12)? What would happen to Tamil and its glorious literature, others demanded, if state funds were redirected towards the support of Hindi? For, as Somasundara Bharati, professor of Tamil and a Congress supporter in his early years, insisted, "clothed with prestige and privileges peculiar to an imperial state language, Hindi is sure to become a dangerous rival to Tamil." Not surprisingly, he wondered if an old "evil," English, was being replaced by a new one, and whether Tamil would continue to suffer in this process (Somasundara Bharati 1937: 17).

Although opposed to compulsory Hindi education, many Indianist devotees like Kalyanasundaram and Sivagnanam continued to extend their allegiance to the Congress's policies into the 1940s, in reaction to the powerful anti-Hindi and anti-India demonology of Dravidianism, and in the face of the Dravidian movement's growing demand for retaining English as the common language. As colonial rule gave way to Congress rule, however, they became convinced that the cause of Tamil would be compromised by the larger cause of the (Hindi-dominated) Indian nation and its needs. Not surprisingly, by the late 1940s, Kalyanasundaram joined forces with the Dravidian movement to oppose Hindi (Kalyanasundaranar 1949). Similarly, in 1946, Sivagnanam formed an interest group called the Tamil1 Aracu Kal1akam, "Association for Tamil Autonomy" (henceforth Tamil Arasu Kazhagam), whose main agenda was to put pressure on the Congress to promote the increased use of Tamil in administration and education, to work towards the creation of an autonomous Tamil state out of a composite Madras Presidency, and to ease up on its pro-Hindi policy. As Sivagnanam wrote in April 1947 on the eve of Indian independence, "The Tamilian is prepared to be Indian. However, he is first and foremost a Tamilian. Only secondarily is he Indian" (Sivagnanam 1981: 105). By 1954, his organization was forced to part ways with the Congress, and in 1967, Sivagnanam even entered into an electoral alliance with the Dravidian movement—the same movement against which through much of the 1950s he had conducted so many campaigns (Sivagnanam 1974: 368-69, 535-55). Most indicative perhaps of Indianism's radical transformation through its dealings with the Hindi question is C. Rajagopalachari's changing stance. The chief promoter of Hindi who made its study mandatory in the late 1930s in the Madras Presidency, he began to insist "English ever, Hindi never" from the late 1950s, and even made electoral deals with his Dravidianist rivals by the 1960s (Rajagopalachari 1962).

The Congress and Indianized Tamil

In 1967, the Congress, the party that prided itself on delivering India from colonialism and that had ruled Madras for the two decades since independence, suffered a stunning defeat at the polls and has never returned to power in the state since. For many a Tamil devotee, the Congress's defeat was its just deserts, for had it not shown, over the years, that it was the enemy of Tamil and Tamil1ttây? Supporters of the Congress have tried to counter such a charge. It was the Congress, more than the non-Brahman elite's Justice Party, that used Tamil from early in this century in party work and popular mobilization. It was under Congress rule that Tamil was extended as medium of instruction in high schools in 1938, and university education in 1960-61. The Congress government also set up, in 1959, the Tamil Development and Research Council entrusted with producing Tamil school and college textbooks in the natural and human sciences, accounting, mathematics, and so on. It also helped finance a series of children's encyclopedias in Tamil, "lucid commentaries" on Cank#am poetry, and an "authentic history of the Tamil people" in 1962-63. And finally, in 1956, it was the Congress that passed the law instituting Tamil as the official language of the state (Karthikeyan 1965-66; C. Subramaniam 1962). Yet, as its critics have been quick to point out, few of these measures seemed to have made any difference to life in the Tamil-speaking land. So, Mohan Kumaramangalam wrote in 1965:

> In practice, the ordinary man finds that the Tamil language is nowhere in the picture....In Madras city, English dominates our life to an extraordinary extent....Corporation property tax, electric consumption and water tax bills are only in the English language; all communications of the Collector are in English; in virtually all trade, including the smallest consumer goods, bills, receipts, etc. are made out in the English language. I think it will be no exaggeration to say that a person can live for years in Madras without learning a word of Tamil, except for some servant inconvenience!

As many of its supporters rightly point out, the Congress government's record on *tamil1ppan#i*, "service to Tamil," is not as terrible or as bleak as its critics portray it. Nevertheless, it pursued Tamil policies that were largely Indianist in complexion at a time when the growing Dravidianist discourse was very persuasively pointing to "India" as the source of many of the Tamil speaker's problems, and at a time when even Indianists within the devotional community were turning away from the Congress. Its Indianist predilections meant that the "improvement" of Tamil under Congress rule proceeded side by side with at least tacit support for the Indian state's Hindi policy. The Congress also resisted a number of devotional demands out of fear that these would open the "Pandora's box" of linguistic "balkanization": the renaming of Madras state as "Tamilnadu," the authorization of Tamil as primary liturgical language in temples, the use of pure Tamil instead of Sanskritized Tamil in school textbooks and administrative manuals, and so on. Above all, Congress policies, like orthodox Indianism's, were premised on the fundamental assumption that "Tamil" and "India" were intertwined, an assumption that it felt compelled to uphold if only to counter the separatist agenda of the Dravidian movement. It would be sacrilegious to think exclusively of Tamil as deserving the absolute allegiance of all its speakers. Thus the Congress, and even the Indianist regime, were never animated by the spirit of total and unconditional celebration of Tamil that characterized Dravidianism's attitude towards the language. In the words of one devotee of Tamil whose own sentiments were contestatory classicist and Dravidianist, "None of the Congress Ministers of Tamil Nad was either a Tamil scholar or a Tamil lover. The Congress leaders of Tamil Nad as betrayers of Tamil, cannot represent the State any more. Blind cannot lead the blind, much less the keen sighted" (Devaneyan 1967: 25). In 1967, the Tamil electorate came to the same conclusion.

LANGUAGE OF THE NATION

And so, finally, I turn to the Dravidianist regime that crystallized in the 1930s, gained momentum through the 1940s and 1950s, and peaked in the mid-1960s. Its primary terrain of activity was a series of anti-Hindi protests which dramatically drew together diverse elements of the devotional community in opposition to the regional and central governments that sponsored Hindi, itself-caricatured as an evil and demonic force out to destroy pure and sweet Tamil (and its speakers). Contemporaries and participants alike marvelled that the common cause against Hindi threw together religious revivalists like Maraimalai Adigal with such avowed atheists as Ramasami; Gandhians like Kalyanasundaram with men like Annadurai who preached secession from India; university professors and elite antiquarians, such as Somasundara Bharati and Purnalingam Pillai, with populist street poets, pamphleteers, college students, and young men like Chinnasami who immolated themselves. Indeed, the poet Bharatidasan, the paradigmatic Dravidianist, had himself been a self-declared devotee of "India" up until the 1920s, and had published some passionate poems on Bhârata Mâtâ before his conversion to Dravidianism and anti-Hindi politics by the 1930s (Ilango 1982; Ilavarasu 1990). Other events of these decades—the creation of linguistic states out of the erstwhile Madras Presidency, the securing of appropriate borders with neighboring states, the struggle to rename Madras state Tamilnadu—also compelled devotees otherwise inclined, such as Sivagnanam, to turn to Dravidianism. Dravidianism is thus the crisis idiom of *tamil1ppar1r1u,* the regime par excellence for mobilizing—albeit temporarily and sometimes reluctantly—diverse, even opposing, devotees under one umbrella, around events that were deemed to be threatening to the future of Tamil and Tamil1ttây.

The most passionate and radical of all the regimes, Dravidianism routinely elicited from its adherents declarations of willingness to give up their wealth, their lives, and their souls for Tamil. It also produced some antagonistic, even violent, attitudes towards other languages and their speakers, as for instance in the following verse published by Bharatidasan, which is fairly typical: "Our first task is to finish off those who destroy [our] glorious Tamil! / Let flow a river of crimson blood!" Its emphasis on fierce, public displays of devotion meant that images of battlefields, of blood, and of death proliferate in Dravidianist discourse. True Tamilians are those—like Chinnasami—who show their commitment to their mother/tongue by putting their very bodies on the line, and dying for it, if need be. More so than the other devotional regimes, Dravidianism's driving imperative was a vision of the Tamil community as an autonomous racial and political entity (*in1am*), even nation (*nât#u*), whose sacral center is occupied solely by Tamil, from which all its members claim shared descent. So, where neo-Shaivism constituted Tamilian solidarity around the shared worship of Shiva and divine Tamil, and classicism emphasized a common ancient, literary past, Dravidianism focused on descent and kinship. Tropes of motherhood, siblingship, shared blood, the home, and the like mark its discursive style, as they do Indianism's. The significant difference between the two, of course, is that Dravidianism made a commitment to only one entity—namely, Tamil. As Tamil1ttây herself insisted, sometime in the early 1960s: "Do not forget that you are all children who emerged from my womb. I *am* your mother. The learned call me Tamil1ttây. You are called Tamilians (*tamil1ar*). You and I have been inextricably bound together for ever and ever through language. That language is what the good scholars call Tamil....If we look closely, we have a home. That its name is Tamilnadu gives [me] great happiness" (Pancanathan n.d.: 9).

In this statement as elsewhere in Dravidianism, descent is reckoned solely from Tamil, which is not merely one among a "family" of languages *in* a putative Indian nation, as it is in Indianism, but is *the* language *of* the nation, imagined variously as "Tamilian" or "Dravidian." No doubt, by the 1970s Dravidianism became more accommodating on the question of India. But the fundamental imperative of this regime continued to be the establishment of the absolute rule of Tamil through the complete Tamilization of the political apparatus and its accompanying ideology, in a territorial space designated as Tamil or Dravidian, which at least into the early 1960s was seen as independent of, and indeed in opposition to, "India."

The political philosophy of Dravidianism was provided by a broad swathe of ideas associated with "the Dravidian movement" (*tirâvit#a iyakkam*). This movement made its impact on the Dravidianist regime when the elitist "non-Brahman" associational politics of the Vellala dominated Justice Party (1916/17-44) was supplemented by the populist call for radical social reform by E. V. Ramasami and his Self-Respect League (founded in 1926) and the Tirâvit#ar Kal1akam, "Association of Dravidians" (the DK, established in 1944). Although many Self-Respecters were concerned with Tamil (e.g., Velu and Selvaraji 1989), Ramasami himself was extremely critical of *tamil1ppar1r1u*, especially of its valorization of the divinity, antiquity, and motherhood of Tamil. This did not stop Dravidianism from lionizing him and selectively appropriating his ideas of rationalist materialism, iconoclastic atheism, radical anti-Brahmanism, and Dravidian nationalism, for he provided the most polemical and sustained attacks on Indian nationalism, which this regime found useful. Ramasami's obvious dilemma was that Tamil devotion threatened his vision of a Dravidian nation that would incorporate all "Dravidians" of southern India, and not just Tamil speakers.

Such a vision had to contend with the resistance of those putative "Dravidians" who were speakers of Telugu, Kannada, and Malayalam. In addition, it was compromised by Tamil speakers who did not necessarily want to participate in a multilingual polity, even if it was "Dravidian." And indeed, as the Dravidian movement itself split, when Annadurai parted company with Ramasami and his DK in 1949 to found his own party, the Tirâvit#a Mun1n1çr1r1ak Kal1akam or "Dravidian Progress Association" (DMK), the inherent tensions between the alternate conceptions of the "Dravidian" and "Tamil" nation came to the fore. By the late 1950s, as the DMK entered the domain of electoral politics, its agenda was primarily formulated in terms of a Tamil nation (albeit one often referred to as "Dravidian"), confined to the territorial space of a Tamilspeaking area, rather than coeval with the more ambitious nation that Ramasami envisaged comprising the speakers of all Dravidian languages.

Like the Dravidian movement, Dravidianism, too, had to contend with the tensions between an exclusive Tamil-speaking nation and a more inclusive Dravidian nation. It adopted various strategies to deal with this, such as suggestions that "Tamil" and "Dravidian" are the same; that since Tamil is the "mother" of all Dravidian languages, the latter are merely extensions of the former; and so on. So, like the other regimes, Dravidianism had its share of contradictions. Notwithstanding these, as a consequence of its discourse, Tamil comes to be firmly "Dravidianized," even as the "Dravidian" category, which had been gaining political and cultural visibility in the region since the 1880s, was unequivocally associated with Tamil. In contrast to neo-Shaivism and classicism, Dravidianism advocated political radicalism and activism as the means to achieve the reign of Tamil: "We have talked enough.... [W]hen are you going to show your sacrifice to [Tamil1ttây]? We are waiting every moment for the honor of being arrested." Under the influence of

Dravidianism, *tamil1ppar1r1u* took to the streets, sometimes quite violently. Petition politics gave way to protest politics, increasingly radical and populist. Antiquarian and elite notions about Tamil and Tamil1ttây, hitherto confined to learned academies and scholastic journals, came to be invoked in street songs, polemical plays, and political speeches at populist anti-Hindi rallies; they were circulated in daily newspapers and street pamphlets, and plastered across billboards and wall posters.

Dravidianism typically catered, like the Dravidian movement itself, to the Everyman, generically designated in its texts as *tamil1an1,* "Tamilian" (Barnett 1976: 114-15). It attracted its following from devotees who were predominantly from middle and lower castes, and from middle or low-income families with limited or no formal education, like Chinnasami and his fellow self-immolators. At the same time, the DMK's support of literature and language also attracted numerous well-educated Tamil scholars and academics to Dravidianism. In turn, many DMK leaders have been devotees of Tamil.

They have assumed titles—*ar1iòar* (scholar) Annadurai, *kalaiòar* (the artist) Karunanidhi, *nâvalar* (the eloquent) Nedunceliyan—which display both their scholarly aspirations and the close links between populist ideology and high literature in the political culture of the region (Barnett 1976: 56-86). Dravidianism's paradigmatic exponents were undoubtedly well-known poets and politicians like Bharatidasan, Annadurai, "Pulavar" Kulanthai (1906-72), Perunchitran (1920-95), Mudiyarasan (b. 1920), Karunanidhi, and the early Kannadasan (1927-81). But encouraged by the Dravidian movement's populism and by Dravidianism's assertion that Tamil belonged to "the people," the Everyman, who remained anonymous or relatively unknown, took to writing and publishing poems, short stories, and essays on the language and on Tamil1ttây. Of all the regimes of *tamil1ppar1r1u,* Dravidianism was thus the one that was truly populist, in spirit as well as constituency.

Dravidianism's fundamental agenda, of course, was to establish the absolute preeminence of Tamil in all spheres of life and being, and to ensure that devotion to the language (and its community) was not diluted by any other passions—for the

Indian nation, for the gods of the Hindu pantheon, or even for the families and mothers of individual devotees. For Tamil is everything; it is the life (*uyir*), breath (*âvi*), and consciousness (*un#arvu*) of every true Tamilian. In its purest form, there were no divided commitments in Dravidianism, no subordination of Tamil to Shiva, to literature and learning, or to India.

Tamil was not a means through which to construct something else, be it an alternate religious or civilizational formation, or allegiance to India. In and of itself, it ought to be the very center of everything in the devoted Tamil speaker's life. Without it, there is nothing. So Bharatidasan wrote in a poem suggestively entitled "Living for Tamil Is the Only Life":

O Tamil! Homage to you!

......

Your well-being is ours as well.

Your victories are ours as well.

We may as well be dead if we live for ourselves.

Living for Tamil is the only life!

For the Dravidianist devotee, Tamil was so much a part of the Tamilian's very essence that it would be impossible to separate the language from its speaker. So Bharatidasan insisted:

We can turn mountains into pits;

We can dry up the ocean bed;

We can fly speedily through the skies.

......

We can even bring the dying back to life.

The Tamilian cannot be separated from Tamil

Even for a moment, by anyone.

This conviction, that Tamil and its speaker devotee had so blended into each other that it would be impossible to separate them, is echoed in other poems as well. Consider this verse by Kannadasan addressed to Tamil1ttây:

Would I ever forget you? Would I cease to sing about you?

Even if they set me on fire,

In the burning flames of the fire,

The world will see only you, O dear mother of mine!

(Kannadasan 1968: 89)

Elsewhere, in 1954, in lines that eerily anticipate Chinnasami's immolation a decade later, the poet wrote, "even in death, Tamil should be on our lips. Our ashes should burn with the fragrance of Tamil. This is our undying desire" (Kannappan 1995: 22).

Given such sentiments, Dravidianism was particularly concerned with all alternate objects of passion that might draw its speakers away from Tamil, such as "India," their gods, and their families. It therefore focused as much energy to convince Tamil speakers of the illegitimacy of these other entities as to emphasize that it is Tamil that sustains their life and consciousness.

Dravidianism and India

While Indianism emphatically asserted that the liberation of Bhârata Mâtâ and Tamil1ttây would have to proceed in tandem, Dravidianism, particularly in its early years, and most especially as expressed by its more radical exponents, saw in the very establishment of the Indian nation the downfall of Tamil. A poem that was published in the *Tirâvit#an1* on 31 August 1947, a fortnight after India was officially liberated from colonial rule, declared: "The foreign Bhârata Mâtâ (*an1n1iyap pâratattây*) has attained glory. / Our own dear Tamil1ttây has been greatly disgraced."

Dravidianism, at its peak, portrayed the newly emergent Indian nation as an imperialist formation, as a tool in the hands of Brahmans and Banias (North Indian merchants), and as an instrument with which the material interests of Dravidians would continue to be subordinated to Aryan Indians (Annadurai 1974: 39-48, 1985: 22-23; Pancanathan n.d.; M. S. Ramasami 1947: 5-6, 19-20). Consider the following verse from a 1947 pamphlet revealingly entitled *Songs of Separation for the Dravidian Nation:*

> *The Brahmans and Banias have united;*
>
> *We are all children of Bhârata Mâtâ, they lie to us[.]*
>
> ......
>
> *Our own Tirâvit#attây [Mother Dravida] is our mother;*
>
> *Bhârata Mâtâ who belongs to the duplicitous, is a deceitful mother;*
>
> *If the Dravidians realize this, they will have no trouble.*
>
> *If we let down our guard, the Northerners will loot and plunder.*
>
> *(M. S. Ramasami 1947: 14)*

Indianism, we have seen, offered Bhârata Mâtâ to Tamil speakers as a mother who would reproduce them as "Indians." In the logic of Dravidianism, however, she was clearly a false mother who sought to lure gullible Tamilians away from their true mother with promises of milk, nourishment, and even jobs. So, in 1958, Bharatidasan, who in his early years had waxed passionately on Bhârata Mâtâ and even declared her his true mother, published a poem in which he ridiculed the Tamilian who is confused about his "real" mother. The poem is addressed to Tamil1ttây:

> *"O glorious Tamilian! What is the name of your nation?"*
>
> *When I ask thus, he sheepishly says "India," O mother!*
>
> *How will this child ever improve if he confuses the evergreen*
>
> *Tamil nation with India, O mother!*

Will he ever change, the one who does not recognize his mother as mother, and declares the evil that destroys his motherland as mother, O mother!

Sitting in [his] mother's lap and nursing on the breast milk of Tamil, how can this child not know [his] mother's name, O mother!

Tamil *is* [his] mother tongue, and Tamilnadu is his motherland.

Does not the Tamilian realize this?

So, while Indianism sought to naturalize "India" by presenting it in the familiar terms of the home and the mother, the Dravidianist logic lay in demonizing it as a "deceitful" or "evil" mother, and substituting Tamil1ttây in its stead as the authentic, *sole* mother of all true Tamil speakers.

Dravidianism's antagonism towards India came to the fore in the numerous protests against Hindi, presented in its discourses as a blood-sucking demoness, lowly maid, seductive temptress, and false mother out to destroy the noble, righteous, but endangered Tamil1ttây. Such Manichean images were deployed to create fear and hatred of Hindi, and to generate sentiments of love, loyalty, and filial piety for Tamil, which its loyal speakers were obliged to protect with life and limb. Just as crucially, the regional state government (in the control of the Congress) and the Indian nation were also rendered into objects that deserved the Tamilians' deepest opprobrium and the withdrawal of their support, emotional *and* electoral. Dravidianism thus seized upon the linguistic fact that Hindi was related to Sanskrit, and translated the assertions of radical neo-Shaivism and contestatory classicism against Aryan Brahmanism into political action against the Indian nation.

For Dravidianism, the battle against Hindi was not only inevitable and natural, but necessary and morally legitimate; it was a "holy war" (*ar1appôr*) fought against evil and on behalf of the good and righteous (Ramaswamy, forthcoming). Although Hindi was in effect legislated out of Tamilnadu government schools in 1968 by the DMK, and although all kinds of accommodations with the North have been made since the 1960s, to this day the threat of Hindi has continued to be effectively used to reiterate the autonomy and uniqueness of a Tamil space within a larger Indian whole, to summon up the specter of non-Tamil elements entering the pure Tamil body politic, and to remind Tamil speakers of the dangers that await them if they cease supporting the Dravidian movement and its Tamil cause.

DRAVIDIANISM AND HINDUISM

In the years between the late 1920s and 1950s, when the influence of the iconoclastic and atheistic Ramasami was at its peak and before the DMK actively entered the fray of electoral politics, Dravidianism also sought energetically to dissociate Tamil from all religious affiliations. Like radical neo-Shaivism, it castigated Hinduism as a Brahmanical, Sanskritic, and Aryan conspiracy hatched to destroy Tamil and Dravidian society.

So, for Dravidianism, a true Tamilian/Dravidian is one who is emphatically *not* a Hindu. "A Hindu in the present concept may be a Dravidian, but the Dravidian in the real sense of the term cannot and shall not be a Hindu" (quoted in Harrison 1960: 127). Tamil speakers were therefore repeatedly called upon to destroy all (Hindu) irrationalisms and foolish beliefs, and to rescue themselves from *ârya mâyai,* "Aryan illusion" (Annadurai 1969). Thus Bharatidasan, who in the 1920s had written passionate poems on Hindu deities and continued occasionally to publish religious verse into the 1930s, insisted in the 1950s that "there is no god" and told the Tamilian that his duty lay in weaning away his hapless fellow speakers from their false belief in divinities.

And here is where Dravidianism parted company with neo-Shaivism: for in its attacks on religion, it did not spare either Shiva or the reformed "rational" version of Shaivism that Maraimalai Adigal and others were attempting to popularize (Sivathamby 1978: 30-31; Venkatachalapathy 1990). Neo-Shaivism may have insisted that Shaivism is the authentic Tamilian religion, radically different from Aryan Brahmanical Hinduism, but Dravidianism was not convinced about this. Nor was it ready to brook neo-Shaivite resistance to reforming and rationalizing the Tamil script, believed by many devout Shaivites to be Shiva's own handiwork (Sivathamby 1979: 71). Dravidianism was also not willing to define the Tamil/Dravidian community as Shaiva, for what would then happen to Tamilians/ Dravidians who were nominally Vaishnavas, Christians, and Muslims?

So Tamil is the life, the consciousness, and the soul of the Tamilian. It is indeed everything, but it certainly is not "divine

Tamil," for to imagine it as such would entangle it with the irrationalisms, inequalities, and idiocies of Hinduism. Tamil speakers, too, consequently would be subordinated and demeaned in an inherently Brahmanical order of things, and they would lose all their "self-respect." In a revealing speech of 1944, Ramasami offered the following advice to his fellow Dravidians: "You may well ask, 'If we give up Hinduism, what religion can we profess to have?' Have courage and claim that religion which will not demean you as untouchable and lowly in society. If there is objection to this, you may always say you are Dravidian and that your religion is Dravidianism. If you have problems even with that, say that your religion is humanity" (Anaimuthu 1974: 446).

Contrary to Marguerite Barnett (1976: 274), who has suggested that "within the Dravidian ideology there was no coherent alternative to religion or Hinduism," I would argue that especially within the Dravidianist regime of *tamil1ppar1r1u,* various efforts were made to create alternatives to both religion and Hinduism. Given the complex entanglements between Tamil devotion and Hinduism, however, such efforts were not entirely successful, nor were they as autonomous as Dravidianism would have desired. Minimally, those devotees of Tamil who turned to active electoral politics as members of the DMK distanced themselves from Ramasami's iconoclastic irreverence for Hindu scriptures, gods, and images. By the 1950s, both the DMK and Dravidianism generated a curious combination of agnosticism ("we do not ask whether there is god or not"), monism ("there is only one god and one community"), populism ("god lives in the smile of the poor"), and humanism ("we must develop that kind of outlook which treats all humanity as one"). This medley of diverse beliefs that Anita Diehl (1977: 29) has shrewdly characterized as "pragmatic, agnostic humanism" opened up a space for the steady incorporation of all kinds of elements from popular as well as the devotional religious practices of the region into the ideology of Dravidianism, such as the celebration of the harvest festival, Pongal; the worship of Murugan; and the apotheosis of Valluvar and his *Tirukkur1al#* (Ramanujam 1971: 168, 175; Ryerson 1988: 108-93).

One other important strategy is followed by Dravidianism in filling up the space vacated by Hindu gods. Consider this 1959 poem by Bharatidasan, addressed to a *tampirân1,* "Shaiva monk preceptor," in response to the opposition of the orthodox to the growing demand for use of Tamil as ritual language in temples:

Is it religion (camayam) that is important, O *tampirân1*[?]

It is fine Tamil that is indeed eminent, O foolish *tampirân1*[.]

Why do you hate Tamil, O *tampirân1*[.]

Why do you hate your mother, O *tampirân1*[?]

Even if religion is destroyed, Tamilians will flourish[.]

If good Tamil is destroyed, can there be a Tamil community[?]

Do service to Tamil! O *tampirân1*[.]

Tamil is the life of the Tamilian! O foolish *tampirân1*[.]

Is it God who is great[?] O *tampirân1*[!]

It is glorious Tamil that is indeed great[!] O foolish *tampirân1*[.]

Even if God disappears, the Tamil community will flourish[.]

If Tamil dies, its community, too, will die, O *tampirân1*[.]

Do you intend to destroy the Tamil creed (*tamil1ner1i*) by invoking Shaivism (*caivaner1i*), O foolish *tampirân1?*

Service to Shaivism is not great, O *tampirân1*[.]

It is auspicious service to Tamil that is eminent, O *tampirân1*[.]

......

Only one thing is greater than [our] mother(s)! O *tampirân1!*

Is that not Tamil, O foolish *tampirân1?*

There are few clearer statements than this of Dravidianism's attempt to displace conventional gods and the religious beliefs associated with them, and to substitute Tamil in their stead. Indeed, Dravidianism sacralized Tamil, even while refusing to participate, at least overtly and consciously, in its divinization. Dravidianism's ambivalence towards religiosity and Hinduism notwithstanding, Tamil was offered to its speakers as an iconic object that deserves all the adulation, adherence, and service they had hitherto reserved for their gods. In this process, even within Dravidianism, Tamil was imagined as desired by the gods, and was every now and then deified. So, in his controversial 1945 poem, *Tamilliyakkam* (The resurgence of Tamil), Bharatidasan asked whether Tamil, "which is life itself," is not dear to the gods (Bharatidasan 1969: 27). On a more personal note, in his autobiography the poet Mudiyarasan, who identifies himself as an ardent follower of Ramasami and Annadurai, asks, "I consider Tamil as god *(kat#avul#)*. How can I be an atheist *(nâttikan1)*?" (Mudiyarasan n.d.: 86-87).

A similar sentiment undergirds the DMK government's institution of the homage to Tamilttây as the state song in 1970. The government may have announced that it was doing this because the song had no "religious or sectarian associations," an assertion it was able to make because it carefully edited out Sundaram Pillai's original title, *Tamillt teyva van#akkam,* "Homage to *Goddess* Tamil." Nonetheless, in its official statement (in English), Tamilttây herself is referred to as "goddess of Tamil," and the hymn is characterized as "prayer song."

Dravidianism and the Tamil Family

Dravidianism did not just have to delegitimize the "other mother," Bhârata Mâtâ it also had to ensure that flesh-and-blood Tamil-speaking mothers themselves did not pose a threat to the absolute devotion and loyalty owed to the sacralized language. This was a very complicated task, for motherhood was the ground on which both Indianism and Dravidianism constituted *tamillpparlrlu.* Indeed, Dravidianism was not content with merely establishing similitude between language and one's mother; more strikingly, it insisted that language *is* that mother:

When I was a child, you snuggled me and placed me on your lap;

You placed flowers in my hair, and adorned me, and admired my beauty;

You are the sweet mother who protected me, in the shade and in the heat;

O my ancient Tamil! May you live long!

(Ulakanathan 1969: 4)

Similarly, the well-known DMK rhetorician R. Nedunceliyan, who later became a key member of the government, insisted in 1960 that there was no difference between one's mother and Tamil:

There is *no distinction at all* between our mother who bore us for ten months, gave birth to us, watched over us, sang lullabies to us, and fed us milk and guarded us, and our Tamil language which taught us about good conduct and tradition, and granted us good values and knowledge, and which is the very reason that we live well and in prosperity. We have the same attachment to our language as we have for our mother; we have the same devotion to our language as we have for our mother; we have the same love for our language as we have for our mother. He who disregards his language...is like he who disregards his mother and forsakes her. Dravidianism may have invited speakers of Tamil to imagine it as their mother. At its most dramatic, however, it elevated Tamil to a position of absolute preeminence, even transcending the status and authority of one's birth mother. For instance, the poet Pulavar Kulanthai declared passionately:

I will never refuse to obey my [own] mother's words;

But if harm befalls my precious Tamil1ttây,

I will not fear to set aside my own mother's words.

I will chop off the head of [Tamil1ttây's] enemy,

Even if [my] mother prevents me.

(Pulavar Kulanthai 1972: 21)

By extension, this kind of loyalty extended to fellow Tamil speakers as well, as is apparent from Bharatidasan's much-cited declaration: "I will not leave alone the man who scorns the greatness of Tamilians / *Even if [my] mother prevents me*" (Bharatidasan 1958: 5, emphasis mine). Indeed, Dravidianism even insisted that service to Tamil and to Tamil1ttây should take priority over the Tamilian's family—over spouses, children, and parents. So Perunchitran demanded as late as 1975: "Are the troubles of your own mother more important than the terrible suffering of our glorious Tamil1ttây? /.../ Are the words of your own mother sweeter than our Tamil language, which is like ambrosia?" (Perunchitranar 1979: 109).

Yet in thus subordinating the family to Tamil, Dravidianism only overtly and consciously articulated a sentiment that was widespread in the devotional community as a whole. As we will see later, in the life stories of individual devotees as these are narrated in memoirs and biographies, their families are typically superseded in favor of devotion to the Tamil cause. The family, which is a primary site for cultivating devotion to the language, is ultimately transcended within the regimes of *tamil1ppar1r1u*. Such a transcendence is deemed necessary, for not even the family can—or can be allowed to—intervene between the devotee and his language.

The DMK and Dravidianized Tamil

Deriving considerable political capital from its self-appointed role as the guardian of Tamil and from demonizing the Congress as an agent of "evil" North Indian interests during the prolonged anti-Hindi protests of the 1950s and 1960s which it spearheaded, the DMK swept the state polls in 1967. Two days after the party's victory was assured, its leading newspaper, *Nam Nât#u,* carried the headline, "Tamil1ttây's Desire of Many Years Fulfilled." The *Muracoli*'s front-page cartoon showed Tamil1ttây, a smile on her face, placing a crown on Annadurai, her "chief son." And it was declared that Tamil1ttây's victory was the fruit of penances undergone by her followers for Tamil's sake: "In order that Tamil1ttây be enthroned, in order that Tamil1ttây should abide with honor, so that Tamil1ttây may be crowned...so many became prey to gunfire, so many drowned in an ocean of red blood, so many martyrs set themselves on fire, so many great ones passed away. This we know. Today, we see Tamil blooming everywhere. You must all go to the Legislative

Assembly. You will hear good Tamil there." The DMK takes great pride that so many of its leaders—Annadurai, Nedunceliyan, and Karunanidhi, among others—have been hailed as great scholars of Tamil and of literature in their own right. So, for many Dravidianists, the DMK's victory finally fulfilled Bharatidasan's dream, voiced years earlier in 1945, that "only the Tamilian who knows Tamil should rule as the chief minister of Tamilnadu" (Bharatidasan 1969: 19).

Regardless of what its opponents may say or statistics may reveal, the DMK has promoted itself as selflessly dedicated to the Tamil cause. Party literature as well as government publications provided details of the measures that it undertook to promote the language: the increasing use of "chaste" and "good" Tamil in administrative and public facilities; the publication of Tamil encyclopedias, scientific manuals, and textbooks; the increasing support of Tamil scholars and Tamil studies both within and outside Tamilnadu; and so on—programs pursued by the Congress government as well to varying degrees.

In addition, under the DMK, Hindi was in effect legislated out of state schools in 1968; steps were taken, although not successfully, to introduce Tamil as the exclusive language of higher education and as medium of worship in high Hindu temples; and the state itself was renamed Tamilnadu, "land of Tamil." DMK cultural policy also focused on creating a new literary and historical canon, by drawing upon the findings of *tamil1ppar1r1u,* especially upon contestatory classicism and Dravidianism. Not surprisingly, the poems of the Cank#am corpus occupy a hallowed place in this canon, Karunanidhi himself offering a new interpretation in 1987 (Karunanidhi 1987a). Similarly, the *Tirukkur1al#,* the new "scripture" of Dravidianism, is valorized, as is the *Cilappatikâram,* as exemplars of the "secular," "egalitarian," and "chaste" essence of true and pure Tamil culture, free from the influences of Sanskritic Aryan Brahmans with their priestly ways.

Correspondingly, a new pantheon of secular icons surrounding the presiding deity, Tamil1ttây, has sprung up. It includes Tiruvalluvar, the author of the *Tirukkur1al#* Kattabomman, who died a martyr's death during the late-eighteenth-century British expansion into South India, and who is considered a paradigmatic symbol of Tamil heroism (Ramaswamy 1994); and Kannagi, the heroine of the *Cilappatikâram,* who is imagined as the ideal Tamil woman, renowned for her chastity and wifely fidelity (J. Pandian 1982). Similarly, Ramasami and Annadurai were lionized for giving Tamil speakers their "self-respect," and many DMK narratives contain laudatory poems on their achievements. And it was under DMK rule that Chinnasami and his fellow devotees who burned themselves alive were immortalized. New mythologies and praise poems on all these figures were written and circulated. Their life stories were narrated and offered as paradigms for Tamil speakers to emulate. Commemorative memorials were set up, and festivals conducted in their honor. In 1968, the government used an academic gathering in Madras, the Second International Conference of Tamil Studies, to treat the populace to a spectacular celebration of Tamil, featuring giant floats of Tamil1ttây, Tiruvalluvar, and other Tamil icons. The party's leaders must believe that such acts carry symbolic as well as political capital, for as recently as 1984, its election manifesto chose to present its achievements to the electorate in the following terms:

In order that Tamil1ttây's jeweled crown should shine,

We built the historic temple to Valluvar whose fame reaches the very skies;

And the world-famous new town of Poompukar with its *Cilappatikâram* museum, seven stories high!

And a fort in the memory of Virapandya Kattabomman at Panjalamkurichi.

We enabled all these, not just one, not just two, but plenty! plenty!

And yet, as critics as well as supporters of the DMK are quick to ask, have such gestures really helped the cause of Tamil? I quote Sivagnanam, who, despite his recent rapprochement with the DMK, lamented thus:

A museum commemorating the *Cilappatikâram* and a memorial celebrating Kattabomman have been built. The names of ministers and homes have been changed. Street names have been changed, and so have the names of towns. But Tamil's fortunes have not changed. Formerly, Tamilttây was worshipped three times a day. Today, she is worshipped six times a day. She is worshipped with great pomp and splendor. But the chains that fetter her arms and legs have not been destroyed.... Tamil will not grow by changing the names of streets, towns, and gardens.

Dravidianism and its Discontents

And this is a lament that we continue to hear to this day, even after about a century of Tamil devotional activity. Sivagnanam's statement points to a fundamental problem with which the Tamilnadu state has had to contend, especially in the past three decades or so, when it has been under the rule of political parties which are ostensibly dedicated to the Tamil cause. In addition to confronting the crucial issue of which Tamil to promote—"classical" Tamil, "pure" Tamil, the "people's" Tamil, and so on—there has been growing awareness that the socioeconomic and political realities of Tamil's status as a regional language within the linguistic economy of a multilingual nation-state, itself embedded within a larger global environment in which English dominates as the world language, preclude the active implementation of public policies that will ensure the supremacy of Tamil in all spheres at all times, the ideal of Dravidianism (on this, see Tamilkudimagan 1990). Strapped by financial and political constraints, it has been easier for the state to indulge in symbolic activities, such as changing street names and instituting official anthems, rather than to ensure high quality education in Tamil studies, or to create job opportunities that would convince Tamil speakers that the study of Tamil is a viable end in itself. Tamil's devotees undoubtedly recognize the value of the symbolic act, but Sivagnanam's lament also reminds us that Tamil devotionalism demands much more, especially from a party that claims to be ruling on behalf of Tamilttây. From the start, Dravidianism, like Indianism, placed its hopes in the political process. The establishment of a Tamil state and the Tamilization of the political apparatus, it was proclaimed, would ensure the triumph of Tamil, everywhere and in everything. And yet, this has not happened. This is a tragedy that casts its long shadow not just on Dravidianism, but on the rest of the Tamil devotional community as well.

This has not been the only cross that Dravidianism has had to bear. The Congress's policies caused the increasing disenchantment of devotees of Indianist sentiment and compelled several to embrace Dravidianism. Similarly, the empowerment of the DMK has accompanied the progressive Indianization of the message of Dravidianism, as its radical separatist vision and its credo that Tamil is everything have been progressively diluted in favor of the Tamil community's coexistence with India. Numerous compromises made by the DMK government on linguistic and cultural policies may be cited to support this claim, but perhaps the most illuminating here is the sanitized version of Sundaram Pillai's 1891 hymn that was instituted as the state "prayer song" in 1970.

Of course, the state song is still loyal to Dravidianism's "secular" recasting of Tamil1tteyvam, "Goddess Tamil," as Tamil1ttây, "Mother Tamil." The lines from the 1891 hymn that likened Tamil1ttây to the primordial lord Shiva—which neo-Shaivism kept alive through the next century—are excised, on the grounds that an appropriate prayer song for a modern Tamil community should have no religious or sectarian associations. This significant erasure is not surprising given radical Dravidianism's antagonism to the divinization of Tamil and to Hinduism. And yet, the government order explicitly refers to Tamil1ttây as the "goddess of Tamil," a slippage that is not accidental. For it indexes the progressive accommodation with religiosity that characterizes DMK cultural policy through the 1950s and 1960s. It also reminds us that within Dravidianism itself, Tamil increasingly took on the mantle of conventional Hindu deities, even as it displaced them.

Next, the recast anthem comes close to compensatory, rather than contestatory, classicism's stance on Tamil, for the government also deliberately excised the much-quoted lines of the original hymn that had referred to Sanskrit as a "dead" language and had declared the superiority of the ever-enduring Tamil (*kan1n1ittamil1*). In his reminiscences, Chief Minister Karunanidhi maintains that these lines were not incorporated into the state prayer song because "it is not appropriate to disparage or ridicule other languages, and to use inauspicious words such as 'ruined' or 'dead' in a hymn in praise of Tamil1ttây to be recited at government functions" (Karunanidhi 1987: 233). Yet, as we have seen, both contestatory classicism and Dravidianism built their arguments on the assumption that Sanskrit was a "dead" language whose very presence had sucked the life out of Tamil.

Finally, Sundaram Pillai's hymn was selected over numerous others precisely because it simultaneously acknowledges the legitimacy of both *tirâvit#a nât#u* (Dravidian nation) and *paratak kan#t#am* (Indian nation). Indeed, the government insisted that the state's prayer song would in no way supplant the Indian national anthem: while the former would be sung at the commencement of official functions, the latter—and no other—would be recited at their conclusion.

Thus the modern Tamil community—as envisioned by the DMK government in this hymn—has been symbolically framed in terms of its dual "Dravidian" and "Indian" heritages, a position that clearly conforms more closely to the Indianist, rather than to the radical Dravidianist, imagining of Tamil. In what ought to have been Dravidianism's paradigmatic moment of triumph—the institution of a daily celebration of Tamil and Tamil1ttây by the DMK—it appears as if it is Indianism, and its vision of Tamil as part of the Indian whole, that wins out.

4

Hinduism Architecture in India

INTRODUCTION

Every civilization's religion too, in the course of its history contributes something to the world in general and in particular to the world of art and architecture. Religious beliefs, ideas and ideals are sometimes given visual expression and sometimes form the subject matter of art and architecture. In a sense art and architecture provide mirrors to reflect a civilization's religion. In this respect Buddhism is no exception.

To contribute means to give. What Buddhism has given to the world is not only a profound analysis of, and a practical solution for the problem of human suffering but also a monumental and rich legacy to the world of art and architecture. Much of this legacy is visible even today in its homeland of India and in much of the eastern world. Today, I would like to give all of you gathered here, a glimpse at what is in a way Buddhism's fourth jewel, its art and architecture.

The beginnings of the Buddhist school of architecture can be traced back to B.C. 255 when the Mauryan emperor Asoka established Buddhism as the state religion of his large empire. Buddhism spread rapidly throughout India and other parts of Asia. Buddhism was, as it were, a graphic creed, and correspondingly its expansion was accompanied by a distinctive style of architecture that expressed the teachings of the Buddha. In India this early Buddhist art was influenced to a large extent by Asoka. He was responsible for the construction of several stupas, which are sacred mounds of brick commemorative of the Buddha. Asoka also constructed stone pillars symbolizing his creed. These were lofty free-standing monolithic columns erected on sacred sites. The most famous of these is at Sarnath.

The Mauryan dynasty crumbled after Asoka's death in 232 B.C; in its wake came the Sungas, who in turn were succeeded by the Andhras. Both these Brahmanical dynasties treated the Buddhists with toleration. The initial steps of the new architectural movement involved enlarging Asoka's stupas. For instance, the stupa at Sanchi was enlarged to nearly twice its size and elaborate gateways were added.

At about the same time that the Buddhist communities were elaborating Asoka's stupas, an entirely different form of architecture was developing in western India. These structures were not, however, built of stone or wood, but carved out of living rock. It is therefore unfortunate that these structures are now referred to as "caves", as though they were natural grottoes in the mountainside, since they are actually large and well planned temples. Some of the finest specimens of this rock cut architecture are to be seen at Ajanta.

Under the reign of the 8th century ruler Lalitaditya, the central Kashmir valley became an important artistic site. A magnificent Surya temple was constructed at Martand. Though now ruined, this remains the masterpiece of Kashmiri architecture. Mahayana Buddhism flourished in the arid valleys of Ladakh, beyond the first high range of the Himalayas. The monasteries at Alchi, dating from the 11th century, have beautiful paintings depicting the Mahayana pantheon. Cave temples were constructed in the 13th to 15th centuries at Saspol and Karsha.

The monasteries at Leh and Phiyang continue to be renovated even today, and the recent resurgence of Indian Buddhism, associated not only with the conversion of lower-caste Hindus to Buddhism under the influence of Ambedkar but with the establishment of Tibetan Buddhist communities, particularly in north India, has introduced a fresh chapter in the history of Buddhist architecture in India.

CONTRIBUTION OF BUDDHISM TO THE WORLD

All civilizations whether primitive, ancient, mediaeval or modem have in the course of their development produced cultures. In the name of Culture they have created art and architecture, language and literature, music and dance social customs, codes of ethics and behaviour, laws, philosophy and religion. It is by examining a civilization's cultural contributions to the world that we can gain some idea and appreciation of its achievements. This becomes more visible when we look into different periods of the art and architecture from around the world.

The very earliest examples of Buddhist art are not iconic but aniconic images and were popular in India after the death of the Buddha. This is because the Buddha, himself did not sanction personal worship or the making of images of the Tathagata, as to have done so would have contradicted his message to mankind. He taught and encouraged people to heed his example and be self-reliant in striving to put an end to human suffering and endless rebirth in Samsara and realise Nibbana for themselves. He was the living proof that this was possible and promised this was attainable by anyone through renouncing worldly and ego-centric desires and by making earnest efforts at mental development and purification as this would help one to eradicate the causes of suffering, greed, hatred and delusion and ultimately result in the attainment of Arahatship and Nibbana. Siddhatha Gotama was a Buddha, a self-perfected, self-enlightened human being and not a saviour of men. He was a human role-model to be followed but not idolized.

Of himself he said, 'Buddha's only point the way'. So this is why the earliest artistic tributes to the Buddha Gotama are abstract symbols indicative of major events and achievements in his last life and in some cases his previous lives. They also serve as reminders of his teachings and provide inspiration.

Some of these early aniconic representations of the Buddha include:

1. The Buddha's footprints which were often created at a place where he was know to have walked or was the scene of one of the Jataka Tales which recount his lifetimes as the Bodhisatta, striving to fulfil the perfections necessary in order to become a Buddha in the future. Such an image exists at Swat in Pakistan and indicates what is believed to have been the scene of the Deer or Migara Jataka Story. Another example of this type of narrative imagery are the depictions of the Jataka Tales at Barhut in India.

2. The Bodhi-tree which is symbolic of Gotama's enlightenment at the age of thirty-five. A cutting of a tree, believed to have been taken from the original Bodhi Tree is enshrined at Bodh Gaya in the grounds of the Mahabodhi Temple. The Bodhi-tree image was retained and used in many later examples of Buddhist art.

3. The Lotus Flower which symbolizes both purity and enlightenment and is a popular motif in much Buddhist art and architecture and is very widely used in Tibetan Buddhist Art.

4. The Wheel which is a reminder of the Buddha's First Sermon. "The Turning of the Wheel of the Law" delivered at Sarnath in Northern India and where stand the ruins of the ancient Dhamekh Stupa commemorating this major event. The wheel has also been adapted to symbolize the wheel of suffering in Samsara in Tibetan Buddhism and many examples of it are beautifully and skillfully depicted in Tibetan Buddhist Art on mandals, a type of meditation-aid and on the cloth paintings known as thankgas.

5. A riderless horse which recalls Prince Siddhattha's renunciation of worldly life for the ascetic life and the beginning of his search for the path to Enlightenment.

6. An empty throne which serves as a reminder of his passing away and attainment of Parinibbana.

After the Buddha's death out of deference to his wishes and devotion to his memory and his teachings, these symbols were widely used in the early days of Buddhist Art in India. Some still survive there and can be seen for example, at the Mahabodhi Temple built at Bodh Gaya, near the scene of the Buddha's Enlightenment. Some of them were also incorporated in later developments of Buddhist art and architecture and featured prominently in places as far afield as for example, the Temples of Thailand. Many of these symbols are used in contemporary Buddhist art and architecture in both the East and West.

To better appreciate Buddhism's contribution to art and architectural we have to take into account the two major schools of Buddhism, the Theravada or Hinayana and the Mahayana as these were to play significant roles in the creation and development of very different types of Buddhist art and architecture. The two schools arose as the result of a rift in the Sangha which had its cause in a dispute over the rule of life for monks. This occurred during the Second Buddhist Council, convened about a century after the first Council was called, in order that the Sangha Elders might recite and agree upon the Dhamma (doctrine) and Vinaya (discipline). This was necessary as the Buddha chose to name no successor. He explicitly stated that the Dhamma and Vinaya was to be his followers' only guide and teacher when he had gone. Later on this fundamental spilt caused the Dhamma itself to be interpreted differently and this brought about the rise of the two major schools of Buddhism with their different beliefs and ideals, which in turn were to have an important influence on Buddhist art and architecture. Despite the schism and the establishing of the two schools neither school's adherents abandoned the Buddha nor the ultimate goal of deliverance from suffering and rebirth culminating in the realisation of Nibbana or Nirvana. However, as the word, 'yana' implies, the vehicle used to reach that goal was different. It is this choice of vehicle which accounts for a difference in the beliefs and ideals which we see mirrored in the art and architecture created by Theravadins and Mahayanists throughout the history of Buddhism.

The Theravada School is the more orthodox and conservative of the two. Its adherents uphold the Dhamma and the ideal of the Arahat and look to the Buddha as the human role-model to imitate in their striving to attain deliverance from suffering and rebirth, and eventually Arahatship and Nibbana. Their vehicle to reach this goal is renunciation of all worldly attachments, the eradication of greed, hatred and delusion through following the Noble Eightfold Path and the cultivation of wisdom and insight. India is the birth-place of Theravada Buddhism and its art and architecture. There the artists and builders of Buddhist structures sought to portray the historical Buddha, and his disciples in the context of Theravadin beliefs and ideals. The chosen medium for this was the Buddha rupa or image and was developed in India. The earliest image we know of is actually a coin struck in the reign of King Kanishak. It shows a robed, standing Buddha. His head is surrounded by a halo, symbolizing his Enlightenment, and his hair is twisted into a top-knot, and one of his hands is raised in the gesture of blessing. The art of Buddhist sculpture and of Buddha images in particular, originated in India, and two distinct styles were created. One in the north, in Gandhara, where the image makers looked to the Greco-Roman tradition for inspiration.

The second style of Buddha image was directly influenced by the earlier Indian style of art peculiar to the south. The first images that we know of appeared in Mathura. The Mathura Buddha images had straight hair tied up in a top knot, and were garbed in the traditional Indian dhoti. The Mathura Buddhas are often shown, smiling peacefully. As these images were most commonly made of sandstone they are much softer in contour and more rounded and curved than those made in the north. Many early Indian Buddhist images show the Buddha as having the thirty-two marks of a Buddha and with his hands placed in various positions displaying gestures of blessing, meditation and teaching. The number of Buddha images and Buddhist architectural structures which survive in India is very great indeed, but in all of the faces of every image, and in the art and design of every stupa. and temple or rock-cave vihara traces of the Buddha-Dhamma are visible.

As Buddhist Art developed and spread outside India the two basic styles were imitated as for example in China where the Gandhara style was imitated in images made of bronze. Gradually the faces on these images were made to look more and more Chinese and are even dressed in long flowing, robes and shawls, after the Chinese fashion. In those countries where Sarvastivada or Theravada Buddhism took hold and remained, such as Afghanistan, Laos, and Sri Lanka, famous for its enormous reclining Buddha. and in Siam, modern Thailand, which is famous for its exquisite and graceful 'Walking Buddhas' or in the temples and shrines of the ancient capital city of Pagan in Burma now known as Myanmar with its many temples, and in the temples of Malaysia, too the Buddha images housed there, show the influence of the early types of Indian Buddha image.

Other notable surviving examples of Buddhist art which mirror the Theravada tradition are to be found at Lumbini in Nepal, the site of the Buddha's birth and in India at Bodh Gaya, Saranath. Kushinagara, Nalanda and at the Shwedagon Pagoda in Yangon, Myanmar, and also at the massive temple complex at Angkor Wat in Cambodia and the very simply, designed yet impressive Temple of the Sacred Tooth in Kandy, Sri Lanka.

The main difference between the Theravada and Mahayana Schools of Art is their subject matter. This difference was a direct reflection of the different ideals and beliefs held by the two schools. For the Theravadins the ideal is the Arahat, who like a Buddha seeks to eradicate suffering and rebirth in Samsara through renouncing the world, and through the eradication of greed, hatred and delusion. This achievement is made possible if one follows the Middle Way and the Noble Eightfold Path as taught by the Buddha Gotama. Nibbana is the Theravadin's final goal and is attainable through the practice of insight. These beliefs and ideals form the subject matter of Theravada Buddhist Art. On the other hand, although the followers of the Mahayana School of Buddhism uphold the goal of Nirvana also and deliverance from endless suffering and rebirth in Samsara, they have a different spiritual hero.

Their hero is not the Buddha Gotama, but the Bodhisattva. A Bodhisattva is a kind of divine saviour, whose role is to aid any being desirous of deliverance and Nirvana. In Mahayana Buddhism anyone can become enlightened and renunciation of the world in order to win Arahatship is not absolutely necessary, but the practice of specific rites and rituals and meditations and visualizations is. These spiritual practices will aid the practitioner in purifying the mind and will also attract the help of the Bodhisattva. The Mahayana School recognised the historical Buddha Gotama, the Shakyamuni, but raised him to the level of a god. He then became but one of many, many divine Buddhas and was eventually regarded as a powerful emanation of the Supreme Essence. It was these celestial Buddhas that were portrayed in Mahayanist Art and very beautifully too in countries such as China, Vietnam, Japan and Korea and of course Tibet where the Mahayana Tradition is followed.

As the Mahayanist school of thought evolved it developed many separate sects which attracted many followers such as the Zen sects of China and Japan. As has been said earlier, Mahayana Buddhism does not uphold the ideal of the Arahat but the Bodhisattva ideal and along with the Cosmic and celestial Buddhas form the subject matter of Mahayanist Art as well as the populous pantheon which surrounds the many Buddhas and Bodhisattvas that belong to the Mahayana Tradition. The word, Bodhisattva, means, 'a being of wisdom' and is a being whose perfections are fulfilled and who stands on the threshold of Nirvana but postpones the attainment of it out of compassion for all other unenlightened beings trapped in Samsara. The greatest virtue of the Bodhisattvas, and there are many, both male and female, is their compassion in contrast to the supreme wisdom of the historical Buddha. This boundless compassion it is what makes a Bodhisattva a saviour and not a human role-model as was the Buddha Gotama. It is also believed that anyone can become enlightened who asks for their help and who practises all the special mediation exercises and performs all the relevant rituals such as chanting.

Mahayana Buddhism is much more mystical than Theravada Buddhism, and therefore so is its art. The figures we see depicted in Mahayanist Art such as Maitreya, Avalokiteshvara, Chenrezig, Manjushri, Tara and Kuan Yin, are all Bodhisattvas. Their beauty and other-worldliness is inexpressable in words, but impressively and well conveyed through the medium of art. We can see them portrayed on wall paintings, on silk scrolls or their images delicately carved of wood, and also notably in the Buddhist caves of China such as those at Longmen, and in the surviving temples of Tibet and the Tibetan exile's place of refuge at Dharmasala in India and in the Mahayanist Buddhist holy places of Nepal, Vietnam, Mongolia and in the Buddhist places of Indonesia, in the east as well as in the many Tibetan centres which in recent times have been founded in the West, such as Samye-Ling, in Scotland.

Throughout the history of Buddhism the supporters of both these major schools have provided countless fine examples of Buddhist art and built magnificent stupas and temples. As one of the functions of Art is to mirror and another is to inspire then most certainly, the ideals and beliefs mirrored in both the major schools of Buddhist Art are a source of inspiration and encouragement to anyone wishing to follow the spiritual beliefs and ideals they reflect.

Both Buddhist Traditions made a huge and impressive contribution to mankind which can be chronicled for over two thousand years and follows the progress the Buddha-Dhamma made as it spread outwards from India in all directions. To better appreciate just how much Buddhism influenced the world and contributed to the world of art and architecture, it is necessary to understand how and why Buddhism spread as far as it did. Buddhism owes its success and its many converts to the catholicity of its appeal and its promise of deliverance from suffering. This is true of both traditions. It also was widely adopted and in some case fully integrated into an existing culture as was the case in Japan. And this success was possible because of the non-coercive approach of its missionaries. However, Buddhists did sometimes suffer persecution and even death and was the case in India, Tibet and China.

Buddhism was also successful because at various times in its history, it enjoyed royal patronage, as for example, that of the great Mauryan King Asoka and some of the later rulers of India including the Pala Kings, the last Buddhist Kings of India. Outside India it was embraced by King Tissa of Ceylon, in 247 B.C.E., the Mon ruler of Thaton. and later in 1056 by the Burmese King Anawrahta the founder of Pagan, in Siam in the eleventh century by King Rama Khamheng and in 1327 by Cambodia's King Jayavarman VII who ruled from his capital at Angkor. It was also adopted by the rulers of Laos and in the eight century in Indonesia by King Sailendra who sponsored the building of the largest Buddhist monument in the world, Borobodur. This devotion to Buddhism and the enthusiasm for Buddhist culture shown by these royal converts and most of their subjects was sincere and the world of art and architecture was all the richer for it.

Another significant factor to influence the spread of Buddhism and indirectly the development of Buddhist Art and Architecture was the tremendous volume of trade which existed in the ancient world most notably along the Silk Road, which was a trade route not only for goods but for ideas as well. The spread of Buddhism in its homeland of northern India began the day the Buddha and the first sixty Arahats went forth to preach the Dhamma. "For the gain of many, for the welfare of many, in compassion for the world." Although Buddhism in India was to die out as a result of the revival of Hinduism and in the aftermath of the Moslem invasions in the seventh century, it was able to spread, and evolve and survive in many other places since. The visible proof of this is to be see in the many examples of Buddhist Architecture.

The size of Buddhism's contribution to the world of architecture is enormous. There are two basic types of structure found in those places where Buddhism spread and developed and they are the Vihara and the Stupa. The word vihara, means "an abode", and its function was two-fold. It was intended to house Buddha images and art and also to serve as a dwelling place for monks. King Bimbisara donated the first Vihara, Veluvana at Rajagaha. to the Buddha himself and his disciples. This was a monastery sited in a Bamboo Grove. Much later on monks would dwell in the shelter of India's caves. One of the most famous cave complexes is the magnificently embellished caves at Ajanta, with its brightly coloured Buddhist murals. Another impressive cave complex is in Afghanistan. As the Vihara evolved in style it was adapted to the climate and terrain of the countries to which Buddhism spread and its design changed and evolved and eventually reflected the cultural characteristics of the lands where either Mahayana Buddhism or Theravada Buddhism had taken root and flourished. The more modern styles of Buddhist temple remain a type of vihara. These structures are made from a variety of materials such as stone in India and Sri Lanka, and from wood as can be see at Kyoto and Nara, in Japan. Brick was also used and some of the surviving temples of Pagan are made of brick. Sandstone is the material used in the building of Malaysian temples.

The second type of Buddhist structure is the Stupa and is itself an object of worship as it was intended to serve as a relic chamber for the Buddha's remains. The earliest examples of the Buddhist stupa were raised in India, as for example the dome shaped stupa at Sanchi, the ancient Dhamekh Stupa at Sarnath and those built inside the caves at Ellora and Ajanta. In time the basic Indian stupa-design evolved into the Dagoba in Sri Lanka, the Chorten in Tibet and the Pagodas of China, Korea and Japan. One of the finest examples of all is the splendid Shwedagon Pagoda in Yangon. As with Buddhist Art, the materials used in the building of viharas and temples and the various types of stupa and pagoda varied and depended on the materials available in the places where they were built. So we find some stupas are built of marble or other types of local stone or brick and even wood, as was the Goose Pagoda at Chagan in China. Happily in the west where Buddhism is becoming a very popular religion, the artists and architects who work on Buddhist building projects turn to the rich and varied legacy of Buddhist Art and Architecture for their inspiration.

All the Buddhist structures that were ever built by their very existence contributed something to the world and are holy places, places of learning and sanctuary for the people who were to use them and the repositories of some of the greatest treasures of Buddhist Art. They were and those that have survived continue to be a source of personal inspiration for all who saw them either in person long ago or even see them depicted in a drawing or a photograph these days. As was said, earlier Buddhist Art and Architecture mirrors the beliefs, ideas and ideals of both the Mahayana and Theravada traditions.

Buddhism in India together with its art and architecture reached its zenith during the Gupta dynasty which was established in northern India in 320 A.D. It was to last into the seventh century. The best known examples of Buddhist Art are from this period and were to form the standard of comparison for all subsequent Buddhist art and architecture both in India and in the rest of the Asian countries where it spread, took root and flourished. The Gupta period also saw the advent of Buddhism's decline in India. It slowly waned for three reasons. First was the rise of Mahayana Buddhism in India which was to bring Buddhism closer to Hinduism. The second reason was that Hinduism enjoyed the support of Kings and underwent a revival. This was so successful that in time it was to absorb the now strongly Mahayana influenced Buddhism. The third reason for Buddhism's decline was the various Moslem invasions, the last of which was waged in the seventh century A.D. and was directly responsible for Buddhism's slow decline and fall. However, at this time as we shall see Buddhism spread out of India to Nepal, later on to Sri Lanka and then eastwards to South East Asia and survived.

In short, Buddhism and its art and architecture was to spread geographically outwards from India in two directions. One was to the northwest into Afghanistan, Iran and then along the Silk Road to Central Asia and then further east to China, Korea and Japan. This development came about not only because of the activity of Buddhist Missionaries, but also because of the work of those Indian traders and the migration of those Indian emigres who settled in Central Asia. These people carried both Hinduism, and Buddhism and much of Indian culture with them wherever they went. This is obvious when we look at the wealth of Indian and Buddhist Art which was created there and can still be seen, today. However, in China, Korea and Japan Buddhism did not supplant the existing cultures but was totally integrated into them.

At the end of India's Gupta period Buddhism was taken to Nepal, Sri Lanka and to the South East Asian Mainland. As I said before, this outward movement was the direct result of the changes taking place in India at the time. Indian commerce also played a part, in Buddhism's spread to these places and were to be greatly influenced not only by Indian culture but also by the work of Indian merchants and monks, who brought with them not only religion but also their country's civilization-writing, art, architecture and methods of ruling as well. The influence of Hinduism was to touch these places before that of Buddhism did, but in time the two coexisted. In the end, however, Hinduism could not endure for long abroad because of the very rigid caste system it supported. Nevertheless, traces of Hindu culture have survived in these places and testify to the great contribution India made over the centuries to all of the Asian world and is still going on. Nowadays India's culture is being carried abroad by the large numbers of Asians emigrating to Australia, Europe, Africa and the United States of America and South America. They are the current carriers of Buddhism and its fourth jewel Buddhist Art and Architecture.

Now, I would like to tell you a true story. The late John Blofeld, a Buddhist scholar and writer of great repute once told the story of how he first became attracted to Buddhism when he was young. One day, he spied a strange statue in shop in Brighton. Sussex and his curiosity was awakened. When he asked what it was, the shop-keeper kindly told him it was a statue of a Buddha. Although, he could not afford to by it then and there, he very much wanted to. For days he could not get the image with its calm and peaceful expression out of his mind. As soon as he was able to afford it he bought it and it became his most treasured possession and kept it with him always. Seeing that statue, was for him a turning-point in his life. Later he began a life-long investigation into Buddhism.

Buddhism has been making contributions to the world's cultures through its teachings. its art and architecture for more than two millennium long. May this continue!

INDUS VALLEY CIVILIZATION

The Indus civilization or the Harappan civilization, which flourished during the Bronze Age i.e. 2500-2000 BC is ranked among the four widely known civilizations of the old world. Extensive excavation work that has been done since Independence has so far identified more than 100 sites belonging to this civilization. A few prominent among them are Dholavira (Gujarat), Kalibangan (Rajasthan), Lothal (Gujarat), Sarkotada (Gujarat), Diamabad (Maharashtra), Alamgirpur (U.P.), Bhagwanpura (Haryana), Banawali (Haryana), Kuntasi, Padri (Gujarat) and Mauda (Jammu).

Extensive town planning was the characteristic of this civilization, which is evident from the gridiron pattern for the layout of cities, some with fortifications and the elaborate drainage and water management systems. The houses were built of baked bricks, which is rare in contemporary civilizations at Mesopotamia and Egypt. Bricks of fixed sizes, as well as stone and wood were also used for building. Buildings in the lower area are rather monotonous, being mainly functional rather than decorative.

But many houses are two storeyed. The most imposing of the buildings is the Great Bath of Mohenjodaro. It is 54.86 metres long and 32.91 metres wide and with 2.43 metres thick outer walls. The Bath had galleries and rooms on all sides. Another important structure was the Granary complex comprising of blocks with an overall area of 55 x 43 metres. The granaries were intelligently constructed, with strategic air ducts and platforms divided into units.

THE MAURYAN PERIOD

If the remnants of the Indus culture are excluded, the earliest surviving architectural heritage in India is that of the Mauryans. The Mauryan period was a great landmark in the history of Indian art. Some of the monuments and pillars belonging to this period are considered as the finest specimens of Indian art.

The Mauryan architecture was embalmed in timber, for rocks and stones were not as freely in use then. The art of polishing of wood reached so much perfection during the Mauryan period that master craftsmen used to make wood glisten like a mirror. Chandra Gupta Maurya had built many buildings, palaces and monuments with wood, most of which perished with time. In 300 B.C., Chandragupta Maurya constructed a wooden fort 14.48 km long and 2.41km wide, along the Ganges in Bihar. However, only a couple of teak beams have survived from this fort.

Ashoka was the first Mauryan Emperor who began to "think in stone". The stonework of the Ashokan Period (3rd century B.C.) was of a highly diversified order and comprised of lofty free-standing pillars, railings of the stupas, lion thrones and other colossal figures. The use of stone had reached such great perfection during this time that even small fragments of stone art was given a high lustrous polish resembling fine enamel. While most of the shapes and decorative forms employed were indigenous in origin, some exotic forms show the influence of Greek, Persian and Egyptian cultures.

The Ashokan period marked the beginning of the Buddhist School of architecture in India. It witnessed the construction of many rock-cut caves, pillars, stupas and palaces. A number of cave-shrines belonging to this period have been excavated in the Barabar and Nagarjuni hills and Sitamarhi in Bihar. These rock-cut sanctuaries, quarried from large masses of rocks called gneisses, are simple in plan and are devoid of all interior decorative carvings. The caves served as the residences of the monks.

There are several inscriptions, which indicate that these rock-cut sanctuaries were constructed by Emperor Ashoka for the monks of the Ajivika sect, who are more closely related to the Jains than to the Buddhists.

The Ashokan rock-edict at Dhauli, near Bhubaneshwar, is considered to be the earliest rock-cut sculpture in India. It has a sculpted elephant on the top, which signifies the Emperor's conversion to Buddhism after his Kalinga victory. The monolithic Ashokan pillars are marvels of architecture and sculpture. These were lofty free standing monolithic columns erected on sacred sites.

Originally there were about thirty pillars but now only ten are in existence, of which only two with lion capitals stand in situ in good condition at Kolhua and Laurya Nandangarh respectively. Each pillar was about 15.24 metres high and weighed about 50 tonnes and was made out of fine sandstone. The pillar consisted of three parts-the prop, the shaft and the capitol. The capitol consisted of fine polished stone containing one or more animal figures in the round. Made of bricks, they carried declarations from the king regarding Buddhism or any other topic. The pillars did not stand in isolation and were usually found near stupas in a spot either unknowingly marked by the Buddha himself or along the royal route to Magadha, the capital.

The Sarnath pillar is one of the finest pieces of sculpture of the Ashokan period. The Ashokan pillars also throw light on the contacts India had with Persia and other countries. Two of the Ashkan edicts have also been found at Laghman, near Jalalabad in modern Afghanistan.

Ashoka was responsible for the construction of several stupas, which were large halls, capped with domes and bore symbols of the Buddha. The most important ones are located at Bharhut, Bodhgaya, Sanchi, Amravati and Nagarjunakonda. The Buddhist shrines or the monasteries were built in somewhat irregular designs following the Gandhara style of architecture. Built on the patterns of a fort and defended by a stone wall, the monastery evolved from the site of an ancient stupa. The principle buildings were housed within a rectangular courtyard with a stupa in the south and the monastery in the north.

Ashoka had also built a number of palaces, but most of them have perished. Ashoka's palace near Patna was a masterpiece. Enclosed by a high brick wall, the highlight of the palace was an immense 76.2 metres high pillared-hall having three storeys. The Chinese traveller Fahien was so impressed by this palace that he stated that "it was made by spirits" and that its carvings are so elegantly executed "which no human hands of this world could accomplish". Made mostly of wood, it seems to have been destroyed by fire. Its existence was pointed out during the excavations at Kumrahar, near Patna, where its ashes have been found preserved for several thousand years.

5

Buddists Temples and Modern Architecture of India

INTRODUCTION

As temples form the backbone of Indian medieval architectural heritage, it would be appropriate to discuss their basic architectural features before we move on to different styles of Indian architecture. Despite the vastness of the land, Indian temple architecture is remarkably uniform. It is, however, often distinguished into two chief styles, each having numerous sub-styles. The Northern or Indo-Aryan style is marked by a tower with rounded top and curvilinear outline while the Southern or Dravidian style has the tower usually in the shape of a rectangular truncated pyramid.

The standard type of the Hindu temple has remained fundamentally same from the 6th century AD to the present day. The construction of temples-whether in the north in the south-essentially followed a similar pattern. There is the sanctuary or the vimana of which the upper and outer pyramidal and tapering portion is called the shikhara, or pinnacle. The vimana is a rather dark place that houses the divine deity. This small area is called garbha griha, literally meaning 'womb house'. The entrance is through a doorway, normally from the eastern side. The doorway is reached through a mandapa or pillared hall, where devotees congregate for prayers. However, earlier temples may have had the mandapa at a little distance from the main temple (the Shore Temple in Mamallapuram near Chennai, circa 700 A.D.), although this practise was done away with in later constructions. Later it became necessary to unite both buildings, making way for the antarala or intermediate vestibule. A porch or a smaller room called ardha mandapa leads up to a hall (mandapa), which in turn goes into a maha mandapa. A tower generally surmounted the shrine-room while smaller towers rose from other parts of the building. The whole conception was set in a rectangular courtyard, which sometimes contained lesser shrines and was often placed on a raised platform. The most perfect examples of temples on this structure are the Khajuraho temples. Here, each chamber has its own separate pyramidal roof rising in gradual steps so that the final sanctum's roof towers up, surrounded by smaller spires, finally forming a graceful, rising stepped pyramid.

In some parts of India, the ascending pyramid roof format was not followed. The roof in such temples was still pyramidal, but was formed of layers that gradually became narrower as they rose. A courtyard was built around the temple, and sometimes a wall would be constructed to ensure seclusion. The outer walls were treated by carving in an orderly group of repetitive miniatures. The shikhara or tapering roof was specifically based on this design, which may have originated f om the domed huts of central and eastern India.

MODERN ARCHITECTURE OF INDIA

After the British left India in 1947, Indian architecture dropped into an abyss. Indian architects, who were relegated to the role of being assistants to the British architects under the British Raj, took their own time to express their ingenuity. Perhaps, there was an identity crisis, a dilemma whether to bask in the glory of the past or move forward with times using new ideas, images and techniques. While in other fields like art, music and culture, the distinct Indian imprint was more enhanced in the post-Independence period; no such thing was discernible in the case of architecture. It is no doubt that the Indian architects were unable to achieve a transformative architecture despite the existence of great potential at the time of Indian Independence.

The post-Independence period saw the emergence of two schools of thought in architecture--the Revivalist and the Modernist. The Revivalists, who advocated "continuity with the past", could not break the shackles of the colonial legacy and left no significant impact on the neo-Indian architecture. The Modernists too depended heavily on the European and American models and tried to adopt them in India without taking into consideration the regional aspirations, diversities and requirements. The contemporary Indian architecture was also beset with problems like population explosion, lack of vision among the planners, lack of support from the government and a less than satisfactory standard of architecture education. The result was that during the initial years after the Independence, foreign architects continued to play a leading role in Indian architecture.

Jawaharlal Nehru, the first Prime Minister, had called for an open architectural competition for the design of the Ashoka Hotel in 1956, which was won by B.E.Doctor, an architect from Bombay. Using technology to create large pillar-less spaces, Doctor created a facade that borrowed from Islamic, Hindu, British and modern architecture.

Indian architecture witnessed a revolution when the Punjab government engaged Le Corbusier to design the new city of Chandigarh. Built in three stages, Corbusier divided the city into three sections. The 'head' consisted of political, bureaucratic and judicial buildings, the administrative parts of the city. The 'body' housed the university and residential complexes in the heart of the city. The 'feet' consisted of industrial sectors and the railway station. Apart from the initial layout of the city, Corbusier also designed several buildings in Chandigarh. The High Court building has a sloping roof, supported by concrete walls which allow air to pass through them. The Assembly is a squarish structure topped with a huge industrial chimney while the Secretariat is made up of hundreds of rooms with an airy exterior.

Taking inspiration from Le Corbusier's creativity, a young Indian architect D V Joshi designed the Institute of Indology in Ahmedabad. Charles Mark Correa, Doshi's contemporary, designed the Hindustan Lever pavilion for the India International Trade Fair in 1961. The pavilion was an exposed concrete structure resembling a crumpled packing case made of concrete with a zigzag ramp to walk along. Correa also designed the Gandhi Sanghralaya in Ahmedabad as a tribute to Mahatma Gandhi.

The Asiad Village in New Delhi, designed by Raj Rewell and built as a colossal complex with more than 800 residential units, landscaped courts, streets, restaurants and shops, all catering to sports persons who had assembled for the 1982 Asian Games, is one of the architectural landmarks of modern India. The lotus-shaped Bahai temple in New Delhi, designed by Fariburz Sabha in 1980 and completed in December 1986, is an awe-inspiring example of the ingenuity of the Indian architects.

However, the fact remains that the contemporary architecture in India has failed to inspire. Even after 50 years of Independence our cities are still symbolised by pre-independence buildings. For instance, Calcutta is symbolised by the Victoria Memorial, New Delhi by the Rashtrapati Bhawan, Mumbai by the Victoria Terminus and the Gateway of India and Chennai by the Victoria Memorial Hall. The post-independence buildings such as the New Secretariat building in Calcutta or the Vigyan Bhawan in New Delhi has nothing much to offer in terms of architectural style.

In contrast most major cities in the world have splendid modern buildings to boast off, like Sydney has its Sydney Opera House, Paris has new Grand Arch and the Georges Pompidos Centre, New York has its World Trade Centre, Chicago has the Sears Tower and Toronto has the C.N.Tower.

Even cities in other Third World countries have several buildings to feel proud about, like Kuala Lumpur has its Petronas Tower, Shangai has the TV Tower, Hong Kong has its Hongkong and Shanghai Corporation building and the Bank of China

Building and even Colombo has its new Parliament building. In November 1998, the media reported that the foundation stone of World Centre of Vedic Learning, the world's tallest building would be laid at Karondi village, in Jabalpur in Madhya Pradesh. The building, which will be built by the Maharishi Mahesh Yogi Vedic University, is being designed according to the Maharishi Sthapatya Veda symbolising the victory of India's ancient knowledge of Vastu Vidya.

The proposed centre for Vedic consciousness, which is modelled on Sao Paulo Tower of Brazil, would be 677 metres (2222 feet) high and 339 metres (1111 feet) wide at the square base. Once completed it will be more than 213 metres (700 feet) taller than the Petronas Tower in Kuala Lumpur and will achieve the distinction of being the world's tallest building. It was also reported that a consortium of architects and engineers who have designed several of the tallest structures in the world is undertaking the design of the building. Indeed, India will have something to cheer about if this building materializes!

Madhya Pradesh seems to be the only state in India which has several grand public buildings and international award winning projects. The New Assembly building in Bhopal and the Madhya Pradesh State Electricity Board office in Jabalpur, The Judicial Academy in Bhopal, the Rajiv Gandhi Jal Grahan Mission in Raipur and the proposed "White House" in Bhopal are some fascinating examples which show that global aesthetics is moving very fast into the smaller Indian cities. Paradoxically, it is the smaller cities and towns like Indore, Raipur, Rajkot, Baroda and Bhopal, with no greatly visible architectural traditions like that of Jaipur, Hyderabad or Lucknow, that are displaying unprecedented alacrity in adapting to 'international styles'. There is a growing brand of young and dynamic architects, which include Charles Correa, Prashant Diwakriti, Ajay Kataria, Anjum Gupta, Vineet Chadha, Nikhil Sompura and others, who do not shy away from experimentation. Most often these architects employ a hybrid style that is a free mix of Roman, English, Gothic, Rajasthani and Mughal styles. This new-age architectural aesthetics has redefined the idea of space. The emphasis now seems to be on having more open spaces, green spaces and natural lighting. It is, however, not possible to term this new trend as a 'representative' architecture of our times as it is highly restricted in geographic terms and also confined to the affluent lot.

SCULPTURE IN INDIA

As far as the origin of sculpture is concerned, it goes back to the Stone Age. The Megalithic people buried their dead and constructed monumental stones over them and worshipped them. The change over from worshipping the ancestral spirits to a personal God is reflected in making icons of the God with his specific attributes. Tiny terra-cotta seals discovered from the Indus Valley reveal carvings of peepal leaves, deities and animals. The famous figurine of the dancing girl of Mohenjodaro bears witness to the fact that the tradition of sculpture and bronze casting goes back to the Indus Valley Civilisation and shows tremendous sophistication and artistry.

The sculpture in India started appearing from 3rd century BC with the stone pillars of Ashoka, the stupas and Toranas of Sanchi, Bharhut, Amravati and the rock-cut viharas of Barabar, Bhaja, Pitalkhoda, Karle, Bedsa, Ajanta and others and continued till the12th century AD. During the reign of the Mauryan emperor Ashoka, nearly 85,000 stupas were constructed. Many awe-inspiring statues exhibiting a serene Buddha, with a glowing face were crafted in large numbers. Though, Buddhism deplored idol worship, human forms of Lord Buddha began to be depicted with features like a halo around the head, the dharmachakra engraved upon his palms and soles of his feet, and the lion throne representing his royal ancestry.

The earliest archaeological evidence of sculpture work in metal, terracotta, wood and stone in the Indian sub-continent is provided by the remains found at the pre-Harappan sites of Baluchistan, the Makran areas of Pakistan and Kalibangan in Rajasthan, dating back to 3000 BC. Literary evidence from the Rigveda states that copper and bronze-smithy was a specialized science and that craftsmen were held in high esteem. Whether it is in wood, stone or ivory, the Indian carver-craftsman has been extremely versatile in applying his techniques and designs to various media. Carved wooden facades and fixtures of dwellings, domestic shrines, temples, churches and palaces of Rajasthan, Gujarat, Kashmir and Kulu in Himachal Pradesh are marked by intricate designs. In Punjab and Haryana, there exists a tradition of clay wall relief in appliqué. India is also famous for producing a startling range of terracotta figures, ritual and secular utility objects and toys for children.

Modern Sculptors: Modern sculpture, like other mediums of art, has experienced a revival. While the traditionalists continue to follow the rhythmic, decorative tradition of the Gupta and Chola periods, there is a growing breed of modern sculptors who are endeavouring to simplify the art form and to bring in contemporary elements and social awareness into their art. Sculptors of this group freely assimilate art forms of Europe and other places to evolve their own individualistic styles. Some of the modern sculptors are Amarnath Sehgal (Conquest of Moon, Collection in White House, Rising Spirit), P. Ramachandra Kamat, Panchal Rajnikant, Dhanraju Bhagat, Jairam, D.P.Choudhury, Sankha Choudhury, Raghav Kaneria, S.Dhanapal, P.V.Janakiram, C.Dakshinamoorthy, P.S.Nandhan, S.Parmavisam, Vidyashankar Sthapathy, S.Nandagopal, Chintamoni, Nandgopal Shankar, Niranjan Pradhan, Pradosh Kusum Das Gupta, Meera Mukherjee and Jashu Shilpi.

WORLD HERITAGE SITES

In 1972, the General Conference of UNESCO adopted a resolution with overwhelming enthusiasm creating thereby a 'Convention concerning the protection of the World Cultural and Natural Heritage'. The main objectives were to: (a) Define the World Heritage in both cultural and natural aspects, (b) Enlist sites and monuments from member countries which are of exceptional interest and universal value the protection of which is the concern of all mankind and (c) Promote co-operation among all Nations and people to contribute for the protection of these universal treasures intact for future generations.

India is an active member State on the World Heritage from 1977. It has been working in close co-operation with other International agencies like International Council of Monuments and Sites (ICOMOS), International Union for the Conservation of Nature and Natural Resources (IUCN) and International Centre for the study of Preservation and Restoration of Cultural Property (ICCROM).

The Department of Culture and Archaeological Survey of India, apart from observing this World Heritage Day on April 18 and the World Heritage Week from 19th November every year. It is specially aimed to involve the youth of the country through NSS/NCC units in such works as protection, preservation and propagation of the great heritage for which our India is world famous.

The various Indian monuments and sites included in the World Heritage List are the Ajanta Caves, Ellora Caves, Agra Fort, Taj Mahal, Sun Temple at Konarak, the Group of Monuments at Mahabalipuram, Kaziranga National Park, Manas Wildlife Sanctuary, Keoladeo National Park, Churches and Convents of Goa, Group of Monuments at Khajuraho, Group of Monuments at Hampi, Fatehpur Sikri, Group of Monuments at Pattadakal, Elephanta Caves, Brihadeeshwara Temple at Thanjavur, Sundarbans National Park, Nanda Devi National Park, Buddhist Monastery at Sanchi, Humayun's Tomb at Delhi and Qutab Minar and associated monuments at Delhi. The UNESCO World Heritage Committee has bestowed world heritage status on the Darjeeling Himalayan Railway in December 1999.

THE PRATHIHARAS

The Pratiharas, who ruled over an extensive empire from Ujjain during the 8th and 9th centuries, were among the significant successors of the Guptas. The Pratihara temples of Central India have their own unique designs and decorative schemes. The important temples of Ujjain include the Mahakaleshwar temple, which has one of the twelve Jyotirlingas of India, Kal Bhairava temple, which finds a mention in the

Skanda Purana, and Mangalnath temple, which is regarded as the birthplace of Mars, according to the Matsya Purana.

THE PALAS

The Pala School of Architecture (8-13th Centuries AD) flourished in Bengal and Bihar under the Pala and the Sena rulers. Nalanda was its most active centre, whose influence was spread to Nepal, Myanmar and even Indonesia. Stone sculptures of this period are found at Nalanda, Rajagriha, Bodh Gaya, Rajashahi and other places. The Pala School of art is seen at its best at Nalanda and several sculptures belonging to this period have been unearthed in excavations.

THE CHANDELAS

The Chandelas of Jijihoti or Bundelkhand were known as great builders during the l0th-11th centuries. It is they who built the temples at Khajuraho justly famous for their graceful contours and erotic sculptures. These 22 temples (out of the original 85) are regarded as one of world's greatest artistic wonders. The Khajuraho Temples do not illustrate a development over a long period of time but were built within a short period of hundred years from 950-1050 A.D.

The Khajuraho Temples have highly individualistic architectural character and are generally small in size. Each temple is divided into three main compartments-the cella or garbha griha, an assembly hall or mandapa and an entrance portico or ardha mandapa. Some temples also contain the antarala or vestibule to the cella and the transepts or maha-mandapa. The Kendriya Mahadev temple is the largest and most beautiful of the Khajuraho Temples. The Shiva Temple at Visvanath and the Vishnu Temple at Chaturbhanj are other important temples at Khajuraho.

CAVE ARCHITECTURE OF INDIA

The earliest man-made caves date back to the 2nd century BC while the latest date to the 7th century AD. The splendid sculpture and lovely frescoes adorning these caves make them one of the glorious monuments of India's past.

Ajanta Caves

The cave temples of Ajanta, situated north of Aurangabad, were first mentioned in the writings of the Chinese pilgrim Huen Tsang who visited India between 629 AD and 645 AD. These caves were discovered by the British officers in 1819 AD. The thirty temples at Ajanta are set into the rocky sides of a crescent shaped gorge in the Inhyadri hills of the Sahyadri ranges. At the head of the gorge is a natural pool which is fed by a waterfall. The excavations spanned a period of about six centuries.

The earlier monuments include both chaitya halls and monasteries. These date from the 2nd to 1st centuries B.C. After a period of more than six centuries, excavations once again revived during the reign of the Vakataka ruler Harishena. The sculptures contain an impressive array of votive figures, accessory figures, narrative episodes and decorative motifs. The series of paintings is unparalleled in the history of Indian art, both for the wide range of subjects and the medium. The caves depict a large number of incidents from the life of the Buddha (Jataka Tales). Overlapping figures suggest that the perspective and colors are harmoniously blended and that the line work is sinuous. However, the identities of the artists responsible for the execution of the Ajanta caves are unknown.

Bhimbetaka Caves

Bhimbetka is located in the Raisen District of Madhya Pradesh about 45 km to the southeast of Bhopal near a hill village called 'Bhiyanpur'. Bhimbetaka, discovered in 1958 by V.S. Wakanker, is the biggest prehistoric art depository in India. Atop the hill a large number of rock-shelters have been discovered, of which more than 130 contain paintings. Excavations in some of the rock-shelters revealed history of continuous habitation from early stone age (about 10000 years) to the end of stone age (c. 10,000 to 2,000 years) as seen from artificially made stone tools and implements like hand-axes, cleavers, scrappers and knives. Neolithic tools like points, trapezes and lunates made of chert and chalcedony, besides stone querns and grinders, decorated bone objects, pieces of ochre and human burials were also found here.

Elephanta Caves

The 6th century Shiva temple in the Elephanta caves is one of the most exquisitely carved temples in India. The central attraction here is a twenty-foot high bust of the deity in three-headed form. The Maheshamurti is built deep into a recess and looms up from the darkness to fill the full height of the cave. This image symbolizes the fierce, feminine and meditative aspects of the great ascetic and the three heads represent Lord Shiva as Aghori, Ardhanarishvara and Mahayogi. Aghori is the aggressive form of Shiva where he is intent on destruction. Ardhanarishvara depicts Lord Shiva as half-man/half-woman signifying the essential unity of the sexes.

The Mahayogi posture symbolises the meditative aspect of the God and here Lord Shiva is shown in his most quiet and serene form. Other sculptures in these caves depict Shiva's cosmic dance of primordial creation and destruction and his marriage to Parvati.

Mahakali Caves

These are rock-cut Buddhist caves situated in the Udayagiri hills, about 6.5km from Mumbai. These were excavated during 200 BC to 600 AD and are now in ruins. They comprise of 4 caves on the southeastern face and 15 caves on the northwestern face. Cave 9 is the chief cave and is the oldest and consists of a stupa and figures of Lord Buddha.

Jogeshwar and Kanheri Caves

Located in the western suburbs of Bombay, it is second largest known cave after the Kailasa cave in Ellora and houses a Brahmanical temple dating back to the 6th century AD.

Excavated between the 1st and 2nd centuries, the Kanheri is a 109-cave complex located near Borivili National Park in

Bombay. The Kanheri caves contain illustrations from Hinayana and Mahayana Buddhism and show carvings dating back to 200 BC.

Karla and Bhaja Caves

About 50-60 kms away from Pune, these are rock-cut Buddhist caves dating back to the 1st and 2nd centuries BC. The caves consist of several viharas and chaityas.

RAJPUT ARCHITECTURE

The Rajputs were great patrons of art and architecture, the finest examples being their forts and palaces. The Rajput palaces are complex compositions built as inner citadels surrounded by the city and enclosed by a fortified wall as at Chittorgarh and Jaisalmer. Some forts, such as those at Bharatpur and Deeg, were protected by wide moats.

The oldest surviving palaces date from the mid-fifteenth century and are found at Chittor and Gwalior. The Man Mandir, the largest palace in Gwalior, was built by Raja Man Singh Tomar (1486-1516). The Man Mandir has two storeys above, and two below, ground level overhanging a sandstone cliff. This gigantic cliff is punctuated by five massive round towers, crowned by domed cupolas and linked by delicately carved parapets. The whole facade is enriched with brilliant blue tiles. The palaces of Jaisalmer, Bikaner, Jodhpur, Udaipur and Kota represent the maturity of the Rajput style. All of these palaces were built predominantly in the 17th and early 18th centuries. The huge fortified city of Jaisalmer is situated far out in the Thar Desert. The buildings are constructed with the local yellow-brown stone and they have been remarkably preserved owing to their remote location.

The city of Bikaner is encircled by 5.63 km long stone wall in rich pink sandstone. There are five gates and three sally ports. The Jodhpur Fort dominates the city, which is surrounded by a huge wall with 101 bastions, nearly 9.5 km long. The Meherangarh fort stands on a cliff with a sheer drop of over 36 metres.

The foundation of Jaipur, the fabled "pink city", in 1727 AD represents the final phase of Rajput architecture. Built by Jai Singh, Jaipur represents a fusion of Eastern and Western ideas of town planning. The city is enclosed by a wall and has bastions and towers at regular intervals. The City Palace is at the center of the walled city and is a spectacular synthesis of Rajput and Mughal architectural styles. The famous building Hawa Mahal, or Palace of Winds, (1799) has a five-storeyed symmetrical facade composed of 953 small casements in a huge curve each with a projecting balcony and crowning arch. The Jantar Mantar, the largest of five observatories built by Jai Singh II in the early eighteenth century, is another interesting example of Rajput architecture.

JAIN ARCHITECTURE

The contribution of Jain art to the mainstream art in India has been considerable. Every phase of Indian art is represented by a Jain version and each one of them is worthy of meticulous study and understanding. Jain architecture cannot be accredited with a style of its own, for in the first place it was almost an offshoot of Hindu and Buddhist styles. In the initial years, many Jain temples were made adjoining the Buddhist temples following the Buddhist rock-cut style. Initially these temples were mainly carved out of rock faces and the use of bricks was almost negligible. However, in later years Jains started building temple-cities on hills based on the concept of 'mountains of immortality'.

Compared to the number of Hindu temples in India, Jain temples are few and spaced out. Surrounded by embattled walls, the temples are divided into wards, guarded by massive bastions at its ends, with fortified gateways as the main entrances. These temple-cities were not built on a specific plan; instead they were the results of sporadic construction. Natural levels of the hill on which the 'city' was being built accommodated various levels so that as one goes higher the architecture and grandeur increases. The only variation in these temples was in the form of frequent chamukhs or four-faced temples. In these the image of a Tirthankara faces the four sides, or four

Tirthankars are be placed back to back to face four cardinal points. Entry into this temple is also from four doors. The Chamukh temple of Adinath (1618 AD) is a characteristic example of the four-door temple.

The great Jain temples and sculptured monuments of Karnataka, Maharashtra and Rajasthan are world-renowned. The most spectacular of all Jain temples are found at Ranakpur and Mount Abu in Rajasthan. Deogarh (Lalitpur, U.P.), Ellora, Badami and Aihole also have some of the important specimens of Jain Art.

THE INDO-ISLAMIC ARCHITECTURE

Indian architecture took new shape with the advent of Islamic rule in India towards the end of the 12th century AD. New elements were introduced into the Indian architecture that include: use of shapes (instead of natural forms); inscriptional art using decorative lettering or calligraphy; inlay decoration and use of coloured marble, painted plaster and brilliantly glazed tiles. In contrast to the indigenous Indian architecture which was of the trabeate order i.e. all spaces were spanned by means of horizontal beams, the Islamic architecture was arcuate i.e. an arch or dome was adopted as a method of bridging a space. The concept of arch or dome was not invented by the Muslims but was, in fact, borrowed and was further perfected by them from the architectural styles of the post-Roman period. The Muslims used the cementing agent in the form of mortar for the first time in the construction of buildings in India. They further put to use certain scientific and mechanical formulae, which were derived by experience of other civilizations, in their constructions in India. Such use of scientific principles helped not only in obtaining greater strength and stability of the construction materials but also provided greater flexibility to the architects and builders. This amalgamation of the Indian and the Islamic elements led to the emergence of a new style of architecture called the Indo-Islamic Architecture.

One fact that must be stressed here is that, the Islamic elements of architecture had already passed through different experimental phases in other countries like Egypt, Iran and Iraq before these were introduced in India. Unlike most Islamic monuments of these countries, which were largely constructed in brick, plaster and rubble, the Indo-Islamic monuments were typical mortar-masonry works formed of dressed stones. It must be emphasized that the development of the Indo-Islamic architecture was greatly facilitated by the knowledge and skill possessed by the Indian craftsmen, who had mastered the art of stonework for centuries and used their experience while constructing Islamic monuments in India.

In simple terms the Islamic architecture in India can be divided into religious and secular. Mosques and Tombs represent the religious architecture, while palaces and forts are examples of secular Islamic architecture. Forts were essentially functional, complete with a little township within and various fortifications to engage and repel the enemy.

Mosques: The mosque or masjid is a representation of Muslim art in its simplest form. The mosque is basically an open courtyard surrounded by a pillared verandah, crowned off with a dome. A mihrab indicates the direction of the qibla for prayer. Towards the right of the mihrab stands the mimbar or pulpit from where the Imam presides over the proceedings. An elevated platform, usually a minaret from where the Faithful are summoned to attend the prayers is an invariable part of a mosque. Large mosques where the faithful assemble for the Friday prayers are called the Jama Masjids.

Tombs: Although not actually religious in nature, the tomb or maqbara introduced an entirely new architectural concept. While the masjid was mainly known for its simplicity, a tomb could range from being a simple affair (Aurangazeb's grave) to an awesome structure enveloped in grandeur (Taj Mahal). The tomb usually consists of solitary compartment or tomb chamber known as the huzrah in whose centre is the cenotaph or zarih. This entire structure is covered with an elaborate dome. In the underground chamber lies the mortuary or the maqbara, in which the corpse is buried in a grave or qabr. Smaller tombs may have a mihrab, although larger mausoleums have a separate mosque located separately from the main tomb. Normally the whole tomb complex or rauza is surrounded by an enclosure. The tomb of a Muslim saint is called a dargah. Almost all Islamic monuments were subjected to free use of verses from the Holy Koran and a great amount of time was spent in carving out minute details on walls, ceilings, pillars and domes.

COLONIAL ARCHITECTURE

European colonists brought with them to India concepts of their "world view" and a whole baggage of the history of European architecture---Neo-Classical, Romanesque, Gothic and Renaissance. The initial structures were utilitarian warehouses and walled trading posts, giving way to fortified towns along the coastline. The Portuguese adapted to India the climatically appropriate Iberian galleried patio house and the Baroque churches of Goa. Se Cathedral and Arch of Conception of Goa were built in the typical Portuguese-Gothic style. The St. Francis Church at Cochin, built by the Portuguese in 1510, is believed to be the first church built by the Europeans in India. The Portuguese also built the fort of Castella de Aguanda near Mumbai and added fortifications to the Bassein fort built by Bahadur Shah, the Sultan of Gujarat, in 1532 AD. The Bassein fort is famous for the Matriz (Cathedral of St Joseph), the Corinthian pillared hall and the Porte da Mer (sea gate).

The Danish influence is evident in Nagapatnam, which was laid out in squares and canals and also in Tranquebar and Serampore. The French gave a distinct urban design to its settlement in Pondicherry by applying the Cartesian grid plans and classical architectural patterns. The Church of Sacred Heart of Jesus (Eglise De Sacre Coeur De Jesus), the Eglise de Notre Dame de Anges and the Eglise de Notre Dame de Lourdes at Pondicherry have a distinct French influence.

However, it was the British who left a lasting impact on the India architecture. They saw themselves as the successors to the Mughals and used architecture as a symbol of power. The British followed various architectural styles-Gothic, Imperial,

Christian, English Renaissance and Victorian being the essentials.

The first buildings were factories but later courts, schools, municipal halls and dak bungalows came up, which were ordinary structures built by garrison engineers. A deeper concern with architecture was exhibited in churches and other public buildings. Most of the buildings were adaptations of the buildings designed by leading British architects of that time like Wren, Adam, Nash and others in London and other places. For instance, the Church of St. John at Calcutta was built in 1787 inspired by St. Stephens Church at Walbrooks, the Government House in Calcutta was built by Capt. Charles Wyatt modelled on the Kedleston Hall of Derbyshire, the Indian Government Mint in Calcutta is a half-scale replica of the Temple of Minerva at Athens and the Pachaiyappa's Hall in Chennai was modelled on the Athenium Temple of Theseus. Unlike Europe, however, these buildings were built mostly of brick and stuccoed with lime or chunam, sometimes "facades" incised to look like stones. Some later buildings were, however, built with stones. Churches, which were symbols of colonialism, were built in great style. Based on London prototypes, several churches evolved with variations as highly original works. The earliest example is the St. Mary's Church in Fort St. George in Chennai.

Neo-Gothic architecture flourished in different parts of India under the British, inspired by the Houses of Parliament in London. Colonel Thomas Cowper built the town hall in Bombay during 1820 to 1835. Governor Sir Bartle Frere tried to give a truly imperial ambience to the city of Bombay. During his reign the old town walls were broken down and the Gateway of India was built in the Gothic style of architecture. The Secretariat, University Library, Rajabai Tower, Telegraph Office and the Victoria Terminus all followed the Victorian Gothic style, similar to buildings in London. Undoubtedly, the Victoria Terminus, designed by the architect Frederick Willaim Stevens modelled on the St.Pancras Station, is the finest example of Gothic architecture with a subtle hint of the Indo-Saracenic motifs, an extravaganza of polychromatic stone, decorated tile marble and stained glass. Stevens also designed other buildings like the Churchgate Terminus and the Municipal Building opposite the Victoria Terminus.

In Varanasi, one of the true Gothic monuments is Queen's College, built in a perpendicular style by Major Kitoe from 1847 to 1852. In Allahabad, the British built a series of edifices including the University, All Saints Cathedral, the High Court and the Mayo College. In Calcutta, a High Court was constructed following the Gothic style. The Howrah Bridge (1943), with its red brick facade surrounded by eight square towers represents a combination of the Oriental and Roman styles. Fort William, the stronghold of the British in mid 19th century that took 13 years to construct at a cost of more than $3.5 million and the Victoria Memorial in Calcutta (1921), designed by Sir William Emerson, are probably the most imposing of all British structures in India.

The passing of power from the East India Company to the British Crown, the rise of Indian nationalism and the introduction of Railways were the watersheds in the British Colonial Indian architectural history. New materials like concrete, glass, wrought and cast iron opened up new architectural possibilities. The British also started assimilating and adopting the native Indian styles in the architecture. All these factors led to the development of Indo-Saracenic architecture towards the end of the 19th century. Victorian in essence, it borrowed heavily from the Islamic style of Mughal and Afghan rulers. In fact it was a pot pouri of architectural styles; a hybrid style that combined in a wonderful manner diverse architectural elements of Hindu and Mughal with gothic cusped arches, domes, spires, tracery, minarets and stained glass. The Indo-Saracenic style was Indian on the outside and British inside since the facade was built with an Indian touch while the interior was solely Victorian. F.S.Growse, Sir Swinton Jacob, R.F.Chisholm and H.Irwin were the pioneers of this style of architecture. The Chepauk Palace in Chennai designed by Paul Benfield is said to be the first Indo-Saracenic building in India. Other outstanding examples of this style of architecture include the Law Courts, Victoria Memorial Hall, Presidency

College and Senate House of Chennai, Muir College at Allahabad, Napier Museum at Thiruvanthapuram, the Post Office, Prince of Wales Museum and the Gateway of India in Mumbai, the Maharaja's Palace at Mysore and M.S.University and Lakshmi Villas Palace at Baroda.

The architecture of New Delhi was the crowning glory of the British Raj. Robert Byron described New Delhi as "The Rome of Hindostan". The British built New Delhi as a systematically planned city after it was made the capital in 1911. The British Viceroy made Sir Edward Lutyens responsible for the overall plan of Delhi. He was specifically directed to "harmonise externally with the traditions of Indian art". Thus, the Western architecture with Oriental motif was realised with chajjas, jalis and chhattris, as stylistic devices in the Viceroy's House (now Rashtrapati Bhawan). Herbert Baker added the imposing buildings of the South Block and the North Block, which flank the Rashtrapati Bhawan. Another Englishman called Robert Tor Tussell built the Connaught Place and the Eastern and Western Courts.

St Martin's Garrison Church marks the culmination of the British architectural ventures in India. The Church is a huge monolith with a high square tower and deeply sunken window ledges reminiscent of Dutch and German architecture.

6

Buddhist Philosophy

INTRODUCTION

'Buddhist' = Peculiar to or originated from the Teaching of the Buddha, in the manifold forms it assumes, all however relating back to the same fundaments.

It will be more difficult to give a definition or even a description of the term 'Philosophy'. It is however very clear that 'philosophy' in its Western (viz. Greco-Christian) context shows a different 'content' than that in the East (predominantly Indian and/or Chinese). From almost every definition of philosophy it goes to show that Western philosophy centers around the question of 'being', the 'first (or last) cause' and the 'absolute'. It tries to find an explanation, analyzes the experiential data and attempts to develop a dialectic around it.

Western philosophy then will be mainly concerned with metaphysics, and especially with ontological questions.

Another facet of Western philosophy (and mysticism) is that it places itself outside the realm of religion, even in those cases where its use lies in giving a coherent structure to religion (viz. Scholasticism).

In the East, philosophy endeavors towards a coherent scheme around which multiple soteriological practices can be weighed, evaluated and structured. The search here is not the search for an explanation (the why-question) but for an efficiency (the how-question). It is not so much the 'absolute truth' that counts, but the effectiveness of a given system or practice.

It is therefore not the question of 'being' but the question of 'knowledge and knowing' (epistemology versus ontology) (viz. Wisdom) that will be the center of philosophical thought in the East. There is the search for understanding the connections and inter-relationships between phenomena and the ability to express them. It is an attempt to translate the non-conceptual (meditative or mystical) into concepts and words, with the clear purpose of describing the salvific process or way to liberation (Enlightenment or Nirvana,...), without however confusing the 'description' with the 'described'.

Emphasis therefore is put on psychology and epistemology as the basis for the development of a soteriology.

Thus, there is no search for the 'absolute' as there is in the West, but an uninterrupted input of relativism and self-critique. It is therefore the religious aspect that is dominant, integrating both philosophy and mysticism. A non-religious philosophy, while characteristic for the West, is conceived as an impossibility in the Eastern context. Even Confucianism, with its initial rejection of all things supernatural takes into account the concept of Heaven (T'ien) and its Virtue (working or effectiveness).

A Buddhist 'philosophy' will make no exception to this rule.

FUNDAMENTALS OF BUDDHISM

The basic principles of the Teaching of the Buddha are found within the Four Noble Truths:

1. The Universality of Suffering
2. The Cause of Suffering
3. The Cessation of Suffering
4. The Way that leads to the Cessation of Suffering

(1) and (2) are situated mainly on the psychological level of the world of experience. Both the 'inner' and 'outer' world

are seen as nothing more than a representation of the mind. Our knowledge originates in the subject. Not the world is illusory, but the glasses through which I see the world makes that the world as it appears to me is an ego-illusion.

If one looks at the meaning of these Four Noble Truths, one comes to the conclusion that the first three Noble Truths point to a theoretical model in which (1) can be taken as consensual, generally acceptable and not necessarily Buddhist; while (2) and (3) are causal: (2) as the cause of suffering, and (3) as the cause of the cessation of suffering. Truth (4) on the contrary is typically Buddhist in its referral to a praxis. The concept 'suffering' is usually misinterpreted, due to a Christian or materialistic point of view. The term 'duhkha', although mostly translated as 'suffering' reaches much further than our ordinary conception of the term suffering: it implies not just our bodily or social torments or vexations, but also-and primarily so-our mental torments. Therefore duhkha would be better described as 'universal unsatisfactoriness' or 'dissatisfaction with the existing situation'. In a certain sense we can also consult philosophers from the West for possible 'better' translations of duhkha. John Locke 1 (1632-1704) speaks of 'uneasiness', thereby remarking that this is the basic feeling, the drive behind every thought or action of humanity. Also found are terms such as 'Unerfülltheit' etc. It is through the use of these, that the term 'suffering' can be taken out of its physical-material context. In a certain sense we could look upon the Buddhist concept of 'suffering' as being the interval, the distance between the existentially experienced and our expectations, on the one hand 'desire' and 'attachment', on the other hand fear:

Suffering here, does not belong to the sphere of salvation or enlightenment-as is often the case in other religions-, but is a characteristic of the existential world in which existence unfolds. This 'suffering' stands loose from the sphere of nirvana: this becomes clear although paradoxically expressed in the 'Heart-Sutra' ("Here, there is no suffering, no cause of suffering, no cessation of suffering, no path that leads to the cessation of suffering."). Duhkha indeed is one of the universal characteristics of that which exists, viz. the 'experienced'. As the locus typicus goes:

- All forms of existence are characterized by suffering;
- All forms of existence are characterized by impermanence;
- All elements of existence are characterized by non-self.

The distinction between 'forms of existence' and 'elements of existence' is of the utmost importance.

All 'things' or 'beings' are compound: these are the 'forms' that existence takes on. (samskara = compound).

This 'compound' is characterized by its composing elements or components (dharma = principle, basic principle, characteristic,...).

If one would use the example of computer science as a metaphor, one could picture a dharma as corresponding to a unit of communication (bit) or a unit of transmission (baud). Samskara than would correspond with a 'message' or 'data'.

Both samskara and dharma have in fact a multitude of meanings that are not always clearly distinguishable. The Monier-Monier Williams Sanskrit-English Dictionary for example gives the following lemma for 'samskara': "...the faculty of memory, mental impression or recollection, impression on the mind of acts done in a former state of existence. Buddh.: mental conformation or creation of the mind (such as that of the external world, regarded by it as real though actually non-existent...". In the Pali Text Society Dictionary on the other hand we read for the same lemma: "1. Aggregate of the conditions or essential properties of a given process or result e.g. the essentials or 'elements' of anything;-essential conditions, antecedents or synergy (co-ordinated activity), mental coefficients, requisite for act, speech, thought. 2. One of the five khandhas, or constitutional elements of physical life...".

'Suffering' is unavoidable since all 'things' are impermanent (not-remaining = Skt. anitya). This impermanence has given rise to a lot of esthetical expressions such as the inevitable withering of a flower, or morning dew, etc. Often this theme of impermanence is emotionally interpreted as the 'transitory nature of all things' through which a sense of doom is evoked, e.g. in poetry. Yet anitya should be understood as objectively neutral: if things where 'doomed' to perish or to disappear, than enlightenment would not be a possibility. Even impermanence can become a factor of enlightenment !

Besides this it is clear that every change in a 'subject' at the same time means a change in the experienced 'object'. In this way anitya in fact becomes a universal experience.

Things are impermanent because there can be no 'permanent' substance ('soul', 'atman', 'self', 'ego'). The 'elements of existence' (dharma)-and therefore also the 'forms of existence' which are composed by these elements-are 'self-less' (P. anatta). All that exists (the world of experience) is self-less, without self, without permanence, without absoluteness. This is the main criterion of the Teaching of the Buddha.

But: if there is no 'self', than who is it that suffers?

That which we call an 'individual', a 'personality', 'ego' or 'psyche', is in fact no more than a convergence of events, impulses, thought constructions, volitional actions, etc. In short, all that is conventionally understood under the term "mental activity". This collection (khandha, skandha) has no permanent substance or essence (atman). Just as no permanent 'house-entity' is found in a constructed house, in the same way no permanent 'entity' can be found within the different forms of existence including sentient beings. This compound nature of the forms of existence explains not only their impermanence but also their 'artificiality', their com-positeness (together + to put) (sam-skri), their polymer character.

The term 'samskara' has, as was mentioned before, a lot of meanings that can not be confused with one another. Each of these possible meanings however point to a compound nature, an aggregate; yet, the context in which the term is used can differ.

It would therefore be wrong to consider each of these skandha's as an 'entity', a 'being'. Not only are they compound (ad infinitum), they also can not exist by themselves but only in relation to and in function of the other skandha's. They are therefore without substance and without autonomy, the two prerequisites for the so-called 'atman'. Thus there is no 'atman'. Or to state it more clearly: concentrating on or around the idea of an atman is (according to Buddhist thought) an inefficient thought-error. Buddhism in all its forms and aspects is an-atman (anatta): non-self.

This strict norm is the main criterion to separate things Buddhist from things non-Buddhist.

Further: the fivefold classification of the personality into skandha's and the twelve-fold classification of karmic existence (see later) are not a "scientific neurological or neuro-psychological" analysis and make no statements concerning an objective, anatomical reality. We are to look upon these classifications as empirical 'expedient means' (upaya) used to gain an insight into the process which leads from an 'existence characterized by suffering' (samsara) to a state of 'non-suffering' (nirvana). We are therefore clearly dealing with a soteriological methodology and not with mere psychological data or metaphysical statements.

The illusion to have or to be an atman-or even to take it into consideration-is the deep origin of suffering. Suffering comes to an end through the destruction of the atman-delusion (avidya = ignorance, mis-conception). This delusion leads to desire (trisna, P. tanha = thirst) and hatred (dosa = aversion), out of which the whole world of dissatisfaction or unsatisfactoriness, in short 'duhkha' comes into existence.

The term 'desire, thirst' should not be interpreted to narrow, in the sense of merely emotional or psychological. Desire encompasses 'all beings'. So for instance we could say that 'the heart desires to beat' seeing that this is the hearts necessary function. We can even speak of a certain 'cosmic' desire, e.g. as is seen in the mutual attraction of two masses (Newton's Law). Seen as such, desire is not only the motive or drive of the individual, it can also be transposed to a collectivity, yes even cosmically as the drive or the motive of the universe. This all leads us to conclude that 'suffering' has its origin in 'desire', which in its turn has its source in 'ignorance'. To often however this is interpreted as "my suffering has its origin in my desire which in its turn finds its source in my ignorance". Such an expression leads to irrelevant questions concerning e.g. the suffering of innocent children. This mistaken shifting of emphasis is based on the input of the concept of 'mine' there where 'it' is meant. The reduction to individuality is in contradiction with the presupposition of anatman or 'no-self' and leads to a methodological incoherence. In our discussion of causality (next chapter) we should continuously take this into account with every step in our train of thought.

This makes that the Third and Fourth Noble Truths should consequently be interpreted in a purely soteriological and pragmatic (i.e. effective) way. A further consequence of the anatman-idea is than that all concepts, all ideas, all forms of thought are anatman, and therefore have no absolute or adequate sense, i.e. they can only be understood as being relative (i.e. in relation to). Further: anatman is also applied to anatman, meaning even anatman is relative: it is only a form of expression in which the content is relative, interchangeable, impermanent. From this the concept of 'emptiness' (sunyata) originated. However, also the concept of sunyata is a mere concept..... therefore..... Buddhist philosophy than will primarily be an epistemology, a philosophy of knowing and Buddhist soteriology will be a wisdom of knowing: seeing things as they are in se, in their emptiness, and not as they appear to our existential consciousness.

The importance of this formulation is that there is no mentioning whatsoever of a permanent entity, of a concept such as atman, 'soul' or 'ego'. The unceasing individuation process that runs through Pratitya Samutpada is none else than the further-becoming or the further-flowing of the pañca-skandha.

The enumeration in addition has no chronological meaning but is a purely causal explanation of existential phenomena. One can therefore picture the 12 nidana's as arising simultaneous and/or overlapping one another.

One could also observe that the first six nidana's form an epistemological structure, while the six latter ones show existential characteristics. This clearly situates the relationship between the functioning of the 'mind' and its effect on 'existence'. In this sense it is understandable that the philosopher Nagarjuna concludes his discussion of the Pratitya Samutpada with upadana, attachment, which he views as the direct cause of suffering in the aspects of the process of becoming, birth, aging and death. After all, attachment has as its objects the five skandha's, which supply the building bricks for the experience of suffering. Hence the mentioning of the term 'pañcopadana-skandhah (P. e.g. Buddhaghosa: pañc' upadanakkhandha) literally the 'five aggregates of attachment', for the relationship that links upadana to the five skandha's. This relationship however also implies that the five skandha's are not only the object of attachment, but that through attachment these five aggregates are made into subject time and again.

The relationship 'ignorance-suffering-enlightenment' often reminds us of the metaphor of the cave, used by Plato to indicate the relationship between the world of shadows and the world of ideas. The beings in the cave, who only see the shadows, are then people chained to ignorance. If they could turn around towards the entrance of the cave, they would experience the light and true reality. But as it is with metaphors and parables, we should not infer to much from the cave-metaphor.

The great importance that Buddhism has laid on Pratitya Samutpada, becomes apparent from the multitude of text referrals which are intended to show that Dependent Origination forms the central core of the Teaching:

- He who sees pratitya samutpada, sees the Teaching; he who sees the Teaching, sees pratitya samutpada." (MN I, 191)
- He, monks, who sees pratitya samutpada, sees the Teaching; he who sees the Teaching, sees the Buddha." (Salistamba-sutra)

- Whoever perceives dependent arising also perceives suffering, its arising, its ceasing and the path [leading to its ceasing]." (Nagarjuna, MMK XXIV, 40).

It has been pointed out above that Buddhism is a religion which does not center around a perception of a god, but in practise can tolerate the belief in any god or gods. Of all major religions of the world, Buddhism is probably the most philosophical one. And there has been in Buddhism a tendency to define Buddha's teachings rather as a philosophy than a religion, at least in the more narrow sense of the term.

As was pointed out by A.B. Griswold in his essay "What is a Buddha Image", published 1962 by the Fine Arts Department of the Thai government, many relevant works representing a tendency to emphasize the philosophical side of Buddhism over the pietistic side were published in the 19th century.

Among them are Henry Alabaster's Wheel of the Law (London, 1871), and the following works by T.W. Rhys Davics: Buddhism (London, 1878), Buddhism, its History and Literature (New York and London, 1896), Buddhist India (London, 1903), Dialogues of the Buddha (translations from the Pali Canon, with explanations, 3 volumes, London, 1899, 1910, 1921), and the article Buddhism in the Encyclopaedia Britannica, 11th edition.

A.B. Griswold states in his essay that the works of Rhys Davics are particularly interesting, as his views are similar to those of many learned Buddhists in Thailand today. Both, Davics and Alabaster, consider that the Theravada is essentially a doctrine of rationalism, paralleling modern scientific and humanistic thought, an ethical and psychological system in which no deity has a significant part. Following Rhys Davics, A.B. Griswold claims that Buddhism has one aim and one only: to abolish suffering. It proposes to do so, not by the aid of divine intervention but by purely human means: that is, by examining the law of cause and effect, and acting accordingly.

Considered the causes of suffering are craving, malice and delusion; if they can be eradicated, Buddhism teaches, suffering will disappear. The remedy sounds simple, but no one supposes it is easy to apply. All Buddhists are expected to play their part in the struggle against craving and malice, by exercising self-restraint and kindness toward all living creatures; but only relatively few are able to participate directly in the struggle against delusion. That task is assigned more to the monkshood (not priesthood, as it is often called), which is expected to lead the struggle against ignorance, bigotry and mental torpor, and to promote good conduct by precept and example.

A.B. Griswold explains that the Buddha lived at a time and place in which nearly everyone believed in the transmigration of souls, taking it for granted that each individual would be re-born again in various conditions on earth, or in heaven or hell for periods of various length. The condition of each re-birth was a reward or punishment for actions committed in previous ones, in accordance with the will of the god in whom one put one's faith; and the gods sometimes tested this faith by requiring the devotee to commit the most outrageous actions.

In contrast to such beliefs, the Buddha taught that retribution does not depend on the will of any god, but on a natural law whose workings can be discovered by the use of human intelligence. There is nothing capricious about it; every man or woman can discriminate between good actions and evil ones, without fear that some god will unexpectedly change the rules; the gods, if such there be, are incapable of setting aside the laws of nature. Favoritism cannot operate; and no act of faith can erase the consequences of an evil deed.

In the interpretation given by A.B. Griswold the Buddha did not deny transmigration, but as he flatly denied the soul it is clear that he interpreted it very differently from most of his contemporaries. The law of impermanence, he taught, applies to all living beings: men, animals, and any other conceivable category. Life is inevitably accompanied by growth, and growth cannot occur without decay. What is commonly called the individual is in constant disintegration, a process which in man and the higher animals begins even before emerging from the womb.

No being, not even a god, is an enduring entity. Each is a compound of elements such as form, matter, perception, and so on; and in each the relationship of the component parts is constantly changing, never remaining the same for any two consecutive moments. It follows that individuality and personality are mere figures of speech and the soul an illusion. Yet that does not mean in the least that good and evil are indifferent; somehow or other, though it is not always easily perceptible, every action brings its retribution; and though there is no soul to be reincarnated, the energy of past action, good or evil continues forever.

This energy, under the impact of craving and delusion, is what is re-born. When simple people, who could not grasp this argument, asked the Buddha whether or not they should believe in transmigration, he advised them to be on the safe side: by acting as if it were true, and doing their best to lead a virtuous life, they would gain the rewards of a tranquil conscience and lose nothing even if they guessed wrong; but if they thoughtlessly rejected it and followed their own evil desires, they would lead a tormented life and finally, if it turned out after all that they were mistaken, they would be "like travellers without provisions".

A.D. Griswold admits that many Indian and European scholars today say that Rhys Davics, Henry Alabaster, and the others who believed the Theravada to be a doctrine of rationalism were all wrong. They say that the rationalist view is a 19th century invention, largely due to King Mongkut (Rama IV, 1851-1868), and that there is no justification whatever to be found for it in the Canon. They assert that the Buddha took transmigration quite literally, just like everyone else; that he was no less superstitious than the generality of educated persons of his time; that he believed firmly in the gods; that he thought himself able to perform miracles; and that he taught his disciples spells to drive away troublesome sprites.

It is true that these scholars can point to a great many passages in the Buddhist Canon that would seem to prove their argument; but A.B. Griswold defends the rationalistic line, saying that the rationalists can point to others, less numerous but somehow more convincing, in which Buddha is seen as a skeptic, gentle but thoroughgoing: he counsels his disciples not to put their faith in tradition or in any honored teacher, even himself, but to rely on their own powers of reason; he limits the meaning of re-birth to an impersonal abstraction; and he not only condemns magic and superstition but even rejects the whole supernatural basis of religion, placing its moral values firmly in human psychology instead.

In fact two contradictory currents of thought, one rational and the other pietistic, run side by side through the Canon, where anyone can see them for him-or herself. The Buddhism that prevailed before King Mongkut's time emphasized the pietistic and the marvelous, just as popular Buddhism still does today. But King Mongkut did not need to invent the current of rationalism: it was already there, though less noticed; he called attention to its importance and shifted the emphasis at the highest level.

In the opinion of A.B. Griswold the two currents of thought are not really as irreconcilable as they at first appear. The contradiction vanishes if passages of the one sort are taken to be factual, and the other as metaphorical. The Buddha knew that teaching is useless unless it is adapted to the capacity of the listener. In addressing sophisticated people he used the technical terms of Indian philosophy, but gave them a new meaning; whereas in talking to simple people he used familiar concepts as allegories and homely anecdotes to point a moral.

Sometimes the simple people remembered the anecdote more distinctly than the moral, or mistook the allegory for the recital of a real event. One does not have to follow their example; and usually there is a clear hint to stop people from doing so. For instance the three daughters of Mara try to tempt the Buddha from the path of virtue, and of course they fail miserably, but not before putting on a seduction scene worthy of Hollywood, the account of which reads as if it were intended to be a real event; but what are the ladies' names? Craving, Discontent and Lust. There could be no clearer warning to the reader who might be disposed to take the story literally. In the interpretation of A.B. Griswold, most people in the Buddha's time believed-as a great many people in India and Southeast Asia still believe today-that a huge population of unseen but powerful creatures haunt the sky and earth, from the great Vedic and Brahmanical gods to the humbler village divinities, from the gods of planets, sun and rain, to the sprites of mountains and rocks, trees and ponds, fields, building-foundations, parasols, and almost any sort of object.

The Buddha did not try to erase these creatures from the general belief-that would have been impossible-but he drastically reduced their importance and at the same time put them to use as figures of speech. So it comes about that Buddhist literature depicts fierce dragons and earth-sprites as being converted to the Doctrine, and Indra, the formerly ferocious Vedic god of thunder and lightning, as little more than a nimble servitor of the Sage.

As A.B. Griswold explains, a person who has extinguished all craving, malice and delusion in himself is exempt from re-birth no matter how it may be defined. In the technical terminology, when such a person dies he "passes into parinibbana", which is the ultimate goal of all Buddhists. It may sound strange to a Westerner who has been nourished on the hope of eternal felicity in heaven; but in Buddhist logic the law of impermanence is inexorable, and a sojourn in any conceivable heaven can be no more than temporary. Since a god is no less subject to craving, malice and delusion than a man, he is just as liable to act in such a way that punishment will follow; and so, if a sojourn in heaven is admitted as a possibility, it will inevitably be followed by more lives of abject misery in other conditions throughout countless millions of aeons.

The only escape is parinibbana, which some people equate with total extinction, and others with a disembodied state of changeless bliss. The Buddha himself refused to define it; but he said that anyone who achieves it "will be no more seen by men or gods." In other words, such a person becomes totally and irrevocably inaccessible to all, and to their prayers.

It is generally agreed that when the Buddha knew his own death was approaching, he told his disciples they must take the initiative and carry on his work without him. The rationalists among them could think for themselves; but it would be harder for the others, less strong-minded but no less devoted, who had relied on him to do their thinking for them. A.B. Griswold states that it can easily be seen how desperate their plight was.

Among people who believed in transmigration, the death of someone whom they trusted and loved would ordinarily leave them some hope that they might meet him again in a future life. But in this case their beloved master, in achieving the goal they were all to strive for, deprived them of any such hope. Only a few of them had advanced so far that they could feel confident of achieving parinibbana themselves when it came their turn to die; the rest including all those to whom transmigration was the most literal reality found themselves facing a hideous eternity of re-births without any possible access to their beloved master.

REMINDERS, REVERED IMAGES

A.B. Griswold, in his essay "What is a Buddha Image", presented an interesting and convincing theory on how a philosophy marked by a considerable disrespect for deities became a religion in which images of the founder of the philosophical school, the Buddha, became subjects of animistic worship, in the sense that the images are considered animated and worshiped as powers in their own right.

A.B. Griswold starts with a rather hypothetical reconstructions of what might have happened at the time of the Buddha's death:

> *"Memory is a frail thing; and unless some means of preserving it could be found, the recollection of the Sage's person, and hence of his priceless guidance, would gradually fade. As the Buddha lay dying, all this was tragically evident to his disciple Ananda, who had served*

him with affectionate care for more than half a lifetime, making up in devotion what he lacked in intellectual power. Could not the disciples, he asked sadly, be allowed to perform some regular act of homage to the memory of the Master in whom they had put their faith? Could they not have some sort of substitute, a reminder of his Person no less than of his Doctrine, to keep them from falling back into the superstitions from which he had rescued them?"

"As a concession to such needs the Buddha replied that the faithful might make pilgrimages to the scenes of the Great Events of his career. When they visited these places they would visualize the Events connected with them, remember his victories over evil and ignorance, and so be inspired to imitate him. If that was not sufficient, they could gather his bodily relics (sariradhatu), such as bones and teeth, after his cremation; they could build stupas, mounds of earth or masonry, to contain them; and the stupas, by reminding people of the Doctrine, would make their hearts glad and happy."

A.D. Griswold explains that according to the orthodox classification, there are four categories of reminder: sariradhatu or dhatucetiya, bodily relics; paribhogacetiya, reminders by association; dhammacetiya, doctrinal reminders; and uddesikacetiya, indicative reminders.

The meaning of the first, sariradhatu or dhatucetiya, is self-evident.

The second, paribhogacetiya, reminders by association, include anything associated with the Buddha himself by physical contact, such as his alms bowl and robes, the footprints he left on river-bank and mountain-top, the benches he sat on, the Bodhi tree at Bodhgaya which sheltered him at the moment of enlightenment, and in a more general way the sites of all the great events. Stupas containing his bodily relics are sometimes placed in this category, some-times in the first category.

The third, dhammacetiya, was originally the whole body of the Doctrine, remembered by word of mouth, but later was extended to include written extracts from the Canon, and stupas built to contain such extracts.

The fourth, uddesikacetiya, indicative reminders, are what might be called "reminders by convention". They are objects, neutral in themselves, which the general opinion might recognize as substitutes for paribhogacetiya, and indeed are usually man-made replicas of them. Trees grown from seeds or cuttings taken from the original Bodhi tree may be put in this category, in the sense that they have come into existence as a esult of human intervention; but sometimes, in view of t eir genetic connection with the original, they are considered to be paribhogacetiya. Replicas of stupas containing bodily relics, when they themselves contain none, are indicative reminders; so are replicas of the footprints; and so are replicas of the scenes of the Great Events, or any essential part of them, in painting or bas-relief or any other suitable medium.

This last category of reminders assumed increasing importance with the spread of Buddhism to distant lands, as they enabled people who lived far away to make pilgrimages, by the power of mental projection, to the holy sites without actually leaving home.

According to A.B. Griswold, educated opinion in India long held the notion of image-making in contempt: images were needed only by the ignorant, who could not grapple with sublime abstractions. In the earliest Indian bas-reliefs depicting scenes from the Buddha's life, the Buddha himself is invisible. He is represented by an aniconic symbol only, such as a stone altar slab or bench, a tree, a serpent, a pair of footprints, or a stupa.

The symbols are depictions of the chief features at the scenes of the Great Events and other incidents: the Bodhi tree at Bodhgaya, and the stone slab under it; the nearby statue of the Serpent King (Naga) who had protected the Buddha from the storm while he meditated; the disk or wheel commemorating the preaching of the First Sermon, the event which "set the Wheel of the Doctrine in motion"; the footprints the Buddha had stamped in rock or clay as souvenirs for the faithful; and the stupas commemorating his parinibbana.

In the bas-reliefs are seen people worshipping these symbols as if they were worshipping the Buddha in person. Some of the worshippers, it may be suspected, had only recently been converted to the Doctrine, and had previously been in the habit of worshipping very similar objects in an entirely different context. In the older cults the solar disk and the serpent had long been worshipped, and so had stones and trees, either in their own right or as the abode of powerful sprites who conferred all sorts of favors when properly approached, but who took terrible vengeance when displeased.

Buddha images, it seems, were first invented about the beginning of the Christian Era, either in Gandhara or at Mathura. A.B. Griswold says that in a curious way they grew directly out of the old symbols, almost as a seedling grows out of a coconut: and just as it takes some time for the coconut shell to rot away, so vestiges of the symbols long clung to the images: the slab as pedestal, the footprints as feet, the serpent or the tree as shelter, the wheel as halo, and various other combinations. And since in the popular mind these symbols were still animated by the sprites inherent in them, people felt that certain images, though representing the Sage of Rationalism (as A.B. Griswold calls the Buddha), possessed the powers and personalities of sprites.

In due course Buddhism was brought from India to Southeast Asia, and the art of image-making as well. One of the most reliable chronicles that have remained, the Jinakalamali, makes it clear what an important role the images had in spreading the Doctrine. Some of them were reputed to possess great magical power, and the timely miracles they performed were a great help in converting the people.

A.B. Griswold recommends that such stories should not be dismissed as fanciful. The power of the images was real enough, he says, though it exerted itself differently at different levels. The staunchest rationalist would admit that Reminders of the Doctrine can start a mental process that will end by dispelling the fear of demons. In the traditional belief, moreover, every Buddha image inherits some fraction of the teja, "fiery energy", which the Buddha himself possessed in incalculable abundance, and which is conventionally represented by a fiery halo, a flame springing from the top of the head, the gilded surfaces of bronze or stone, and so on.

It is not difficult to guess why some images were thought to possess much more magical power than others. One that was believed to be very old would seem to have demonstrated its unusual potency by its unusual power of survival; and if it was thought to be directly copied from one of the original authentic images it would naturally hold more teja than those whose resemblance to the Buddha's person, transmitted through copying at many removes, was less perfect.

Old local beliefs played their part in a variety of ways. If statues of the Buddha sheltered by the Serpent King were particularly popular in Cambodia, and in Thailand during the Khmer period, it was surely because converts from the old serpent cults saw them as inheritors of the serpent's power. Images carved from certain stones, or the wood of certain trees, which had previously been worshipped as the abode of sprites, were still instinctively felt to be animated by those terrifying creatures. And if a particular image happened to be present when a very striking and unusual event occurred, people might easily think it responsible for the "miracle".

Such beliefs now and than produced incongruous results. Siamese chronicles make no attempt to veil the fact that ambitious rulers resorted to unscrupulous tricks and even the threat of open warfare to get hold of the most powerful images, or to cause political rivals to loose the images which were thought to protect them. Each city needed at least one powerful image for its protection, and if the enemy got hold of it he would very likely be able to take the city, too. Thus certain images became deeply involved in political affairs.

As A.B. Griswold pointed out, the chronicles dealing with events from the 13th to the 16th century record that allegedly some images themselves did not always behave very well. Some of the most famous ones were very unpredictable, and often downright cranky, acting in a way the Buddha himself would have condemned in the strongest terms. Like powerful sprites, they gave material rewards when flattered, but in moments of annoyance inflicted disease, set buildings on fire, and caused earthquakes.

The feeling that certain images behave in so un-Buddhist a way lasted right down to modern times. Two of them, the Emerald Buddha and the Phra Bang, were said to have detested each other; and towards the end of the 18th century, when they were brought to Thonburi together, it is believed that they caused all sorts of trouble, including a brief revolution, so they had to be separated. As late as 1867, when they were both in Bangkok (occupying separate buildings, but still not far enough away from each other), their alleged jealousy was said to have caused two disastrous crop-failures within three years.

One still hears of Buddha images that bring bad luck to their owners. The only remedy in that case is to present them to a monastery, where their mischievous tendencies will be kept in check.

A.B. Griswold relates that not many years ago he experienced an amusing example of misplaced piety. In the gallery of a monastery at Ayutthaya there was a long row of apparently identical images, one of which had been singled out for particular favors by an admirer. He had presented it with a silk scarf, and he spent a good deal of time in front of it in a reverential attitude, with palms pressed together as if in prayer. Why had he singled out this particular image, which differed in no way from the dozens of others in the same row?

A.B. Griswold relates that upon inquiry he found that a week earlier it had inspired the man to place a bet on a certain horse, which won the race handily and paid off well; so now he wanted to express his gratitude and at the same time seek further inspiration. A.B. Griswold judged that the supposed personality of the image reminds one more of a Neapolitan saint than of the Buddha; it is hard to believe that the Founder of the Doctrine himself would have given such encouragement to gambling. Tradition explains such eccentricities by saying that they are not caused by the Buddha image as such, but by the sprite inhabiting it. The old belief that almost any noteworthy object is animated by its particular sprite has already been cited, and Buddha images are no exception. When they are made of certain sorts of wood or stone, those worshipping them may believe that the sprites were already in them before they were carved into Buddha images, and the process of carving did not wholly change their original nature.

States A.B. Griswold nonchalantly: "In any case the trouble-makers are rare. Most images behave with perfect decorum."

A.B. Griswold points out that not only old animistic believes are responsible for the widespread opinion that Buddha images are actually alive. The Brahmanical rite of "opening the eyes" of inert, inanimate objects that have to be brought to life by a particular ceremony also plays its part.

Siamese chronicles contain a large number of records which indicate the extend to which Buddha images have long been believed to be animated. One of the most famous and beautiful images in Thailand is the Jinaraja Victorious King at Phitsanulok, cast when that city was part of the Kingdom of Sukhothai. Not long afterwards Sukhothai, including Phitsanulok, was conquered by the rival Kingdom of Ayutthaya. The annals record a curious event: in 1438, when the Crown Prince of Ayutthaya proceeded to Phitsanulok, to become Viceroy of the conquered provinces, tears of blood were seen to flow from the eyes of the statue.

Until today, images are often presented with cloth robes to wear, and some are presented with gem-studded golden crowns and costly garments. The Emerald Buddha has three changes of costume: a princely attire for the hot season, a monastic robe for the rainy season, and a mantle of gold mesh for the cool season.

The old laws of Ayutthaya provided severe punishments for anyone mutilating a Buddha image. To cut off its head was to commit murder, to scrape the gold leaf from its surface was to skin it alive; and anyone who would commit so evil an act was a criminal of the worst sort.

During the long years of warfare that ravaged northern Siam in the late 18th century, many images were broken and others fell into ruin from neglect. As soon as peace was restored, the ruler of Chiang Mai set about restoring the damage; an inscription tells "he thought of the old images, lying broken in field and forest, neglected and exposed to sun and rain; and he took pity on them in his heart".

A mission with a similar purpose was performed by Prince Wang Na at the command of his brother, King Rama I (1782-1806). He proceeded to Ayutthaya, Sukhothai, Phitsanulok and other cities to rescue the images that had been neglected during the Burmese wars, and brought many hundreds of them, of life-size or larger, to Bangkok by raft. The colossal image called Sri Sarbejna ("the Omniscient One"), which had been the object of the deepest veneration at Ayutthaya, proved to be too badly damaged to repair; so it was reverently entombed in a large stupa built for the purpose at Wat Pho. The others were distributed among various monasteries in Bangkok and Thonburi; more than half of them were deposited at Wat Pho, where they may still be seen.

They were given a curious restoration treatment: they were covered with a thick coating of plaster and gilt lacquer, which completely obscured their beauty but did not prevent their teja from functioning. In recent years the plaster has been removed from many of them, revealing the beauty of the patinated bronze; but they were then almost immediately given a new coating of gilt lacquer, though not thick enough to disguise them as completely as before. Those at Wat Benchamabophit, also known as Marble Temple, can be seen to better advantage: at the suggestion of Prince Damrong, they were left ungilded so as to serve as examples of style to students and archaeologists.

At Phitsanulok there was a companion image of the Jinaraja, named Jinasiha, Victorious Lion. Both images were objects of particular veneration to King Rama I; before ascending the throne he used to go to Phitsanulok as often as he could spare the time from his campaigns against the Burmese and in the civil war, and there he would offer homage to the statues. The monastery where they were located had fallen into ruins, but when peace was restored a new Vihara was built for the Jinaraja, and in 1829 the Jinasiha was brought to Bangkok.

The raft which bore it, towed by hundreds of gilded and gaily decorated barges, stopped at the landing-stage of the Prince Wang Na's Palace; and after three days of rejoicing it was conveyed by land to the Excellent Abode Monastery (Pavaranivesa), a vast throng of people pulling the many ropes that were required for so heavy a burden.

In his essay "What is a Buddha Image", published by the Fine Arts Department of the Thai government, A.B. Griswold presented some more curious stories connected with the belief that images have a life of their own. In a monastery in Ang Thong Province there is a colossal reclining Buddha image of masonry, which, according to historical records, on one occasion during the reign of King Rama V (1867-1911) manifested the power of speech. One afternoon, in the presence of the abbot and a large group of monks and novices, deep muffled sounds were heard to issue from its bosom. "Are you not well, Sir?" the abbot asked politely. The image replied: "Thank you, I am quite well; and you?" "Sir, I am well." "But trouble is on its way," said the image; "within two months, there will be a bad outbreak of cholera." Upon being asked what counter measures could be taken, the image provided a recipe to be compounded from certain herbs; and when the cholera came, exactly as predicted, the medicine proved to be an effective cure.

A.B. Griswold outlines that the belief that miniatures worn around the neck confer invulnerability can be explained in more than one way. Some people would say that the teja inherent in the image transmits itself to the wearer and makes him immune from harm; others might argue that by reminding the wearer of the Doctrine, and particularly that part of it that counsels constant alertness, it enables him to keep out of harm's way.

Critics of such an opinion may point out that in the manner of this explanation, any irrationalism could be rationalized. The may be reminded that irrationalism, rationally explained, does not turn irrationalism into rationalism. Furthermore, those wearing images in the belief they are amulets protecting them from harm do not understand them simply as reminders to keep them alert. And by rationalizing amulets as reminders, the question remains unanswered whether or not the images worn as amulets protect the wearer on account of their own power.

In spite of such arguments, A.B. Griswold sees the rationalizing of images as reminders as sufficient to defend the opinion that Buddha images are somehow animated. He states in his essay cited above: "We can now begin to see why such miniatures were made in huge quantities to be buried away inside stupas and colossal images. They were a sort of electric charge, suffusing the stupa or the statue with teja: even if most of them proved to be inert, or nearly so, on the basis o probability at least a few of them would turn out to be pa ticularly effective. Lo

ked at in another way, they were intended to assure th durability, the invulnerability, of the Reminder that contai ed them: and even if they failed in that, and the Reminder was ever broken open, they would pour forth in an explosion of fiery energy, teja, conferring their benefits as reminders and protectors far and wide upon future generations."

"We can now see, too, why images inspire such fervent devotion. They fill the function for which the various sort of reminder, cetiya, were designed, but they also do rather more. They act as substitutes for the Buddha himself in a sort of mystical worship that reminds us of the bhakti of Hindu religions; and some people have a feeling that although the Buddha himself is inaccessible, he can be worshipped through his substitutes and somehow answer prayers through them too. At a less sublime level they are magical protectors, jealous gods who must be kept in a good humor, since they are

equally capable of bestowing enormous favors and of bringing on a general disaster."

MAKING MERIT

According to A.B. Griswold, the most obvious reason why Buddha images have been created in Thailand in such stupendous quantity is simply the intent to make merit (tam boon). And he explains that by doing good deeds, those who believe in transmigration lay up a store of merit for the future, like prudent people making deposits in a savings bank. To enter th

monkhood for several days or months; to help in the construction or maintenance of a monastery; to contribu e to education; to make gifts to the needy; to give alm to monks; to perform any act of kindness, great or small: a l such things, and many others, are recognized as acts of m rit. And of course it is an act of merit to create any sort of reminder, uddesikacetiya, from a great monument to a little heap of sand in the form of a stupa, from a colossal image to a tiny votive tablet. □The amount of merit acquired, it is felt is a function of the effort expended by the donor in roportion to his means. That explains why the rich lik to commission images of gold or precious stone, and why King Rama III (1824-1851) founded the vast reclining Buddha, over 4 meters long, at Wat Pho. Great efforts are expected of the possessors of great sources; but a poor man may earn as much merit by creating a simple reminder of clay.

It has been explained that in spite of the fact that Buddhism doesn't consider the Buddha a god, Buddha images seem to rank higher in Buddhism than crucifixes in Catholicism. Buddha images are considered animated in their own right, while crucifixes are symbols and symbols only. As A.B. Griswold pointed out, Buddhist may believe that a Buddha image can miraculously talk, and in this case, the spirit of the Buddha image is considered the talking force.

Catholicism also knows images that miraculously talk but Catholicism interprets such occurrences as the Holy Spirit talking through the medium of the image, and not the image talking on its own. A.B. Griswold in his essay "What is a Buddha Image" named the Buddha "Sage of Rationalism". His essay also indicates that he sees himself on the side of those who attempt a rationalist interpretation of Buddhism. In spite of this, he defends what appears to be image worship even by Buddhist rationalist, and he does so with a seemingly rationalist explanation. The more this appears to be contradictory, the more interested one may be in his chain of arguments.

A.B. Griswold:

"But what of the rationalists? Would they not view all such notions, if not with contempt, at least with a mildly amused skepticism? Yet we often see modern-minded Buddhists, including the leaders of the rationalist movement, prostrating themselves before an image and making offerings of flowers and incense."

"The usual answer is that they are expressing their gratitude to the memory of the Teacher who conferred the priceless gift of the Doctrine on mankind. While this answer may seem strange to a Westerner, I am sure it is right. In all countries that take their forms of politeness from India, the manifestations of respect accorded to a teacher looks very much like worship."

"Still, we might think it an exaggerated way to express gratitude to a Master who long ago passed into Total Extinction, or at least far beyond the range of human behavior, and who can consequently derive no possible satisfaction from such homage. But the rationalist knows that the expression of gratitude is really for the benefit of the living, reinforcing the power of the Reminder in his own feelings and in the feelings of others; and even in the West it sometimes occurs that the most skeptical writers, who have no belief in any sort of future life whatever, will dedicate a book to the memory of some deceased friend."

"There is still another reason for such outward acts of piety on the part of Buddhist rationalists. Though they

are indeed atheists, in the sense that they allow no significant place for a god or gods, they are not at all bigoted; and unlike the atheists of Communist countries they have no thought of undertaking a crusade against religion. Though for their own part they consider faith to be rather a hindrance than a help to clear thinking, they freely admit that many people need faith as a support for good morals. Tolerance is a cardinal principle of Buddhism; they recognize the good features of all religions, and in particular they respect the traditional forms of Buddhist worship."

"And they believe that good manners are the counterpart, in small things, of good morals in large ones. This is a good thing for Westerners to bear in mind, even those Westerners who have no particular sympathy for Buddhism."

"Among the souvenirs a tourist takes home with him from Bangkok there will very likely be a few Buddha images. [The export of Buddha images has been prohibited only after A.B. Griswold's essay was first published.] They should not be used as door-stops or decorations for a bar, placed on the floor, made into lamps or coffee-tables, dressed up in humorous costumes, given nicknames, turned over to the children to play with, or treated in any other manner that does not befit objects of religious significance. To put them in unsuitable places is not only bad manners, which would hurt the feelings of any Buddhist who happened to visit the house; it is also a singularly unsatisfactory way to bring out the beauty of a work of art. No one in his right mind, no matter how little he might care about Christianity, would hang a crucifix on his wall upside down. Buddha images were made with the expectation that they would be placed in a position of honor-generally speaking, at such a height that their legs are at the level of the spectator's eye-and that is the way they can be seen to best advantage."

"Buddha images, however, are not 'works of art' in the ordinary sense. The purpose in making them was not

to delight a connoisseur or to win praise from a critic; nor was it, except in a secondary way, to please the eye at all. As we have seen, they are religious mechanisms of a very peculiar kind. Nevertheless a great many of them are also objects of beauty by any standards; and there is certainly no harm in a non-Buddhist seeing them as such, provided he remembers that that is not the whole story. Unfortunately Western taste often seems to prefer a severed head or hand, rather than the complete image, and instances have been recorded of thieves mutilating images in monasteries to obtain such fragments for sale. I would not go so far as to say that we should refuse to display a detached head or hand that has been dug up, if the body has been lost-though in the eyes of an old-fashioned Buddhist such a display is rather gruesome and indeed likely to bring bad luck-but we should always remember that the whole image is much more valuable, and more worthy of display, than a mere fragment; and we should do everything we can to discourage the mutilation of images."

"Apart from that, we can only sense the inner beauty of a Buddha image by discovering what it means to Buddhists on different levels of understanding."

"Its surfaces and silhouette may please the eye, or even cause a gasp of surprise by their beauty. But they exist only as the capsule that contains the fiery energy; without that, whether we define it as magic or as psychological power, the image would not even have come into existence."

EPISTEMOLOGY

Siddhartha Gautama the Buddha is portrayed in Buddhist literature as ridiculing the sacrificial rituals of the Brahmans and accusing the priests of fabricating them for no better reason than to make money from the wealthy and to manipulate the powerful. Attacking the sacrificial practices of the Brahman priests in this way eventually led to challenging the authority of the Vedic literature that the priests considered sacred. An early Buddhist philosopher who challenged the authority of sacred texts was Nagarjuna, whose arguments called into question the very possibility of justified belief. In a text called Vigrahavyavartana (Averting Disputes), Nagarjuna argued that all opinions are warranted by an appeal to experience, or to various forms of reasoning, or to the authority of tradition. Now among the opinions that one may hold, said Nagarjuna, is the opinion that all opinions are warranted in one of those ways. Nothing, however, seems to warrant that opinion. If one should claim that that opinion is self-warranting, then why not grant that all other opinions are also self-warranting? On the other hand, if that opinion requires substantiation, the result will be an infinite regress. Therefore, concluded Nagarjuna, no opinion can be grounded. Realizing that one can never arrive at certainty thus becomes for Nagarjuna the most reliable way of freeing oneself from the various delusions that cause unhappiness in the world. Dispelling delusions is therefore not a matter of discovering truth, but a matter of realizing that all opinions that pass as knowledge are not really knowledge at all.

Although Nagarjuna's scepticism managed to capture the spirit of some passages of Buddhist literature that depict the Buddha as questioning the authoritarianism of other teachers, it did not leave adequate room for distinguishing truth from error. Most Buddhist philosophers who came after Nagarjuna, therefore, placed an emphasis on both eliminating error and securing positive knowledge. Dignaga, modifying theories of knowledge that Brahmanical thinkers had developed, argued that there are just two types of knowledge, each having a distinct subject matter unavailable to the other: through the senses one gains knowledge of particulars that are physically present, while the intellect enables one to form concepts that take past and future experiences into consideration.

In an important work called Klambanaparakra (Examining the Support of Awareness) Dignaga developed an argument that his predecessor Vasubandhu had made. Here Dignaga argued that a cognition is accurate only if the subject matter of the cognition is identical to that which causes the awareness to arise. So, for example, if one sees a dead tree in the dark and takes it to be a man, then the subject matter of the cognition is a man, which is not identical to the dead tree that is causing the cognition; the cognition is therefore inaccurate. Given this principle, said Dignaga, it follows that none of our sensory cognitions is accurate, because each of them is really caused by atoms massed together; nevertheless, we are never aware of anything as a mass of atoms. Instead, what we are aware of is such things as human beings, elephants and trees. These notions of things as human beings or elephants, however, are purely conceptual in nature and are not in accord with the realities that exist in the external world. Therefore, he concluded, the only objects of our awareness are concepts; we are never directly aware of realities as they occur outside the mind.

Dignaga's essays rekindled an interest in epistemological questions among Buddhist philosophers that lasted for several centuries. As influential as his theories in logic and the sources of knowledge were, there was little in them that explicitly referred to previous Buddhist doctrine. It was left to the systematic philosopher Dharmakarti to draw out the implications that questions of logic and epistemology had for people interested in the traditional Buddhist preoccupation with eliminating delusions concerning the nature of the self in order to win freedom from discontent.

Dharmakarti's system of epistemology was centred around his criticism of the Brahmanical doctrine of the special authority of the Veda, which the Brahmans supposed had been revealed to humanity by God. He combined this criticism with a defence of the doctrine that the Buddha was a source of knowledge. The Brahmanical claim of authority for their scriptures is based upon the notion that God is omniscient and compassionate; this idea, said Dharmakarti, is extravagant and laughable. The Buddhist claim for the authority of the Buddha, on the other hand, is based on the modest claim that the Buddha was an ordinary man who could see the root cause of discontent, knew how to eliminate the cause, and took time to teach other human beings what he had discovered. Moreover, argued Dharmakarti, the Buddha taught nothing but principles that every human being could confirm. Full confirmation of the Buddha's teachings was said to be impossible for a person whose vision was still clouded by delusions. On the other hand, to a person who had learned to listen to wise counsel, reflect on it and then put it into practice, all the teachings of the Buddha on the question of winning nirvana would be confirmed.

The form of reflection that Dharmakarti recommended was based upon a systematic study of the principles of legitimate inference; most delusions, he contended, stem from forming hasty generalizations from limited experience. Most doctrinal matters about which philosophers dispute, he said, cannot be decided with certainty. In this respect, Dharmakarti adopted the cautious attitude of the Buddha and Nagarjuna towards unwarranted opinions and assumptions. At the same time, he tried to show that the extreme scepticism that had characterized the work of such thinkers as Nagarjuna was also unwarranted. This epistemological 'middle path', consisting of modest claims about the extent of the Buddha's knowledge and yet insisting that the Buddha's doctrines were true and distinguishable from falsehoods, set the tone for most of the Buddhist philosophy that evolved in India until the time that Buddhism stopped being an important factor in the philosophical milieu of the Indian subcontinent. The focus on epistemological issues enabled Buddhists to set aside the sometimes bitter disputes over the question of which Buddhist scriptures were authentic.

METAPHYSICS

Given the emphasis in Buddhist teachings on the role of erroneous belief as a cause of unhappiness, it was natural that Buddhist philosophers should focus on questions of ontology and the theory of causation. Ontology was important, since a kind of intellectual error that was supposed to lead to unhappiness was being mistaken about what exists. The theory of causation was important, since the eradication of the cause of unhappiness was supposed to result in the removal of unhappiness itself. The earliest attempts to systematize the teachings of Buddhism were in the genre of literature known as 'Abhidharma', in which all the factors of human experience were classified according to a variety of schemata. The study of the relationships among these classes of factors eventually evolved into a detailed theory of causality, in which several types of causal relationship were enumerated. There were many schools of Abhidharma, and each had its own set of schemata for the classification and enumeration of the factors of experience. Indeed, each had its own interpretation of what the very word 'Abhidharma' means; among the possible interpretations of the word, a common one is that it means a higher or more advanced doctrine, or a doctrine that leads to a higher form of wisdom. The variety of approaches taken in Abhidharma literature makes it difficult to discuss this literature in any but the most general way. Among most schools of Abhidharma, there was a commitment to the idea that the best strategy for coming to an understanding of any complex being is to analyse that being into its ultimate parts. An ultimate part is that which cannot be analysed into anything more simple. Most Buddhist systematists held to the principle that the ultimately simple building blocks out of which things are made are ultimately real, while complex things that are made up of more simple parts are not ultimately real; they are held to be real only through the consensus of a community. As was seen above in the section on human nature (§1), for example, there was a strong tendency for Buddhists to accept that a person's character is the product of many components; these components were held to be real, but the person was held to be ultimately unreal. The idea of a person may be a fiction, but it is one that makes the running of society more manageable, and therefore it can be regarded as a consensual reality, in contrast to an ultimate reality.

The philosopher Nagarjuna questioned the whole attempt to make a distinction between consensual and ultimate truths. One interpretation of his philosophical writings is that he was trying to show that every attempt to understand the world can only be an approximation on which there may be some degree of consensus; there is, however, no understanding that can claim to have arrived at an adequate description of things as they really are. Along with this radical criticism of the very enterprise of trying to discern ultimate from consensual realities, Nagarjuna criticized the doctrine that the simple constituents that serve as causes of more complex beings are more real than the complex beings themselves. This principle had rested on the assumption that the more simple a being is, the closer it is to being independent. In fact, he argued, the apparently simple constituents are no less dependent than their apparently complex effects. To this fact of being dependent upon other things, Nagarjuna gave the name emptiness; since all beings are dependent for their existence on other beings, he said, all beings are empty.

Later Buddhist philosophers, beginning especially with Dharmakarti, devoted their energy increasingly to refuting the claims, advanced by some Brahmanical thinkers, that the whole universe can be traced back to a single cause. Dharmakarti argued that if all things in the history of the world had a single cause, such as God or some type of primordial matter, then there would be no way to account for all the formal variety in the world at any given time, nor would it be possible to account for the fact that events unfold in sequences. If all the formal and temporal diversity are already inherent in the cause, he argued, then the cause is not a single thing after all. One might argue that the diversity exists in the single cause only as a potential of some kind; this, however, only raises the problem of explaining how that potential is actualized. If the potential is activated by something outside the cause that possesses it, then the outside agency must be counted among the causal factors along with the primary cause, in which case there is no longer a single cause. Besides general arguments directed against the view that all things could have any single cause, Dharmakarti also gave arguments against the existence of a creator God in particular. The universe, he observed, shows no signs of having been designed by anyone intelligent. Even if it were conceded for the sake of argument that the world might have been made by some intelligent being, there is still no sign that this being had any concern for any living beings. Later generations of Buddhist philosophers expanded upon

Dharmakarti's arguments against the existence of a single intelligent creator, but most of these expansions took the form of replying to the objections of opponents rather than formulating new arguments (see Causation, Indian theories of §6).

During the last five hundred years that Buddhism was an important factor in Indian philosophy (600-1100), criticism of Buddhist doctrines by Brahmanical and Jaina religious philosophers, as well as from anti-religious materialists, forced Buddhist thinkers to refine some of their arguments and even to abandon some of their doctrinal positions. Arguments among Buddhists became much less a feature of Buddhist philosophy than arguments against non-Buddhist opponents. Within Buddhism itself, there was a tendency to try to reconcile differences that in earlier centuries had divided Buddhists against each other, at least doctrinally. This new spirit of overcoming sectarianism resulted in several ingenious attempts to fuse the old Abhidharma schools, the Madhyamika schools, the Yogachara schools and the Buddhist epistemologists. Few new issues were raised in this last five-hundred-year period, and not many new arguments were discovered to defend old positions. Careful scholarship tended to replace philosophical innovation as the principal preoccupation of later Buddhist intellectuals, such as antarakaita, Kamalala, Jñanaramitra and Ratnakarti. It was during this period of the decline of Buddhism in India that Buddhist philosophy was introduced into Tibet. Once established there, it received a new impetus from a range of Tibetan intellectuals who were able to study many of these doctrines with a fresh perspective.

DOCTRINE AND TRUTH

When early readers began to understand Buddhist texts as expressions of doctrines, and implicitly to grasp written language as signs signifying ideas, they came to understand the world in terms of formerly unseen relations. The Buddhist categories they applied were Chinese translations of Sanskrit terms, and this usage remained predominant even after modern Japanese scholars turned to Indian sources. The categories included names for the basic factors or elements of existence and the relations of cause and effect, conditioned and unconditioned, part and whole, relative and absolute.

The first systematic study of these categories and relations occurred in the so-called six schools of Nara, during the historical period of the same name (710-81). These 'schools' were more bodies of doctrine than independent sects with their own adherents. Often the doctrines were studied together in the same locale, such as the great temple Tadaiji. The Japanese version of the Indian Abhidharmakona school stressed the analysis of some seventy five conditioned and unconditioned constituents (dharmas) of existence and some ten types of direct and indirect causes that give rise to the conditioned factors.

As abstract as it appears, this analysis was intended as a kind of psychological examination to remove obstacles on the path to liberation. The Jajitsu (Establishment of Truth) school proceeded to show the emptiness, or lack of substantial reality, of all constituents. The Ritsu (Precept) school conveyed very specific ethical and administrative rules to regulate the ordination and life of monks and nuns, and taught that the observance of precepts was one purification necessary for enlightenment. As discussed below, however, it did not provide an ethical theory or general principles for determining good and evil.

The Sanron (Three Treatises) school derived from Indian Madhyamika philosophy (see Buddhism, Madhyamika: India and Tibet). It practiced the refutation of all claims of the existence or non-existence, truth or falsity, of separate elements and doctrines. The discursive language used to refute all views ultimately pointed to its own limit, beyond which lay absolute truth. The Hosse school formed the scholastic counterpart to Indian Yogachara or 'consciousness-only' philosophy. It criticized the Madhyamika tendency to absolutize emptiness, explained the role of consciousness in the appearance of self and world, and taught that enlightenment requires a conversion of the deep unconsciousness, called the 'storehouse' consciousness. It rejected the teaching that enlightenment is equally attainable by all. The sixth school, the Kegon (Flower Garland), was historically no more influential than these last two, but introduced a principle crucial to an understanding of the treatment of doctrines and truth in subsequent Japanese Buddhism.

The Nara schools took over doctrines and analyses from their Chinese counterparts virtually without change. These doctrines were partially incompatible with each other, but the discrepancies seemed little cause for dispute. Various doctrines and categories show up in later Japanese Buddhist philosophy, often as a foil for more innovative ideas. An example is the way the Abhidharma breakdown of reality and time forms the springboard of one chapter of Dugen's Shabgenz, 'Ocean Reflecting Samadhi'. This work first accepts the Abhidharma analysis of the causal arising of all elements but then disrupts it to proclaim the totality and sufficiency of each moment. In general, the failure of scholastic doctrines to challenge later generations of Japanese Buddhist thinkers is a sign that the latter have been more at home with practical reasoning and reconciliation than with formal argumentation and adjudication of claims. Indeed, until its introduction from the West there was in Japan no formal logic, where the rules of validity are separable from the content of the argument. This lack does not necessarily point to a deficiency in the ability to reason, however, but may have to do with a way of relating absolute and relative, universal and particular. The philosophy of the Kegon school best epitomizes that way.

The Kegon school accounted for the variety of doctrines by placing them in a scheme of increasing difficulty and comprehensiveness. The level of the teachings matches the hearer's capacity to understand. Partial teachings, in other words, are 'skillful means' designed to lead one to more difficult and comprehensive teachings. The Kegon school typifies the inclusion characteristic of much of Japanese and Chinese Buddhist thought. One Buddhist school would incorporate rather than exclude the doctrines of rival schools, but would regard them as incomplete and place them on a lower level. To be sure, the hermeneutic of inclusion was often politically motivated, intended to increase a power base by incorporating and not alienating other groups; but it also followed the dialectical principle that rival or alternative beliefs were partial truths that fit into a larger scheme.

The Kegon scriptural hermeneutic privileged its own source sutras and was rivalled by a similar scheme offered in the tremendously influential Lotus Sutra, but it developed a philosophy of totality and interrelation crucial for understanding most Japanese Buddhist thinking. According to this philosophy, each part or constituent of reality perfectly reflects the whole, and the whole depends upon each and every constituent part. All individual parts are therefore equivalent as conditions of the whole, and at the same time they are distinct and interdependent. The implications of this philosophy of nature for a theory of truth are the key to approaching Japanese Buddhist thought. There is no whole, universal or absolute, without its manifestation in concrete, distinct and re ative particulars. In the twentieth century, Nishida Kitara reformulated this principle paradoxically: the more relative a truth is-that is, the more deeply embedded or embodied in particulars-the more absolute it is. The absolute must encompass the relative, not stand in opposition to it. In general, Japanese Buddhist philosophy developed through a kind of synecdochic argumentation that appealed not to a priori reasons or empirical evidence, nor simply to scriptural sources of authority, but to this mutua accommodation of relative and absolute.

UNIVERSAL AND PARTICULAR

Three interrelated themes display the mutual accommodation of relative and absolute, universal and particular: the locus of liberation, its actuality and the equality of beings.

Indian Mahayana sutras introduced the idea that liberation does not lead to a transcendent realm different from this world, but they often spoke of the 'three immeasurable eons' required for its attainment. In contrast, many seminal Buddhist thinkers in Japan developed one Chinese view of the locus of liberation:

the idea of becoming a buddha in this very body (sokushin jubutsu). For Saichu (767-822), the founder of the Tendai school, it meant only a partial realization of buddhahood; but by the time of Tendai scholar Annen (841-89?) it referred to buddhahood attained in this very life. Kukai (774-835), founder of the rival Shingon school, taught that yogic practices involving body (mudras or symbolic hand gestures), speech (mantras) and mind (mental concentration and visualizations) could unify the practitioner with the Buddha Mahavairocana. Such practices made it possible to attain buddhahood in this very body. This doctrine, popularized by Kukai, provided a theoretical basis for the bodily aspects of practice and the enactment of rituals that were important especially in the esoteric traditions of Tendai and Shingon Buddhism.

In summary, the idea of becoming a buddha in this very body or life involved a temporal and a metaphysical reduction. First, it collapsed the various stages of the path to enlightenment that were so important in various Buddhist traditions, and reduced the 'three immeasurable eons' to one lifetime. Second, it collapsed any remnant of a difference between the physical reality of life on earth and a transcendent realm, between the transient human body and the transcendent dharma-body. The body we are born with is the site of realization and symbolically embodies the entire universe, the 'truth-body' of the Buddha. Dugen modified the idea further and proclaimed that 'this very mind is buddha' (sokushin zebutsu) when the discursive mind was disengaged. Although Dugen speaks of 'mind' and not body, no psychophysical dualism is implied here.

Other Buddhist reformers of the Kamakura period (1192-1333) qualified the idea that liberation was possible in this world or life. Hunen and Shinran placed this possibility in the Pure Land, which they usually considered as immediately accessible if intermediate between this world and the realm of final enlightenment. Even where it was imagined as a different world, this Pure Land was not nearly so remote a goal as Indian views of nirvana, and was sometimes in effect made immanent in this world. Ippen explicitly stated that the Pure Land was indeed identical with this world. Nichiren too emphasized this world as the locus of salvation.

The affirmation of this world in Japanese thought is often called phenomenalism (see Phenomenalism), but this description neglects the principle or absolute said to interpenetrate all phenomena. One tenet of Kegon philosophy was that 'principles are not impeded by things' (rijimuge). Tendai Buddhism stressed the Mahayana doctrine of the 'identity of the phenomenal and the real' (genshazoku jissa), and proposed that the phenomena of the world are aspects of Buddha. Dugen wrote that the 'true reality' (jiss) is in fact all things, and that birth and death (impermanence) (see Muju) is Buddha or nirvana. To understand these developments in Japanese Buddhism, however, one needs to consider the question of the actuality of liberation.

Many Indian Mahayana sutras teach that all sentient beings possess the nature of Buddha. The Lotus Sutra proclaims further that the historical Buddha is not a man who attained awakening but rather is a manifestation of the universal buddhahood that is available to all. It rejected schemes that differentiated levels of potential in beings and that excluded the lowest level from eventual enlightenment. Saichu advocated universal buddhahood, based on the language of the Lotus Sutra. Universal buddhahood and 'becoming Buddha in this very body' are ideas based on the notion of hongaku, the Chinese doctrine that all beings are 'originally or inherently awakened'. Inherent enlightenment, in contrast to 'acquired enlightenment', is timeless and independent of spiritual development. For some contemporary scholars such as Tamura Yoshira, the hongaku idea is definitive not only of Buddhism in medieval Japan but of Japanese culture in general, since it underlies the ideals of equality, harmony and conformity (Tamura 1987).

The ideas of inherent and acquired enlightenment do not form logical contraries, since both depend upon the buddha-nature in all beings, but rather pose a practical question: how is this innate enlightenment related to practice? Legend has it that Dugen encountered this question in his boyhood Tendai training and made it an existential problem: why undergo rigorous practice when we are endowed with 'dharma nature' by birth? Dugen's answer is thought to be a criticism of the hongaku idea, but can also be seen as its limit. He proposed 'the unity of practice and realization': 'The dharma [truth] is not manifested unless one practices; it is not attained unless there is realization'. The practice of concentrated mind-body, epitomized in zazen or seated meditation, is a way to actualize our inherent nature. In §1 above, Dugen's words were quoted: 'As for the Buddha Way, not to voice it is impossible... ' and this sentence concludes: 'not to study [practice] it is remote.' Dugen thus collapses the distinction between practice as means and enlightenment as end. Instead, zazen, the practice of awakening, becomes the manifestation of enlightenment.

Like Dugen, other Kamakura Period Buddhist reformers reacted against the complacency encouraged by the idea of original enlightenment, but modified rather than rejected it. For Hunen and Shinran the only 'practice' that counts is the nembutsu or invocation of the Buddha Amida. In his form as the Bodhisattva Dharmakara, Amida enunciated a primal vow that made his enlightenment contingent on that of all sentient beings. Those with sincere faith in Amida's vow were assured of rebirth in the Pure Land, where final enlightenment will be possible. In the original story, countless lifetimes elapse before Dharmakara becomes Amida Buddha, but the logic of the conditions may suggest a non-dual, timeless relation: since Amida Buddha is indeed here to save us, our liberation need only be actualized in this moment. Some writings of Shinran explicitly suggest that to recollect Amida Buddha with a believing mind (shinjin) is already to actualize buddhahood, without waiting to be reborn in the Pure Land. Moreover, this entrusting invocation is strictly speaking not a practice at all; that is, it is not accomplished through one own efforts or 'self-power' but rather is a gift of Amida, a result of Amida's 'other-power'. Ippen stated that 'the nembutsu is what recites the nembutsu'. Although faith in personal effort is considered futile, as in some interpretations of inherent enlightenment, true reality must be activated by personal faith. This again is a variation on the theme of the actualization of reality.

The idea of universal buddhahood supported both syncretistic tendencies in Japanese Buddhism and the equality of all beings. The first undermined any ultimate difference between Buddhist and Shint? objects of veneration, and the second any difference between the human and natural worlds, or what we today call culture and nature.

Syncretistic tendencies were formalized in the theory of honji suijaku. This theory regarded indigenous Shintu deities (kami) as trace manifestations (suijaku) of buddhas and bodhisattvas, who were their original ground or true nature (honji). The theory appears to establish a hierarchical relationship, with the bodhisattvas as more basic and important than the kami, and thus Buddhism as more fundamental than Shintu. This interpretation implies that the Shintu gods cannot exist without the Buddhist ideal beings. It not only reverses the historical order of their appearance in Japan; it misplaces the emphasis. In fact, the honj-suijaku theory often worked to set the two realms and their objects of veneration on a par with one another. If a kami functioned as a trace or attribute of a bodhisattva, the particular bodhisattva was best manifested in the kami. The reality of the one depended upon that of the other. This interdependence was explicit in a Tendai version of honji suijaku theory according to which the true nature could only be perceived in its manifestations. A fourteenth-century Shintu school simply reversed the order of bodhisattva and kami. Moreover, specific Buddhist and Shinta ideal beings are sometimes identified with one another and then contrasted with other pairs. In the twentieth century, a 'new religion' called Gedatsukai in effect identifies the Buddha Mahavairocana and the Shinta deity Tenjinchigi as honji, and gives other Buddhist-Shinta deities the status of suijaku. These examples illustrate that the accessibility of ideal beings was more important than any rank order, which was historically variable.

The theory of original ground and trace manifestation was developed in the late Heian Period (794-1185), contemporaneous with the idea of inherent enlightenment. Yet the underlying association of Shintu and Buddhism is evident much earli r and lasted until much later. At the very beginning of Japanese Buddhism, the Nihon shoki (Chronicles of Japan) report that the Emperor Yamei (d. 587) 'believed in the Law of the Buddha and reverenced the Way of the Gods'. Yet the name 'Way of the Gods' (Shintu) was a Chinese, quasi-Buddhist concept. In effect, Buddhism prevailed and was established as the state religion, at least temporarily, through the efforts of Yamei's sister, Empress Suiko, and especially of his son, Prince Shutoku, who wrote commentaries on sutras and built temples. In the Nara Period (710-81), Shintu shrines were incorporated into Buddhist temples in order to protect land interests, and Buddhist altars built near shrines ensured the protection of Shintu.

At one locale the god of war, Hachiman, was named the Bodhisattva Daijizaiten in 783; at others he was associated with different bodhisattvas. In the ninth century, Kakai proposed a 'dual aspect' theory that, for example, identified the sun goddess Amaterasu with Mahavairocana, the Buddha of Great Illumination, whom Kakai further identified with the dh rmakaya or truth-body of Buddha. Although Tokugawa Period (1600-1868) nativists such as Motoori Norinaga reasserted the superiority of indigenous Shintu, the Buddhist inclusion of Shinta was not effectively challenged on a national scale until the early Meiji government's policies (in the 1870s) of 'separating gods and buddhas', persecuting Buddhism and establishing State Shintu. Religion and state have had separate legal tatus since the Second World War, but Buddhist and Shintu eachings and customs still coexist in Japanese family life.

panese Buddhist thought extended the idea of universal buddha ood to the equality of all beings. In particular, the id a of inherent enlightenment lent support to the doctrine of the Bu dha-nature of non-sentient beings that is often alluded to in me ieval Japanese literature. It was both Tendai and Nichiren doctrine that the grass and trees-in other words, beings not possessed of a sensitive mind-can become buddhas: 'Grasses, trees, mountains and rivers all attain buddhahood' became a frequent saying in medieval Buddhist texts. A chapter of Dugen's Shabgenz quotes the enlightenment verse of Chinese poet Su Dongp
.

The sounds of the valley streams are His long, broad tongue;

The forms of the mountains are His pure body.

At night I heard the myriad sutra-verses uttered

How can I relate to others what they say?

(Cook 1989: vii)

For Dugen, this verse provides one answer to the questions, 'where is buddha?', 'what is buddha?' and 'how does he preach?' The preaching of nonsentient beings, a frequent theme in Dugen, is echoed earlier in the poetry of Saigy?. It expands Dugen's view of 'expression' to the world of nature. Whether the traditional Japanese love of nature preceded or succeeded the absolute significance accorded to the phenomenal world cannot be determined.

THEODICY AND ETHICS

Japanese Buddhist treatments of theodicy and ethics also reveal ways in which Buddhism was transformed in Japan. Theodicy is meant here in Max Weber's general sense of an explanation that make the injustices of life intelligible and accounts for evil in the world. In classical Indian thought, the notion of karma answers the problem of both moral and natural evil. Karmic retribution means that every deed or action has consequences and evil deeds bring about suffering. Suffering is not punishment by a God who is free to punish or not, but rather is an inevitable consequence of evil actions. There are accordingly practical reasons to avoid evil and do good. In early Indian thought the notion of karma entailed that of transmigration. Karma is, as it were, the momentum of our actions that propels us through samsara, the continuous cycles of birth and death. This transmigration occurs through various lifetimes and life forms, mythologized as the six realms of hell, hungry ghosts, animals, fighting demons, humans and gods. The Buddha taught a way of liberation that is a release from transmigration and its cause, karma, whether good or evil. In later Japanese Buddhist philosophy, attachment to self and the concomitant ignorance of the reality of no-self were stressed as the root cause of samsara.

After Buddhism was introduced to Japan, people easily accepted the notion of karmic retribution but not the literal belief of rebirth as animals or lower life forms. Transmigration through the six realms of samsara played a larger role in Japanese literature and theatre than in philosophical discussions, which focused more on the practical path to liberation. Good deeds were not the means to liberation; they did not, for example, ensure rebirth in the Pure Land, whether taken as the physical abode or spiritual state wherein final liberation is possible. Hunen, and later Shinran in his Tannish? (Lamenting the Deviations) went so far as to state that: 'If a good person attains birth in the Pure Land, how much more so the evil person'.

The apparent incompatibility between any notion of rebirth and the Indian Buddhist doctrine of no-self or no-soul was not an issue in traditional Japanese Buddhist thought. Moreover, even after the Japanese understood this doctrine they, like the Chinese, continued to believe in the spirits of ancestors who remain somehow present among the living. That folk belief has played a stronger role in everyday life and religious practices than has Buddhist doctrine.

Logically, the disassociation of good deeds and liberation would seem to compromise the theodicy offered by the notion of karmic retribution, and ancestor veneration to compromise the doctrine of no substantial self which is the basis of compassion with all living beings. In effect, however, the compromises have meant little more than finding a middle course, or superimposing the two metaphysically incompatible beliefs. Belief in karmic retribution has encouraged the avoidance of deeds conventionally deemed evil, and thus supported conventional ethics; but karmic retribution does not entail any final resolution to misery.

Only religious practice, whether conceived as self-power or other-power, holds out the prospect of final liberation, or at least the actualization of one's inherent enlightenment. In the meantime, one is to do good and avoid evil; more specifically, one is to adhere to conventional Buddhist precepts such as not killing, stealing, lying and so on. Similarly, veneration of ancestral spirits, including Buddhist patriarchs, has encouraged a respect for tradition and social order, while non-ego has been extolled as the basis of right action in both Japanese Buddhism and Confucianism. If we seek in Japanese Buddhist philosophy a coherent theory of ethics as a separate branch of philosophy, we find instead a variety of practical reasons; for a moral theory, we would have to refer to Confucianism.

This general description receives closer definition in the views of Shinran and Dugen. Dugen's ethical views reflect both the penchant to practical reasoning and the transcendence of ethics in the realization of enlightenment. Dugen's sermons to monks training under him admonish them to keep the precepts while recognizing that their content is relative to the situation. Ultimately, the practice of keeping precepts is subsumed into zazen or the practice of realization. Dugen's more philosophical writings transform practical admonitions such as 'do good' and 'do no evil' into proclamations of the realized state: 'the non-production of evil, the performance of good'.

Ultimately, both Dugen and Shinran would have us transcend the duality of good and evil to manifest, through uncontrived actions, absolute non-dual reality or 'suchness', which is perfect as it is. There is no cause-effect relation between morality and enlightenment, and so the issue is not the situational relativity of morality but, once again, the problem that the absolute is not complete without its manifestation in the phenomenal. Here ethical issues would give way to the problem of inherent enlightenment. The contemporary interpreter D.T. Suzuki advocated Zen enlightenment as the solution and simply proclaimed it to be 'beyond good and evil' (Suzuki 1964). On the other hand, the idea of inherent enlightenment has come under attack in the 1990s as perpetuating the status quo of society and blinding Japanese Buddhism to the need for reform guided by a social ethics.

BUDDHISTIC ETHICS AND SOCIAL CRITICISM

Buddhism arose in India during a period of intense intellectual and social ferment. It was a period during which the authority of the Vedas had been placed in doubt, the concept of god as a supreme being and creator was in question, the hereditary restrictions on caste mobility were under attack, and the efficacy of Brahminical rituals was being challenged. The authors of the Upanishads had opened the door for various heterodox currents to emerge in society, and amongst the most significant of these were the Lokayatas who polemicized against religious charlatans, and the Nyayavadis whose rational epistemology created the foundation for intense philosophical debate and encouraged the investigation of the real world based on reason and logic, freed from the burden of superstition and irrational adherence to burdensome rituals. Various ideological sects competed for the attention and acceptance of the ruling elites and the public. The most important amongst these were the Jains and the Buddhists. Although each of the various sects made original and interesting contributions to philosophy, it was the early Buddhists who attempted to provide a unified philosophical system where ethical conduct and social criticism lay at the very core of their ideological system.

Although today, Buddhism is viewed as a religion by many of its followers, the early Buddhists sects were either strongly atheistic or agnostic. The atheists believed that rather than "God having created man in his own image" it was man who had created "God" in his image. In their view, the liberation of humanity was contingent upon humanity shedding the delusion that "God" existed.

Other parables from surviving Buddhist texts indicate agnosticism. For instance, there is a suggestion that Buddhist followers ought not to waste their time on unsolvable metaphysical questions such as "does god exist". The search to identify the "one true god" or to speculate on the nature of god was seen as an exercise in futility.

But the most frequently cited argument against god by the Buddhists was that if an omnipotent and omniscient being such as "God" truly existed, and who was also all good, there could not be the kind of dukkha (suffering) that was so widespread in the real world.

These shlokas (verses) from the Bhûridatta Jataka illustrates this point:

If the creator of the entire world they call "God" be the lord of every being, why does he order such misfortune, and not create concord?

If the creator of the entire world they call "God" be the lord of every being, why let prevail deceit, lies and ignorance, why create such inequity and injustice?

If the creator of the entire world they call "God" be the lord of every being, then an evil master is he, knowing what's right did let wrong prevail!

Unlike religions that ascribed earthly miseries to human sinfulness that brought upon the wrath of a vengeful god who needed to be feared, Buddhism saw the root of human suffering in ignorance that could only be ended through the acquisition of wisdom. Rather than expect some supernatural entity to end human suffering, the Buddhists argued that it was in human hands to end their sorrows through conduct and action driven by knowledge and correct understanding of human nature and the physical world. Hence, the aspiration for knowledge (jigyasa) was seen as the answer to blind faith. Although the Buddhists were not alone in developing this view, the elaboration of this point of view became pivotal to early Buddhist philosophy.

Central to Buddhist philosophy was an understanding of human nature and what caused dukkha-i.e. human suffering. They saw human personality as constituting five attributes, i.e. body, feeling, perception, disposition and consciousness, and used this framework to develop their understanding of human suffering. Citing examples of conditions that led to human suffering, such as aging, sickness and death, or association with the unpleasant, (or separation from the pleasant), or the inability to get what one wished-they concluded that suffering was a condition of stress and conflict inherent within human existence and interaction with the world.

They also connected suffering to the very impermanence of things. They observed how people lamented over the loss of a loved one, or experienced sorrow when something or someone that had once given them happiness became separated from them. They noted that even human pleasures were not immune from suffering because they didn't last forever, and the loss of pleasure inevitably left people feeling deprived. Seeing as how clinging to things (that were necessarily impermanent) was one of the primary causes of dukkha, they cautioned against excessive attachment.

At the same time, they recognized a recurring and more general type of existential unease and anxiety (aniccha) that arises from the very transience of life, and our inability to control or comprehend all worldly phenomenon, which they characterized as viparinama-dukkha.

But the Buddhists did not see dukkha only emanating from the difficulties of an individual. They also saw suffering emerge on a much larger scale from hostile social conditions such as poverty, war, and social oppression which they described as dukkha-dukkha.

As a formula (char-mulya) for addressing these different types of suffering, the Buddhists advocated a four-fold scheme of a) recognizing the problem i.e. suffering (dukkha); b) identifying the cause of the suffering-such as craving stemming from ignorance (samudaya); c) establishing the goal of ending the problem (nirodha)-i.e. the cessation of suffering (nirvana); d) conducting life in a manner that was consistent with the cessation of suffering-following the right path or engaging in the right practice (marga).

Followers were thus goaded into developing both a sense of personal ethics and a social conscience:

> *"He who has understanding and great wisdom does not think of harming himself or another, nor of harming*

both alike. He rather thinks of his own welfare, of that of others, of that of both, and of the welfare of the whole world. In that way one shows understanding and great wisdom." Anguttara Nikaya-(Gradual Sayings)

"By protecting oneself (e.g., morally), one protects others; by protecting others, one protects oneself." Samyukta Nikaya (Kindred Sayings)

Human actions (kamma, kaama, or karma) in the Buddhist framework were to be judged based on both the intention or motive (chetanaa) and the consequences (vipaaka) of the action. Altruistic actions which helped in the establishment and promotion of a just society were encouraged in the dharmaniyama (moral duty code).

{The discourses, or suttas in the Digha Nikaya, illustrate how there was deep concern with the creation of social conditions favorable to the cultivation of Buddhist values and the expansion of social equity and justice. These views undoubtedly influenced the creation of a "welfare state" during the reign of emperor, Ashoka (B.C. 274-236)}

In their theories of causality Buddhists challenged the view that human destiny was unaffected by the ethics or morality of human actions. They countered the doctrine of amoral causation (akriyavaada) whose adherents argued that there was no merit in doing good and no demerit for doing evil. (An extreme expression of such thinking was seen in philosophers who denied all morality and saw no crime in the killing of any person.)

Realizing that such a world-view could lead to the rejection of moral distinctions and personal responsibility for ones actions, they argued strenuously against such beliefs. They also argued against the theory of Makkali Ghosha (or Ghoshala) who believed that human fate was predetermined, and therefore denied that human actions had any bearing on the results of things (ahetuvaada) and maintained that human intention and effort were essentially powerless in changing human destiny, and therefore advocated fatalism (niyati).

They also countered philosophers from the school of "absolute skepticism" who doubted everything and never committed themselves to any specific position in doctrinal debates. Philosophers from this school such as Sanjaya Belarthaputra (who was known as a theorist of endless equivocation or an equivocationist (amraavikkhepavaadin)) were criticized in the Brahmajaala Sutta (or Sutra) as "eel-wrigglers" who were incapable of taking a definitive stance on the vital philosophical questions of the day. Such skepticism was seen as emanating from both the fear of being in error and the lack of knowledge (or inability) to provide reasonable answers to question put forward for discussion. Such all-pervading doubt coupled with a cynical skepticism (vichikicchaa) was viewed as a serious mental hindrance, a fetter in the path to wisdom.

Other theories that contradicted the notion that human actions mattered were theories of accidentalism (ahetu-apachayavaada), theistic determinism (ishvaranimmaanavaada) and past-action determinism (purvaketavaada or purvekatahetu). All of these were were opposed by the Buddhists. Accidentalism was an indeterminist theory which held that whatever was experienced was uncaused and unconditioned by human intervention. Theistic determinism was a determinist theory, which held that whatever was experienced was due to God's will or by plan of a "Supreme-Being". Past-action determinism was also a determinist theory, but it held the belief that whatever was experienced, whether pleasurable or painful or indifferent was entirely due to ones past actions (from a previous life), and ones present actions had no relevance.

The danger in each of these theories was highlighted in these words: "Thus for those who fall back on these three erroneous views as essential dogma, there is neither the will to do what is ought to be done, or not to do what is ought not to be done, nor necessity to do this deed or abstain from that deed. No moral improvement or intellectual culture can be expected from them."

Some of the theories in circulation at that time built on a germ of truth but generalized to the point of absurdity. For instance the accidentalists were correct only to the extent that certain things did indeed appear to happen by random chance or accident. But they failed to recognize that sometimes what may have seemed to be accidental was more due to inadequate understanding or improper or incomplete perception, and that other activities had a clearly discernible cause. To deal with the extreme generalizations of such theorists, they introduced a middle standpoint for their epistemology and ethics.

They thus rejected the theory admitting that everything exists (sabba atthii ti) and in permanence-i.e. the extreme of eternalism (sassatavaada), and its opposite which advocated that nothing actually exists (sabba natthii ti) i.e. nihilism (the denial of all reality in real-world phenomenon) or the extreme of annihilationalism (ucchedavaada). Related to their critique of the eternalist and nihilist philosophies was their rejection of both hedonism and self-mortification (attakilamathaanuyoga) which they viewed as painful, fruitless, unprofitable and ignoble.

Buddhist texts also expressed suspicion about claims by heretical teachers of being constantly "all-knowing" and "all-seeing" and in possession of "all-embracing knowledge-and-vision." Such claims were countered with arguments relating to the actual behaviour of such charlatans in different situations. For instance, they wondered why such "all-knowing" and "all-seeing" spiritual teachers lost their way in an unfamiliar place or why they were unable to escape from trouble while countering a fierce animal such as dog, elephant, horse or bull. Moreover, if they were really omniscient, they wouldn't need to ask for people's names, clans, or the name of a village or market town or make enquiries about anything. That they did such things indicated that their knowledge was evidently limited just like that of any average worldly person (puthujjana).

Unlike religions that were based on revealed truth or the sanctity of every word in a holy textbook, the Buddhist belief system prescribed reasoning based on investigation as the means of determining ones dhamma, (or dharma as in Hindu practise).

In a parable in the Kaalaama Sutta, followers of Budhism are advised not to accept any moral codes on the following ten grounds: (1) Vedic authority (anussava), (2) tradition (paramparaa), (3) hearsay or report (itikiraa), (4) textual authority (pittakasampadaa), (5) apparent agreebility of the view (sama o no garu), (6) authority of the holder of the view (takkahetu), (7) apparent logicality of the view (nayahetu), (8) the fact that the view is an accepted standpoint (aakaaraparivitakka), (9) inadequate reflection on reasons (bhabbaruupataa), or (10) the fact that the view agrees with one's own (ditthinijjhaanakkhanti).

In this manner, the Buddhism developed a very sophisticated philosophical system in which social ethics were integrated with rational investigation of human nature, social organization and the physical world. Buddhist ideas and concepts left a powerful impression on other Indian philosophical and religious belief systems, and over time, many commonalities developed amongst the competing ideologies.

However, there were also certain problems with the Buddhist world view which prevented its complete acceptance by intellectuals committed to the scientific method. For instance, although the Buddhists rejected the theory of past action determinism, they did posit the existence of a soul which survived a person's death and carried with it the merits and demerits of a person's past lives. Presumably this concept was essential to the Buddhist goal of encouraging right conduct but it was rejected by those who considered the soul as inseparable from the body and did not believe that the soul survived death. Those who rejected the concept of transmigration of the soul naturally couldn't accept the idea that human destiny had anything to do with merits and demerits accumulated in previous incarnations of the "soul". In their view, morality and ethics were entirely social constructs and had to be dealt with accordingly. The realists (such as the Nyayavadis) who shared the Buddhist concern for morals and ethics in society argued that while morals and ethics ought to be encouraged, they could only be enforced through societal laws and judicial codes.

Another problem facing the Buddhists was that in many ways, their views were too advanced for their times. Society had not yet developed to the point where education was universal, and knowledge of the real world sufficient to prevent superstitions and irrational beliefs from being completely abandoned by the masses. In an era where society had only limited control over nature, it was inevitable that sections of society would continue with beliefs in deities and supernatural phenomenon in the hope that they may be spared from natural disasters or that their crops might withstand attacks from pests and disease. Thus although the Buddhists had a very important and salutatory effect on Indian society, the most advanced Buddhist concepts could be understood and practised by only a minority in society.

Over time, the spirit of inquiry and rational investigation that had spurred the early Buddhist scholars towards dialectical thinking and critical social analysis became more and more replaced by narrow and literalist interpretations of the earlier texts. For instance, advice against accepting something that appeared "logical" without personal verification was taken to mean that logic could be rejected. Advice against wasting ones time on unsolvable metaphysical questions was also taken too literally and many Buddhist scholars remained aloof from the metaphysical debates pursued by other philosophical schools such as those of the Jains and the Nyaya Vaisheshikas. What they didn't anticipate was that some of these debates might lead to useful advances in mathematics or deeper understanding of human thought processes and new insights on human memory and psychology. These led to valuable advances in the interpretation of moods and emotions-thus benefiting Indian art, literature and music.

In addition, later Buddhist monks lapsed into some of the very things that had been attacked by the early Buddhists such as indulgence in unnecessary and elaborate rituals, belief in supra-natural phenomenon, and alienation of the priests from the masses. Activities such as meditation which were encouraged as a means to gaining wisdom became ends in themselves, and were turned into idealistic fetishes. Although Buddhist monks dutifully delivered sermons on right conduct and right action, they often failed to engage in relevant and timely social criticism-and did not always connect the textual suggestions to concrete practice. Intra-Buddhist disputes developed around less significant details, even as some of the most important ideas that had initially shaped the philosophy were pushed into the background. As a result Buddhism as it was practised came to be associated with idealism and inaction. Whereas the early Buddhists saw no merit in worshipping god or its images, later Buddhism developed a pantheon of deities not very different from other Indian religions.

Thus even as Buddhism had spread almost throughout Asia by the 5th-6th C AD, it gradually began to lose its distinct edge and liberating influence on much of Indian society. Within the Indian subcontinent, strains of Buddhism survived in Sri Lanka, Bengal, Bhutan, Sikkim, parts of Bihar and Nepal, and parts of Sindh, Punjab, Kashmir and Afghanistan. In parts of Orissa and adjoining regions (such as Chhattisgarh and Telengana), Tantric (and other) influences reshaped the practice of Buddhism. Yet, Buddhism continued to have an impact outside India and developed pockets of influence as far West as Syria, as well as in much of Central Asia (including what is now Uzbekistan, Tajikistan, Kyrgyzia, Kazakhstan) and Tibet. In the East, its influence was felt on virtually every nation including Burma, Thailand, Malaya and Indonesia, Laos, Cambodia, Vietnam, China, Korea and Japan.

As noted earlier, the vast literature of Buddhism (like much of Hindu or Jain literature) was not a literature of revelation and authority. Its essays on social ethics and moral responsibilities, its treatises on philosophy and science, its art and poetry were but pointers to a path to wisdom. This gave Buddhism both flexibility and adaptability. Owing to its non-hegemonic character and humanist appeal, Buddhism was adopted without coercion or force. It was also successfully fused with Hinduism in many parts of South East Asia just as elements of it had been integrated into Hindu practices in India. In

China, it was integrated with Taoism and Confucian principles; in Japan with Shinto beliefs. For several centuries, within India and outside, several people followed multiple faiths and identified as both Buddhists and Hindus, or as both Buddhists and Tantrics, (or Buddhists and Taoists) and so on. During the Gupta period (and in other reigns), philosophers from various schools of thought received royal patronage and temple grants were conferred for the construction of Buddhist and Hindu monuments alike.

It is also important to recognize that the form of Buddhism that was embraced in each nation was often quite different. For instance, in Western and Central Asia, it was not the philosophical or intellectual aspects of Buddhism that were popularized, but rather, its personal moral codes. Buddhist prosletysers imbued their stories of the Buddha with examples of miraculous healing and super-natural compassion so as to win more followers.

While such tendencies were also to be seen as Buddhism travelled within India or outwards, in Burma, Sri Lanka and Thailand, Buddhism developed organizational structures that appear to have been much more resilient. It was perhaps realized that the development of Buddhist virtue would require leadership and constant interaction with the community. In these nations, Buddhism did not degenerate into the extremes of mysticism or retreatism that became commonplace in certain parts of India (such as in the foothills of the Western Himalayas). Burmese and Thai monks maintained a practical and benevolent connection with the community, and thus retained a measure of respect within the community. This also appears to be the case in Japan. In Korea, the emphasis on gaining wisdom was taken very seriously, and Buddhist monks took the lead in promoting mass literacy. This propelled the growth of technologies associated with the production of paper, writing instruments, inks, and furniture. And unlike in India, (where due to Upanishadic influences, "inner" wisdom came to be favored over outer wisdom), Buddhist concern for disseminating the writings of the Buddha had significant positive secular impact. In Korean (and other Eastern) Buddhism, there was the correct realization that a Buddhist mindset, or that a Buddhist society could not be constructed overnight. There was thus the emphasis on the (helical) upgradation of individuals and society towards greater "Buddhahood". This philosophical element was perhaps signficant in that it prevented the sort of philosophical stagnation that occurred in India, where followers too often sought immediate succuor, and thus not only became divorced from reality, but also lost sight of the strategic potential of the philosophy.

In addition, it ought to be noted that Buddhism in India also had to contend with strongly anarchic and ultra-democratic tendencies. Precisely because its philosophical structure emphasized the relative and changing nature of truth, different tendencies under the Buddhist mantle competed for leadership through argument and debate. Initially, this led to important advances in democratic practices within the Sanghas. But over time, it also led to clashes of egoes, hair-splitting and deadlock. While some Buddhist sects compromised and fused with other tendencies (even alien tendencies), others remained fiercely autonomous. To survive, Buddhism had to confront both the tendency to be co-opted, as well as the tendency to atomize.

However, the catastrophic demise of Buddhism in India was triggered by the onslaught of Islam which first obliterated the remnants of Buddhism in Central Asia, and then later in Afghanistan and India. By and large, Buddhism survived only in those countries that escaped invasions by Islamic conquerors. As a gentle faith that encouraged its followers to abjure violence, it was perhaps unable to protect itself from iconoclasts and proselytizers who intended to enforce a new religio-political order. Accustomed to centuries of peaceful co-existence, India's Buddhists had not anticipated the need to develop viable strategies for self-defence that could have combated the violence of India's Islamic conquerors who virtually obliterated Buddhism from the land of its birth.

Yet, it also appears that (in large part) later Buddhism had deviated considerably from the rational principles outlined in the early texts. Monasteries often became isolated from mainstream society, and monks who focused exclusively on meditative practices and idealistic or esoteric philosophical speculation contributed little to social progress. Some have even argued that the monastic orders had degenerated into sheer parasitism and were becoming a heavy social drain. Consequently, value judgements on the demise of Buddhism and the rise of Islam in India need to be made with a measure of caution.

Nevertheless, it must be acknowledged that the ascent of Islam was concomitant with the eclipse of Buddhism, and since the influence of Buddhism was greatly dependant on the existence of the monastic orders, the destruction of monasteries and their conversion to mosques and institutions of Quranic learning simply lead to mass conversions to Islam.

In the long term, this could have had the effect of stunting India's future intellectual development, since the destruction of important institutions of Buddhist learning also led to a notable decline in the opportunity (and social sanction) to study secular subjects such as logic and epistemology (which were also taught at Buddhist universities-such as Bhagalpur).

It might also be observed that the destruction of Buddhist centers of learning coincided with the destruction of extremely valuable textual materials-which could have been potentially rediscovered, and revived or reinterpreted by future generations of Indians so as to achieve a society that was more thoughtful and learned. Islamic texts did not offer anything comparable in terms of causality or epistemology. Nor did they offer the psychological, sociological, or moral insights that had been developed under the ambit of Buddhism. Nor was there any comparable stress on seeking knowledge or constantly updating ones understanding of nature and human society.

One can, therefore, only speculate as to the full consequences of this profound sociolgical and cultural loss (and discontinuity).

But East of India, Buddhism did survive, and in countries such Korea, Thailand and Burma, it continued to enjoy a loyal popular following. Philosophical innovations also took place, and as noted earlier, Buddhist scholars in China, Korea and Japan offered their own commentaries and somewhat individual interpretations of Buddhist concepts and formulations outlined in later (5-7th C.) Indian texts. And although the sacking of monasteries and centers of learning (such as Nalanda and Vikramshila in Bihar) led to records of the original Buddhist texts being permanently destroyed, it has been possible to reconstruct some of them from translations that survived outside India such as in Thailand and Tibet. Notwithstanding the virtual erasure of Buddhism in India, it is possible to infer from these reconstructed texts and other archaeological records (and surviving monuments and artifacts) that Buddhism had a very powerful impact in shaping the destiny of India, and in triggering a social and cultural renaissance that would take Indian and other Asian civilizations to a higher level of social, cultural and material development.

DIVERSIFICATION

The diversification of the Buddhist streams-reaching several climaxes between the 2nd Century BCE and the 5th Century CE-did not so much result from schisms concerning the fundamental doctrines-such as the Four Noble Truths or the doctrine of Dependent Co-Origination-as from the additions of elements not mentioned by the Buddha, or even elements which the Buddha refused to discuss.

At first, these additions remained peripheral, later however they became more far-reaching and radical (e.g. in the Pudgalavada-tradition where the concept of anatta was 'bypassed'). The diversification on the philosophical level concerns mainly two themes:

- dharma: principle, supporting characteristic, basic element of cognition;
- buddha: as historical figure, as transcendental being, as cosmic principle.

It is and remains agreed upon however that both are in fact identical, and thus interchangeable: "He who sees the Buddha, sees the Teaching; and he who sees the Teaching sees the Buddha", the Buddha more than once proclaimed. (e.g. in SN, IV-120)

Broadly speaking however, it could be said that the 'dharma-theme' was more emphasized within circles of monks and philosophers, whereas the 'buddha-theme' (certainly at the outset) was more appealing to lay-people, preachers and artists- as is apparent from the oldest archeological Buddhist findings in India. Also a lot of the early 'biographical' literature, e.g. Lalitavistara, Jataka's and Buddhacarita, refers mainly to the exemplary function of the 'buddha-theme'. The diversification can (but therefore doesn't have to) happen by way of diverse, interactive points of view, coming from diverse angles, which will require us to look upon it in the light of a multidimensional complexity.

Apart then from disciplinary and/or soteriological problems, we can determine the following important points of view concerning the Teaching of the Buddha, without however being able to pinpoint in how far they are simultaneous or consecutive. Their chronology remains very uncertain.

Diversification According to the "Addressee"

In the scriptures of the different schools we see that the Buddha addresses a great diversity of social and spiritual categories of listeners, thereby each time adapting his use of language and terminology in function of the social and/or educational level of his audience.

Grosso modo we can reduce this to three main groups of listeners:

- the monks: with a strong emphasis on meditative states and levels;
- lay-people: mainly concerning ethical questions;
- the "specialists" (e.g. brahmins, sramana's, muni's, etc.): questions regarding worldview and metaphysics.

A strong and definitive demarcation between these three groups is however impossible, since the Teaching of the Buddha starts out with the anatta-criterion, a criterion that covers all further consequences.

Tensions between (1) and (2) have led to the first known 'schism' (during the so-called Second Council at Vaisali, be this historically correct or not...) whereby-for purely disciplinary reasons-the Elders (Sthaviravada) who strongly held to the letter of the Vinaya, parted with the Greater Community (Mahasanghika) which consisted for a great part, if not the majority, of lay-people. Tensions between (1) and (3) could have been the cause for the origination of the "pre-Mahayana".

Diversification According to Abhidharma

The Abhidharma (Pali: Abhidhamma) in its broadest meaning is the "Extended Teaching", viz. the systematically and philosophically structured envelopment of the actual soteriology. This later 'extension' differs strongly from school to school as becomes apparent from the transmitted Abhidharma-pitaka's. Certain schools even went as far as rejecting every form of Abhidharma. (e.g. Sautrantika)

The two extremes of this diversification according to importance given to, or rejection of the Abhidharma are:

- Buddhist 'Scholasticism', is most strongly represented by the Sarvastivada (e.g. their discussion concerning the dharma's, their classification, their existence and their time-value). Mostly practiced by monks and based on scriptural texts and commentaries. Leads towards abstraction and reduction to conceptual forms (e.g. buddha (buddhata)
- 'Devotion' and especially 'popular devotion', most strongly emphasized by the lay. Traces of this can be found back in the oldest Buddhist archeological monuments (e.g. Bharhut and Sanchi) and in the Edicts of Emperor Ashoka. Institutionally they are mostly represented in the Mahasanghika-stream (e.g.

Lokottaravada, with its emphasis on the transcendence and the "deification" of the historical Buddha)

The synchronicity of diversifications A and B leads to new perspectives apart from the distinction between the Smaller Vehicle (Hinayana) and the Greater Vehicle (Mahayana). (Philosophically very artificial at first). The distinction between the two streams is in fact much more complex than conventionally presented. Many correlations and interactions have played an important role in this process.

Further we see an evolution in the thinking and living of the Teaching, in which the distinction between Smaller and Greater Vehicle has given way to the emphasis of either Buddha or Teaching (Dharma).

Diversification According to Dharma and Buddha

In connection to A and B we see the inclination towards an emphasis on either the expression of the Teaching or the 'person' of the Buddha:

Dharma: The historical Buddha is 'only' the bringer of the Teaching, which makes him 'subordinate' to the Teaching. This emphasis will be expressed the strongest in those currents that give importance to discussion and polemics, to scholasticism, ethichs and psychology, such as there are

- Sarvastivada and Theravada (i.e. Smaller Vehicle)
- The Prajñaparamita schools in India and China (i.e. Greater Vehicle) E. Conze uses the term "Wisdom-schools".

Buddha: The Teaching is the manifestation of Buddhahood, with its inherent, open to human experience, characteristics of Wisdom and Compassion. Here we notice however again a distinction between:

- Gautama Buddha as exclusive Buddha, be it as a historical figure or as manifestation of an "Eternal Buddha": e.g. Theravada (Smaller Vehicle); Lotus-sutra, Zen (Greater Vehicle).

- Non-historical (so-called 'meditative') Buddha-figures who assume a cosmic scale (up to present only Mahayana): e.g. Vairocana in Avatamsaka and Tantra; Amitabha in Sukhavativyuha.

We need to underline however that within this complexity the actual soteriology remains centered around the Four Noble Truths, of which the coherence should be looked upon as exclusively soteriological, certainly not ontological. Most 'additions' or 'extensions' are of a cognitive and explanatory nature. Within Mahayana philosophy they are regarded as 'expedient means' (upaya-kausalya), as are all forms of appearance of the Teaching.

NIRVANA

If there is one term in Buddhism that has given rise to a lot of confusion and misunderstanding, it must be nirvana. Nirvana, "the Great Nothing or Void as Supreme Bliss", is such an image that has more become-from Schopenhauer until present-a western pseudo-myth than the central concept of Buddhist soteriology.

The negative appreciation of nirvana as destruction of existence is in fact the result of a dichotomous approach. Although it is true that nirvana is in a sense a negative expression, it must be said that that which is negated does not belong to the domain of ontology, not even the domain of general metaphysics. It is most certainly not a negation of "being", nor of "non-being". In Buddhism, 'being' and 'non-being' can neither be affirmed nor denied: they are concepts that do not belong into the soteriology. Sakyamuni Buddha himself classified questions of this nature in the category of theoretical irrelevancies.

The sense of nirvana therefore must be searched for within another domain. Time and again, the Buddha-and many masters after him-has emphasized that nirvana should be approached and interpreted in an (in a certain sense) epistemological, and primarily in a pragmatic-soteriological sense.

If we look at the etymology of the term we find that nirvana is a compound of the prefix ni[r]-(ni, nis, nih) which means "out, away from, without", and the root vâ[na] (P. vâti) which can be translated as "blowing" as in "blowing of the wind", but also as "smelling, etc"

The compound 'nirvâna' therefore undeniably has the meaning of "blowing out, putting out, extinguishing (of a lamp or of fire), setting (of the sun)". Used as an adjective it can mean "quiet, stilled, tamed, departed". MMW adds to this lemma that for Buddhists and Jains the term means "the absolute extinction or annihilation of individual existence or of all desires and passions". Nirvana thus means the "settling of the wind, the extinguishing of the fire". As a medical term it is also used as "stopping of the fever or stress".

Although all Buddhist schools in a way agree on this basic meaning of the term, diverse interpretations and connotations appear. Grosso modo we can make a distinction in interpretations between those of the Hinayana (especially the Sautrantika and Sarvastivada schools) and those of the Mahayana schools.

The Smaller Vehicle sees nirvana primarily-and almost exclusively-as an ethical event, attainable in this life (at least in theory) through the practice of morality, contemplation and insight. It is only within the Abhidharma-literature that the meaning of nirvana will somehow extend to a certain realm of existence of passionlessness, peace, etc.

Such an approach must necessarily lead to a strictly negative formulation, e.g. that of Udana viii. There, nirvana is described as the realization of the fourth proposition of the logical tetralemma: "neither [this]....nor [not this]....", with by the way a truly Nagarjunian sense for expression.

This negative formulation will be less the case in Mahayana-texts. Often, nirvana is here equated with sunyata (emptiness), which-one should keep in mind-for a Buddhist is a positive term, equivalent to 'availability' and even-especially in later Mahayana-'totality'. Nirvana in this sense can be approached in a positive way as 'Enlightenment' (bodhi), Buddhahood (buddhata), etc.

The situation becomes more clear when nirvana is in the first place seen as the opposite of samsara: the world of suffering as the cycle of birth-and-death. Since samsara is in a sense "propelled" by karma-formations (volitional activity conditioned by desire, aversion and delusion), nirvana means-as the opposite of samsara-the halting of these (causative) karmic formations and therefore also the exhaustion of their karmic 'fruit' (results of volitional actions). The realization of nirvana is therefore the cessation of the karma-causality.

Mostly the commentators agree when it comes to the 'attributes' that can be ascribed to nirvana, this despite the fact that they-paradoxically enough-keep stressing that nirvana is "inconceivable, unthinkable, indescribable'. So, it is said that nirvana is the 'unconditioned' (asamkrita), peaceful (santa), unarisen (anutpada), etc.

Moreover distinctions were made between a 'temporal, created nirvana' (nirvana seen from the human condition, and therefore as a relative truth), and the 'perfect, definitive, uncreated nirvana' which belongs to the experience of ultimate (absolute) truth.

Or, a distinction is created between a 'place bound' nirvana (pratisthita-nirvana), which is realized in this existence and with this present body, and the 'nirvana of no-abode' (apratisthita-nirvana). Only this nirvana is complete as the realization of Buddhahood.

D.T.Suzuki (in his translation of the Kyogyoshinsho, note 90) says that nirvana "....is the annihilation of the notion of ego-substance and of all the desires that arise from this erroneous conception. But this represents the negative side of the doctrine, and its positive side consists in universal love or sympathy (karuna) for all beings."

Nirvana then is not an 'individual' event or state, but the cessation of every illusion or conceptual form of (individual) personality. The Lotus Sutra states: "But he (the Buddha) does not teach a particular Nirvana for each being; he causes all beings to reach complete Nirvana by means of the complete Nirvana of the Tathagata."

Among the Buddhist philosophers there were-and still are-those who held/hold different, sometimes diverging opinions concerning the nature of nirvana. Yet, there remains a unanimity concerning the 'nirvanic' nature of the cessation of the condition of suffering. Remarkable however is the fact that it is exactly the European Buddhologists (among whom we find names as de la Vallée-Poussin and Theodore Stcherbatsky) who have started the polemics on the subject.

RELATIONSHIP HINAYANA/MAHAYANA

Taking into account the different diversification criteria, we can conclude that the Smaller Vehicle (Hinayana) and the Larger Vehicle (Mahayana) have (1) a lot of themes in common and (2) that they overlap each other on a number of topics. It should be noticed here however that to look upon these two streams as 'whole units', viz. completed and closed-off systems, is a fiction.

1. A lot of the so-called 'typical' Mahayana doctrinal points appear in the Pali-Canon, which is seen without a doubt as the Hinayana document par excellence. A great number of these doctrinal points are found in the oldest layers of the Pali-Canon and cannot be taken to be later interpolations.
2. Another remarkable fact is that within Indian Buddhism there rarely is any mention (not until very late) of separate Mahayana communities. Apparently the monks of the divers streams lived among one another, following more or less the same Vinaya rules. Witness to this are the writings of the pilgrim monk Hsüan-chuang (600-664) who gives a detailed description of the situation of Buddhism in India. There is therefore no reason to speak of a 'schism' in the Christian sense of the word.

> It is impossible, given the present archeological research, where India is concerned to draw a sharp demarcation line between the two streams. It is only in China that the institutional separation of Hinayana/Mahayana becomes truly noticeable.

Also remarkable is that, on the doctrinal level, we notice an evolution (or better yet, an extension) of the original anatta-teaching. With the transmission of the term from Hinayana to Mahayana, we notice that the emphasis on its non-ontological character is preserved, whereas the dualism between self/non-self is transcended in the sense of the logical tetralemma (viz. the fourth lemma 'neither-nor').

At first, the term 'Mahayana' did not have the implication of being sectarian or schismatic, but it referred to a 'different approach' of the salvific problem.

The adjective maha(n)t, in compounds 'maha', does not just mean 'great', but also 'broad' or 'large'. It is exactly this meaning that lies at the basis for the term 'Mahayana': the 'broad or large vehicle'.

In this sense 'Mahayana' points primarily to a soteriology that is 'broader' [than for monks alone]; namely, that there is also a possibility for salvation outside of the strict observance of the Vinaya rules or the monastic discipline. The 'Way' (or path, Skt. Marga, Ch. Tao) is 'Broad' ! It is in this sense that the term appears, probably for the first time, in Asvaghosha's "Mahayana-sraddhotpada-sastra" 1(The Awakening of Faith in the Mahayana).

In a somewhat later evolution, the Mahayana evolves towards a stronger contrast in regards to the 'Smaller Vehicle', which emphasizes the effort towards individual salvation "Diligently strive towards your own salvation". In contradistinction to this the Mahayana posits "the salvation of all beings, regardless their numbers". This will go as far as the Mahayana accusing the 'Smaller Vehicle' of mere self-concern and a lack of compassion.

This polemic will appear most clearly in the controversy Arhant/Bodhisattva as the proposed ideal set to be followed by the 'adept'.

Arahant (P.)-Arhant (Skr.)

It is stated that the adept meditator has to transgress four stages on his way to enlightenment:

- sotapanna: the 'stream-enterer'
- sakadagami: the 'once-returner'
- anagami: the 'none-returner'
- arahant: the 'praiseworthy' or the 'holy one'

The arahant, the final stage of this evolution, is the one who is no longer subject to the cycle of birth-and-death. By overcoming the fundamental ignorance he has become desireless and has been freed of every ego-illusion. Because he gives no more rise to desire, no more karma-formations (volitions, acts of will) arise and he is no longer reborn.

He has reached this state through his own efforts by practicing the Dharma, the Vinaya and the "Four Levels of Meditation" (P. jhana; Skt. dhyana). When he experiences suffering as a result of past karma, there is no more mental reaction against this suffering in him. He lives in a state of 'emotional non-reaction'3, equanimity an invulnerability, a state to which every being should strive.

This ideal state is difficult to describe, and even more difficult to realize. The subject in any case brought along a lot of discussion within the different Hinayana-schools (e.g. concerning the question whether the Arahant can 'regress' to a lower state or not).

In the Mahayana-schools the Arahant-ideal was mostly the subject of sharp attacks. He was blamed for working exclusively towards his own salvation. It is true that he functions as an example and that in this way he arouses the desire in others to walk the same way, but besides this he is inactive. He sits alone in a 'small vehicle' and lacks the element of Compassion.

Difference between Arahant/Buddha

- The arahant needs the Teachings (Dharma) set forth by the Buddha, whereas the Buddha discovered the Dharma.
- The arahant puts the Teachings into practice, whereas the Buddha established the practice.
- The arahant has put an end to the causes of suffering, but is not necessarily capable of transmitting this experience to others; whereas the Buddha necessarily shares his experience with others.
- The arahant has a passive knowledge (jñana) of the Teaching, but lacks Wisdom (prajña); whereas the Buddha has (is) active Wisdom.
- The arahant misses compassion (karuna); whereas the Buddha has (is) Great Compassion (maha-karuna).

Pratyekabuddha (P. paccekabuddha)

At a certain moment, another distinction between a Buddha or 'Sammasambuddha' versus a 'pratyekabuddha' is introduced. A pratyekabuddha or a 'solitary Buddha' discovers the Teaching by himself, and fathoms its Wisdom, but he dies without having proclaimed it (viz. the Compassion-element) to others. A lot of interpretations concerning the pratyekabuddha are possible ! (e.g. the possibility of enlightened beings outside the realm of Buddhism).

Bodhisattva (P. bodhisatta)

Enlightenment-being-Being towards Enlightenment-Being focused on Enlightenment.

This term is difficult to translate, even more difficult to describe.

Evolution of the Term

The term bodhisatta is already found in the Pali-Canon, be it with a limited meaning: Bodhisatta is Siddharta Gautama before he realized Enlightenment. Therefore we see two phases in his biography: bodhisatta before, and Buddha after his Enlightenment.

Therefore Bodhisattva is the stage that precedes Enlightenment; however, the way of the arahant excludes Perfect Enlightenment (sammasambodhi). The arahant realizes Complete and Final Nirvana5 at the moment of his death, not being reborn again he does not pass through the stages of the bodhisattva. The way of the bodhisattva leads towards Enlightenment; not just his own enlightenment, but the Enlightenment of all beings indiscriminately.

In the Mahasanghika-school a more liberal interpretation of the bodhisattva-idea will come to light and gradually the ideal of the bodhisattva will become the Mahayana counterpart of the arahant ideal in the Hinayana. The bodhisattva is a 'being' that refuses to remain (some would say 'enter') in Nirvana because of its vow to help others; the bodhisattva chooses to remain in the world of suffering and rejects Complete and Final Nirvana (in the sense as stated before).

This will become the 'leitmotiv' for Mahayana Thought: the bodhisattva chooses Enlightenment for himself and all other beings over his own, individual Enlightenment (cfr. the anatta-doctrine). Besides this, every being (and therefore every human being) has within itself a conscious or unconscious drive towards Enlightenment: the Mind of Enlightenment (bodhicitta), through which it has the potential to realize the bodhisattva within itself.

Different 'Kinds' of Bodhisattva's

It doesn't hold to classify bodhisattva's into different 'kinds' or 'categories'. If we do so, than it is exclusively with the intention to smoothen the approach of the problem. Because, every distinction lies exactly within the approach. So it goes that the Buddha-characteristics of Wisdom and Compassion in se are not different, and yet we experience them as two separate characteristics. It is important to keep in mind that the bodhisattva does not have a separate existence; he is mainly an ideal-projection of-and in-our mind.

BODHISATTVA-MAHASATTVA

The "Great Being Bodhisattva's" traditionally number about 10. They are in fact manifestations of a Buddha 'quality'. The two most important 'qualities' we ascribe to a Buddha are 'Wisdom' (prajña) and 'Compassion' (karuna). Thus we see two kinds of manifestations:

'Wisdom Bodhisattva's' such as Mañjusri (cognitive wisdom) or Mahasthamaprapta (intuitive or emotional wisdom). The Wisdom Bodhisattva's have multiplied almost infinite in number, especially in Tibetan Buddhism.

'Compassion Bodhisattva's' such as Avalokitesvara (the most popular, spread over the divers Buddhist cultures, very important in popular devotion); Samantabhadra (active compassion); Maitreya (the Peaceful, Buddha of the future).

'Human' Bodhisattvas

Since all beings have bodhicitta within them, human beings are also potential bodhisattva's. Here we distance ourselves from the metaphysical structure of the term and emphasize more the emotional element: every human being can be bodhisattva in the perception of every other human being. In this way a human relationship can through the capacity of wisdom and compassion rise above ordinary human standards.

Some typological examples:

* The sages and teachers that brought new insights to the Teaching and thus brought human beings closer to Enlightenment, are often called bodhisattva. E.g. we speak of the philosopher Nagarjuna as Nagarjuna Bodhisattva.
* A strong, spiritually colored relationship through which a normal human relationship is elevated towards a higher level. E.g. Shinran Shonin (1173-1262) saw in

his wife Eshin-ni the embodiment of Kannon Bosatsu (Avalokitesvara Bodhisattva). On the other hand, Eshin-ni, after Shinran's death mentioned in a letter to her daughter Kakushin-ni, that-although she had never told him-she always was convinced of the fact that Shinran was an embodiment of that same Kannon Bosatsu.

* Meritorious people who have made a continuous effort for the spiritual, mental and physical welfare of other people are at times-by way of silent consensus-titled as bodhisattva's. E.g. In Hiroshima's Peace Park there is a sober almost inconspicuous monument in memory of a doctor who died of the effect of radiation, after treating other victims of the atomic bomb for 3 or 4 days. The inscription calls him 'bosatsu' (bodhisattva).

This 'seeing' of a bodhisattva in another human being is a religious act.

The 'Cosmos' as Bodhisattva

When all beings can become bodhisattva, the term bodhisattva will gain an strong expansion. So the feeling of interaction will arise through which all beings out of their true nature are inclined to bring all beings to Enlightenment. Through contact with all beings, any being can experience the Teaching of the Buddha.

From the limited understanding of 'bodhisattva as manifestation of Buddhahood' we will arrive to the embracing of the totality of human occurrences and from there to the embracing of the totality of existence in all its manifest forms. All beings and things participate in each others bodhisattvahood. Certainly in Chinese Buddhism this thought has found a vivid expression, maybe through interaction with Taoism.

DIFFERENCE BUDDHAHOOD/BODHISATTVA

Buddhahood surpasses the existential and is related to 'true nature': availability, totality, sunyata.

The bodhisattva stands in relative existence and is subject to anatta. He has no objective 'being'. He is the existential reflection of Enlightenment; he outlines and objectivates Enlightenment in this relative, relational existence. Besides this he offers man a kind of spiritual ideal, in which man can project him/herself as a being on the way to Enlightenment.

His function, both in Buddhist popular devotion as in the doctrinal development and experience, is therefore not to be underestimated. But also in the personal, intimate approach of the Dharma, the bodhisattva-on whatever level he is situated-is an important element.

MADHYAMAKA AND NAGARJUNA

The philosopher Nagarjuna is the first Buddhist thinker with a vision that transcends the "theological" i.e. the Abhidharmic. He implements the convergence of the various Mahayana-streams and unites them in one coherent system, without neglecting elements from Hinayana-literature.

The starting point of his philosophy is the return to the main tenets of the Teaching as they were proclaimed by Gautama Buddha, thereby thoroughly rejecting the Abhidharmic elaboration. His basic point of view is-just as the historical Buddha's view-mainly empirical, epistemological and not ontological (as e.g. De la Vallee Poussin and partially also Stcherbatsky had claimed), emphasizing the 4th lemma of the Logical Tetralemma (see before), by which it obtains a negative aspect. His point of view is that the Mahayana-acquisitions continue the original themes of the Middle Way (Madhyamaka is the equivalent of Madhyama-pratipad).

Biography: Legend has made itself master of Nagarjuna's biography and is therefore highly unreliable. He is supposed to have lived during the 2nd or 3rd century, as a Brahmin or the son of a Brahmin, in the Middle and/or Southern India. It is even suspected that several "Nagarjuna's" are processed in the legend. Nagarjuna ('snake-white') is a very common name in India.

Works: A great number of works are attributed to Nagarjuna, but textual criticism (already in India, China and Tibet) has rejected the authorship by Nagarjuna of several of these works.

According to the latest research results1 the following works could be authentic:

Mula-madyamika-karika

Sunyata-saptati

Vaidalya-prakarana

Catuh-stava

Suhrillekha

Yukti-sastika

Vigraha-vyavartani

Ratnavali

Pratitya-samutpada-hridaya

Sutrasamuccaya

Some important other works attributed to Nagarjuna are less certain, e.g. Maha-prajñaparamita-sastra and Dasabhumika-vibhasa. All other works are unanimously considered to be inauthentic.

CONTROVERSY: NAGARJUNA, HINAYANA OR MAHAYANA?

Nagarjuna reverts to what he sees as the original teaching of the Buddha, and certainly not to the 'Hinayana'-developments of it. It is by means of original data that he systematizes the pre-Mahayana and Mahayana themes and that he refutes the propositions characteristic for the Sarvastivada and Sautrantika-schools.

We can thus determine notable differences between Nagarjuna and the traditional Hinayana doctrines. So, e.g. Nagarjuna emphasizes sunyata (emptiness) over anatmya (P. anatta-non-self); he posits dharma-sunyata instead of dharma-svabhava (Sarvastivada) and pudgala-sunyata (Sarvastivada, Sautrantika, Theravada).

Yet, it is claimed by some that Nagarjuna is not a "factual Mahayanist" (Warder), or even that he is a Theravadin (Kalupahana). Against these opinions we can bring up the following arguments:

1. The presupposition that only the Pali-canon reflects the 'original' Teaching of the Buddha cannot be maintained. The final redaction of that Canon dates from Buddhaghosa, ± 2 centuries after Nagarjuna.
2. Kalupahana's argument that in MMK only the Katyayanavada is mentioned as a reference; and that this agama appears in the Pali-canon as Kaccayanagotta-sutta, is not convincing, since that same text is also found in the Chinese ("Mahayna") canon.
3. Kalupahana states that "Assuming that Nagarjuna was a Mahayanist and, therefore, must have rejected any literature that came to be preserved by the Sthaviravadins,...). This is contrary to the reality that Mahayana has integrally absorbed the Hinayana-texts into its own scriptural canons.
4. Nagarjuna introduces-also in his MMK-themes that are completely strange to both the Pali-canon and the Hinayana-tradition, e.g. upaya (expedient means) or the Three Levels of Truth with the impossibility to attain absolute truth by way of discursive thought.
5. The traditional transmission within Hinayana rejects the propositions of Nagarjuna (not withstanding the influence they had on their teachings); in Mahayana on the other hand, Nagarjuna is looked upon as the 'second Buddha' who "set the Wheel of the Dharma in motion for the second time." In some cases Nagarjuna was even deified!
6. We should not take MMK out of the context of other undeniably Nagarjunian works, but should recognize their mutual interrelation.

Nagarjuna is without doubt the systematizer of the Mahayana and the starting point of Mahayana philosophy. This is probably why J. Takakusu in his 'Essentials of Buddhist Philosophy' describes Madhyamaka as 'Quasi-Mahayana'.

It is generally accepted that Nagarjuna was especially inspired by the Prajñaparamita literature. This is undeniably so, but also a link with the Avatamsaka way of thinking can not be denied. Typically 'Nagarjunian' sayings can often be found in the Garland-Sutra, e.g.:

"Samsara and nirvana are both ungraspable. Deceiving teachers preach a difference between samsara and nirvana." Or,

"The bodhisattva clearly sees that all existence has only a non-self nature and therefore he understands that it is completely empty and without substance. There is neither body, nor is there no-body, neither thought nor no-thought. There is neither being nor no-being. The entire existence is without possession and without being. It is neither being nor no-being."

One cannot get more 'Nagarjunian' than this...

Emptiness, Concepts and the knowledge of Truth.

Already the historical Buddha stated that:

all forms of existence are characterized by unsatisfactoriness;

all forms of existence are characterized by impermanence;

all elements of existence are characterized by non-self.

Within the existential experience we can therefore not speak of permanent or autonomous values.

But how then should we interpret this existential experience?

In Buddhist terms this is samsara, the 'world of suffering'. 'To exist' is what each separate being perceives for itself. Existence is that which takes place-again for each separate being-between the moment that has passed and the moment that is not yet here, i.e. the transitional process from past (karma = the acts of the past) towards future (phala = karmic results). The present therefore is always a 'becoming'. This 'becoming' is none other than pratitya samutpada, namely, a process of causal conditions.

That which is 'true' therefore remains beyond being (permanence) and non-being (annihilation).

Nagarjuna consequently extends this train of thought.

He calls this 'neither being nor non-being' sunyata (emptiness). Emptiness is not a negative concept (as in 'nothing'), but affirms the possibility, in function of eventual relational conditions, of manifesting all imaginable characteristics.

Since all that is knowable (the phenomenal world) is 'empty', also all our knowing which is made relative by the relation (subject/object) is 'empty'. We reduce the perception into elementary concepts (dharmas), who in their turn can be again regarded as cognitive objects. Nagarjuna stresses the 'emptiness' of each dharma on every level of our cognitive abilities.

Concepts (dharmas) are empty, i.e. without substance. Our discursive thought, which uses language to attach concepts to what is perceived, is therefore irrelevant when it comes to adequately knowing reality in-itself, i.e. independent from perception.

The only thing that can be said with sense, is that all experience and expression of that experience, is 'emptiness'. 'Emptiness' is, where our powers of cognition are concerned, the only reality that all things (subjects and objects) have in common.

But also this concept of 'emptiness' is 'empty' and in the final analysis irrelevant-yet, it remains the ultimate point of what is expressible.

Conceptual thought is necessarily dualistic since-when reduced to its simplest expression-it can only exists in the mutual relationship of a 'conceiver' (as subject) and a 'concept' (as object). Neither 'conceiver' nor 'concept' can be regarded as separate entities. By way of discursive thought, which works with concepts and their language expressions, we therefore can never go beyond what is relative (or relational).

Here, Nagarjuna manifests himself clearly as an empirical epistemologist. He comes to the conclusion that there are three levels of truth. The first two are mutually related and form a bivalence: something is untrue/something is true. Which gives us:

1. asatya-untruth (lie or mistake), e.g. "a hare has horns"
2. loka-samvriti-satya-'world speech truth', 'relative truth', e.g. "a hare does not have horns" the third level of truth is non-conceptual:
3. paramartha-satya-'ultimate truth, absolute truth'. Since this third level can neither be conceptual nor discursive, it is a truth which is inconceivable and inexpressible.

Traditionally these three levels of truth are illustrated by the metaphor of the snake:

At dusk a man walks along a path in the forest. Suddenly on the road in front of him he sees a snake. He is terrified and runs off. Next morning he walks the same path and discovers that what he took to be a snake is, in broad daylight, just a rope.

1. the perceived 'snake' is untruth
2. the 'snake that is a rope' is a relative truth.

   Nagarjuna adds to this that both 'rope' and 'snake' are only concepts and concludes:
3. in 'absolute truth' there exist neither snake nor rope, only the empty concepts of them.

Concepts that are untruth, belong to the world of ego-illusion (aham iti = I am) and are characterized by ego-thought: subject 'untrue' object 'untrue'

Concepts that are relative truth, are forms of expression from a non-ego perspective. They are 'true' in the system in which they appear: subject 'untrue' object 'true'

Concepts can never be 'absolute truth', since on this level every duality falls away. Every knowledge of absolute truth therefore has to be non-conceptual i.e. 'im-mediate' (without mediator)

In the forms of mediate knowledge, which makes use of ideas, thoughts, words, etc., things are only knowable as concepts, i.e. within the relations in which they appear. Subject and object are reducible to dharmas, thus, 'emptiness' is the only 'true' nature we can attribute to them.

Where there is dualism present, the "true nature of things" or "true reality" remains beyond knowing; the "knower"-at best-remains at the level of relative truth.

Some examples of dualisms or dichotomies: good/evil, creator/creation, the Enlightened One/the foolish being, transcendent/immanent, suffering/joy, duality/unity, samsara/nirvana.

Applied in relation to the Buddhist teachings this gives:

- untruth: adharma, the non-teaching
- relative truth: buddhadharma, the teaching as it was proclaimed by the historical Buddha Sakyamuni.
- absolute truth: saddharma, the Teaching seen beyond time and space.

What then, is the relation between the Four Noble Truths and the levels of truth established by Nagarjuna?

To the level of relative truth belong the first two Noble Truths (Suffering and the Cause of Suffering), since they take place on the samsaric level. They form as it where the transition from (a) to (b) and their result is relative knowledge (jñana: knowledge).

To the level of absolute truth belong the last two Noble Truths (Cessation of Suffering, and the Noble Eightfold Path), since they take place on the nirvanic oriented level. They form as it where the transition from (b) to (c), and their result is absolute knowledge (sarvajña: omniscience or prajña: wisdom). We can note here that each of these transitions is nothing else than a process of dependent causation, which takes place according to the paradigm which is pratitya-samutpada.

Nagarjuna's point of departure is clearly negating. The introductory verses to his MMK e.g. are (from the Sanskrit Version):

> *"I salute him, the fully enlightened, the best of speakers, who preached the non-ceasing and the non-arising, the non-annihilation and the non-permanence, the non-identity and the non-difference, the non-appearance and the non-disappearance, the dependent arising, the appeasement of obsessions and the auspicious."*

The Chinese translation of the introductory verses by Kumarajiva is even more powerful, and is known as the Eight Negations.

No Arising,

No Extinction,

No Annihilation,

No Permanence,

No Unity

No Diversity,

No Coming,

No Going.

NAGARJUNA AND BUDDHIST SOTERIOLOGY

Nagarjuna's thought reflects itself mainly on the soteriology. For, only this is truly important to the being subject to suffering, impermanence and delusion. In a nutshell we can say that Nagarjuna-just as the historical Buddha-was before all an empiricist and a pragmatic, whose goal it is to free man from [wrong] views.

The problem of conceptual dualism and the rejection of it has several consequences:

It is not through conceptual, discursive thought that Enlightenment can be realized. Intellectuality (including philosophy...) cannot offer a perspective on Enlightenment; only direct or immediate experience, among others on the meditative level, whereby the activity of the ego-forming consciousness (manas) is neutralized, offers access to absolute truth, which in turn stands for nirvana.

Good and evil are dualistic, i.e. relative concepts which can only be used on the level of relative truth. Salvation or Liberation lies beyond these concepts. Nagarjuna here emphasizes the subordinate function of morality and moral discipline (sila) in relation to the soteriology. He however underlines the input of concepts as 'wholesome' (kusala) and 'unwholesome' (akusala), certainly on the level of relative truth, as actions that are carried by the karmic law. This law stands in function of volition. In this perspective the pairs 'good' (punya) / 'wholesome' (kusala) and 'evil' (papa) / 'unwholesome' (akusala) are only 'expedient means' (upaya kausalya).

In the end, even samsara and nirvana are only concepts and therefore only applicable on a relative level, e.g. in relation to each other or in relation to the situation of the suffering being. Seen from the 'absolute', they are both sunyata, both with the identical characteristic of emptiness. Their difference resides in the wisdom-approach. As is stated in the MMK, XXV.19-205

There is no difference at all

Between Nirvana and Samsara,

There is no difference at all

Between Samsara and Nirvana.

What makes the limit of Nirvana

Is also then the limit of Samsara.

Between the two we cannot find

The slightest shade of difference.

Should therefore be seen in its proper context of MMK, XXV.23-24:

What is identity, and what is difference?

What is eternity what non-eternity?

What means eternity and non-eternity together?

What means negation of both issues?

The bliss consists in the cessation of all thought,

In the quiescence of Plurality.

No (separate) Reality was preached at all,

Nowhere and none by Buddha.

The difference and/or equality that we ascribe to samsara and nirvana are thus in no way to be interpreted as an ontological difference, as if this world of suffering would be different or identical to the world of enlightenment. Difference and/or equality are empirical, epistemological statements: we regard an eventual 'objective' world only through experiential data. Discriminating between, and conceptualizing about samsara and nirvana are therefore constructions of our consciousness and thus only valid on the level of relative truth.

Nagarjuna has prevented that Buddhism would end up as a static teaching. That risk was real, e.g. in the Sarvastivada school with its leaning towards scholasticism. Also, through relativating philosophical and even soteriological concepts (ideas) he has opened, from an originally a-metaphysical Buddhism, a way towards a wider-and in a certain sense even a metaphysical-research, even towards a so-called horizontal mysticism.

Through the rejection of all dogmatic interpretations he offers the Mahayana the possibility of numerous non-conflicting ways as long as they remain relative 'worldly speaking' expressions of a "inconceivable, unthinkable and inexpressible Teaching". It is therefore only fair that Nagarjuna is looked upon as a founder and patriarch by almost all Mahayana and Vajrayana schools, be it sometimes for quite different sayings from the Master.

It probably happens that an exclusively negativistic view is ascribed to Nagarjuna. This is however countered by his stand in relation to the possibilities that man is offered towards the realization of Enlightenment. Because what Nagarjuna has refuted in the first place is the possibility of realizing Enlightenment by way of conceptual thought.

Opposite to that however he puts the so-called Three Gates towards Liberation (trini vimoksa-mukhani, Ch. san-chieh-t'o-men, J. sangedatsumon), namely the meditations on:

- emptiness (sunyata, Ch. k'ung, ku)
- the non-substantiality of phenomena, their signlessness (animitta, Ch. wu-hsiang, J. muso)
- the undesirability of things (apranihita, Ch. wu-yüan, J. mugan), i.e. the being-free of desire and meaning.

In this way Nagarjuna gives his philosophy a positive direction, even when this is aimed against conventional, worldly 'knowledge'. We could look for analogies in Lao-tzu.

MADHYAMAKA AFTER NAGARJUNA

Nagarjuna's way of thought was undoubtedly a great influence and has been carried on by a great number of philosophers after him. Thus it could be said that his philosophy (together with the Prajñaparamita-literature and the Lankavatara-sutra) has laid the foundation for the later Ch'an-schools, be it however with a strong influence from Taoism and Yogacara-thought. Yet, the impact of Nagarjuna goes further, and it is no miracle that he is recognized as a patriarch in practically all Mahayana-schools.

In the 5th century Madhyamaka was split up in two currents who each attempted to represent the 'true' Madhyamaka. It is undeniable that also the blooming of Buddhist Logic-e.g. Dinnaga7-was unthinkable without the impulse given by Nagarjuna. The two schools in which the Madhyamaka was divided are:

Svatantrika: 'School of the Independent Grounds', most known representative is Bhavaviveka (6th century). 'Svatantra' refers to a more positive position: the negations characteristic for Nagarjuna are exclusively the refutation of wrongly held views. The pratitya-samutpada is the middle position between affirmation and negation.

Prasangika: 'Teaching of the Undesired Outcome'. The origin of this school is attributed to Buddhapalita (5th century), but its most important exponent is without doubt Candrakirti (6th-7th century), also the most famous commentator on MMK.

According to him Nagarjuna aimed at a polemic reductio ad absurdum, a demonstration that each statement, each conclusion must lead to the falling away of any/every presupposition. Emphasis is put on the pratitya samutpada as the proces of the origin of suffering.

Often this school is associated with 'radical empiricism'. It is this current that has had the most success in China (thanks to Kumarajiva 344-413 and Chi-tsang 549-623). To this day it remains the dominating philosophy of the Tibetan Gelug-pa.

But also outside of Buddhism Madhyamaka had a great influence:

- on Hinduism, and especially on the 'New Vedanta' (Nava-Vedanta) of Sankara (8th-9th century). Even a century earlier a certain Gaudapada was accused by Kumarila, a Mimansa-master, of conceding too much to Buddhism. Ramanuja (± 1050-1137), the main exponent of theistic Vedanta, accused even Sankara of being a crypto-Buddhist...
- More recent however we can note the great interest of present-day philosophers and physicists for Madhyamaka. In this way, Nagarjuna had no small influence on existentialists such as Karl Jaspers and Martin Heidegger, or theoretical physicists such as Heisenberg and Schrodinger.

Yogachara and Vasubandhu

Yogachara: Teaching in Discipline Vijñanavada: Path of Consciousness Also the name Vijñapti-matrata is sometimes used: "System of Consciousness-Only". This name was mainly used in China (Wei-shih) and in Japan (Yuishiki).

This current follows both chronologically and logically on Madhyamaka.

Nagarjuna postulated the double negation: negation even of negation. Religiously seen this is an attitude which is difficult to manage, since it forces the adept to go to the most extreme possibilities of his (everyday) thought. Opposite this conceptually negativistic attitude of Nagarjuna, one will however keep on striving (empirically) towards something affirmative. It was thus to be expected that there would follow a psychological reaction against the philosophical negation.

This however is not a step back; only a shifting towards an empirically more understandable realm: from the 4th lemma back towards the 3rd lemma, in the form of "being and non-being".

The Yogacara will then not systematically refute Nagarjuna, but on the contrary, will apply some of his thought to come to a stage where a positive formulation becomes possible and useable.

Yogacara, just as Madhyamaka, accepts the impossibility of an adequate formulation of an 'absolute' truth. On the other hand however we have to our disposal the use of cognitive elements (whether they are objectively-realistic or subjectively-idealistic...). This presupposes that we have cognitive experiences, even if these are limited by the limits of our consciousness. And it is within this consciousness that logical and critical inquiry belong to the possibilities.

A clear sign of this idea we find for example in Dhammapada (I, 1-2):

"Everything (all dharmas) has mind in the lead, has mind as a forerunner, is made by mind (...)"

The Lankavatara Sutra (of which the date of origin is not clear, but which was already translated in Chinese by Gunabhadra in the 5th Century) is one of the texts on which Yogacara-philosophy will be based. The first figure that in a certain way can be related to the Mind-Only School is Asvaghosa in his work 'The Arising of Faith in the Mahayana' (Mahayana-sraddha-utpada).

The definitive formation of the school however rests with Asanga, in his 'Clarification of the Teachings of the Mahayana' (Mahayana-sutra-lamkara) and his 'Exposition on the Stages of the Practice of Discipline' (Yogacara-bhumi-sastra').

It is his brother, Vasubandhu, who firstly from a Hinayana point of view (Sautrantika, and not Sarvastivada as is sometimes claimed) wrote the impressive Abhidharma-kosa-bhasya ('The Treasury of the Abhidharma'), but later went on to the Mahayana-thought of his brother and than wrote the Vimsatika-vijñapti-matrata-siddhi ('The Exposition on Consciousness-Only in 20 volumes') and the Trimsika-vijñapti-matrata-siddhi ('The Exposition on Consciousness-Only in 30 volumes').

The two brothers, Asanga and Vasubandhu, are dated somewhere between 280 and 500 (?) CE.

Starting Point: It is a fact that we cannot 'know' in an absolute way, but even our relative thought presupposes an 'instrument of thought'. This 'thought-instrument' is called vijñana, mostly-but unjustly-translated as 'consciousness'. This 'consciousness' is therefore the only reality that is undisputable.

To situate the concept of 'vijñana' more clearly, we have to take into account the etymology of the word. The prefix "vi-" points to separation (according to MMW vi = *dvi = two), to discrimination or distinction, and sometimes it even has a meaning opposite to the thought expressed in the word that follows it. The Lankavatara-Sutra describes it as "The cutting of the whole in its parts and than applying a selection to it". It becomes clear that we have to approach the term 'consciousness' with great reserve. This will certainly be the case in the compounds of vijñana in the sense that they are used by the Yogacara. Every progress in mind-concentration (i.e. a 'single-mindedness') is an approaching of absolute reality.

Things are nothing but convergences of perception. Consciousness is the ability to take in sense-impressions and by sifting through them come to the formation of concepts. The activity of consciousness has its origin in a beginningless drive. All skandhas and sense-functions (ayatanas) are reducible to vijñana.

Being-in-itself is denied, but not so the possibility of introspection.

The accepting of the reality of vijñana is by the way an empirical necessity, for without consciousness the universe would fall into a state of complete 'blindness' (not 'blinding'!), and every form of knowledge-even of wrong or relative knowledge-would be impossible.

Only vijñana exists and functions and is knowable; its 'objects' ('consciousness-content') however are delusional through the working of ego-activity. The point concerning the objective 'being' of the world outside of the experiencing consciousness however was never stated very clearly, neither by Asanga nor by Vasubandhu. The Hindu Nava-Vedanta will extend this point in deciding that the world outside of consciousness is a total illusion (maya).

THE STRUCTURE OF 'CONSCIOUSNESS'

In this context we can search for an analogy with the empirical idealism of e.g. Locke, Berkeley and Hume. Yet, we should not to easily come to the conclusion of an identit of vision. Once more, we should point out the fact that the E piricists' conclusion ends up on the level of metaphysics there where the Buddhist Yogacara's conclusion is situated on the level of epistemology and soteriology.

Asanga and Vasubandhu will in their writings consequently extend the classical Buddhist structure of 'consciousness'. In this way the intellect (mano-vijñana) will lead towards self-reflection (vijñana-vijñana), i.e. the knowing subject will look upon itself as the knowledge-object. The personality experience that culminates through this in our consciousness is nothing other than the consciousness of 'being ourself'.

This is where the fundamental 'error' known as avidya (wrong-knowing, ignorance) is situated: the consciousness of consciousness is interpreted as 'being-ourselves'.

Out of this distortion originates manas, the 7th form of consciousness, that function of the mind by which we experience the nama-rupa (viz. 5 skandhas) as an atman, a permanent entity that constitutes our "self-ness".

Manas is therefore the source of ego-thought (aham-kara), of the "I am" illusion (asmi-maya). In relation to modern psychology the manas-activity will be mainly situated in the sub-conscious, which makes it so difficult to point to or to fathom.

> *Manas is therefore an ego-differentiated and differentiating aspect of alaya-vijñana, just as a wave appears to be distinct from the great ocean. The bijas are 'perfumed', i.e. they receive impressions through knowing and acting, through which they are manifested within the karmic process, i.e. they take on form in manas; this leaning towards formation of karmic results lays the 'seeds' in a 'seedbed', from which they 'spring' at the 'appropriate moment', i.e. when a causal condition (hetu pratyaya) creates the possibility for it to arise.*

There are those bijas that are present from time immemorial (the so-called 'primal or original' bijas), and there are those that are newly acquired, which are re-perfumed, i.e. re-activated. Both kinds together create all manifestations of the existential delusion and are therefore cause of the 'defilements'.

But, there is also an 'unstained seed', that through sprouting and growing absorbs and suppresses the delusional and bewitching nature of alaya-vijñana and so leads towards ultimate enlightenment. This unstained seed is none other than Buddha-nature. When this seed has transformed the totality of alaya-vijñana into Buddha-nature

(= Enlightenment !), there arises-at least according to the later Vijñanavadins-a 9th form of consciousness: the 'Stainless Consciousness' (amala-vijñana), which is identical to Suchness (tathata). Once alaya-vijñana is freed of its defilements related to its content, it becomes the source of Buddhahood: the "Womb of the Tathagatas" (Tathagatagarbha).

A lot of commentators and authors have attempted to describe the nature of this 'storehouse-consciousness'. As the basis from which all bijas of consciousness spring. As the container-intellect; as the basic consciousness seen as totality of both the absolute and the relative, impersonal and personal; as the fundamental mind-consciousness of sentient beings who as it where confiscate all experiences of individual existence; as the seedbed of all events; as the root of all experience, i.e. of the skandhas on which all beings are dependent for their conscious existence; as the source of the cycle of birth-and-death, etc. Each of these descriptions are at the same time right and wrong.

Concerning the complexity of 'consciousness' and 'total-consciousness' we could refer to the holographic model of consciousness in the holistic theory developed by e.g. John R. Battista.

THE THREE TRUTHS

Following Nagarjuna the Yogacara also knows a threefold structure of truth, viz. untruth, relative truth and absolute truth. Nagarjuna, however, did not show a lot of interest in the relative truth, since this is merely situated on the level of conceptual thought. Yogacara on the other hand thinks that it is exactly through this relative truth that the possibility exists to arrive at the absolute truth.

This absolute truth is called parinispanna by Asanga: the complete fulfillment, not subjected to impermanence.

The relative truth (samvriti), also called laukika-satya or worldly truth' by Dharmapala (439-507), is however subdivided in:

- parikalpita (established in the mind, imagined): purely subjective, without self-existence, yet empirically experienced as truth, however by the yogin recognized as untrue since it is not-adequate, i.e. leading towards enlightenment.
- paratantra (dependent on other things): resulting from causality (hetu-pratyaya), what arises and is recognized as the subject/object dichotomy; "the manifestation is in fact untrue, but that which causes the manifestation is true". From there also the connotation of 'consensual truth', i.e. a truth which is valid within a certain 'consensus', a certain 'system of coordinates'.

Absolute truth stands beyond every subject/object dichotomy and is therefore subjectless and objectless (= emptiness). Paratantra is the overlapping of parinispanna by an infecting parikalpita. By removing this infection from paratantra, parinispanna is realized.

We can mention here that this teaching of Three Truths (Trayasatya) has given rise to the formation of a full-grown Buddhist Logic.

TRIKAYA: THE THREEFOLD BUDDHABODY

The three levels of truth reflect in the three 'body' forms of Buddhahood.

At first Buddhism knew of two so-called 'Buddha-bodies':

- buddhakaya: the corporeal manifestation form of the historical Buddha.
- dharmakaya: the spiritual message as it was proclaimed by the Buddha.

Slowly these concepts developed however, e.g. through the abstraction procedure in the Sarvastiva, and through the import of the concept "Eternal Buddha" (e.g. in the Lotus Sutra).

Asanga states in his Mahayanasutra-lankara and in his Mahayana-samgraha that a threefold body can be attributed to Buddhahood:

1. Nirmanakaya (also nairmanika-kaya): an appearance-body, manifestation-body or transformation-body, the body that can assume an infinite number of worldly forms and which mainly exists for the benefit of all beings. This body can be historical, e.g. Buddha Gautama. It is then the manifestation in time and space of Infinite Buddhahood. This form appears within the samsara/nirvana duality and therefore is sometimes called the 'nirvana-body' (nirvanakaya). In later centuries (in China, and probably under the influence of Taoism) the nirmanakaya comprises the whole manifested world.
2. Sambhogakaya (also sambhogika-kaya): the 'glorification-body', the 'bliss-body', 'reward-body': the ideal image of Buddhahood conceivable to beings. It is in this way that bodhisattvas 'see' Buddhahood. The glorification-body is a) the radiance of Absolute Buddhahood in a conceivable form, and b) the projection of the human ideal ('the ideal human') in the glorified forms of bodhisattvas and Buddhas. It is certainly in this sense that the sambhogakaya can be seen as a 'transitional' object', an 'expedient means'.
3. Dharmakaya: (also svabhavika-kaya = body of own-nature): The Body of the Teaching, Absolute Body of Wisdom/Compassion, Principle Body: the ultimate reality as Suchness (tathata), Enlightenment, True Reality (dharmata). According to the later Vijñanavadins the Absolute Self. The Dharmakaya is totally situated beyond the conceptual (after all, dharmata equals sunyata or emptiness) and is consequentially "formless, colorless, inconceivable, unthinkable, inexpressible".

Avatamsaka-Hua-yen

"Avatamsaka" (Flower Wreath) is the name for both the scriptural cycle and the philosophical current based on this literature. The sutra cycle probably dates from the 2nd or 3rd century CE. It mostly deals with the mystical teachings concerning Maha-Vairocana-Buddha, i.e. the "Cosmic Buddha". As scriptural source we know mainly the Buddha-Avatamsaka-Sutra (Discourse on the Buddha Flower Wreath), a collection of texts of which most of the Sanskrit originals have been lost. Still extend are:

Gandavyuha-sutra: The story of the young man Sudhana who goes on a quest for the absolute (dharmadhatu). Determined to find it he becomes the student of 51 (or 53?) teachers (kalyana mitra, lit. "good friends") all of a distinguished character: sages, kings, men, fools, women (even a prostitute), gods, bodhisattvas, etc. After many kalpa's of searching throughout an innumerable number of universes, he ends up with Manjusri Bodhisattva, the Supreme Wisdom of Buddhahood. Manjusri shows him to a place where "the" Wisdom can be found: a tower high upon a steep mountain. After a journey full of dangers Sudhana arrives at the tower: it is empty!

Also the Dhasabhumika-sutra (Sutra on the Ten Stages) is traditionally counted among the Avatamsaka texts.

In India there doesn't appear to have been a separate Avatamsaka school. The story of Sudhana is however also told in Divyavadana (preserved in the Sanskrit and Tibetan translations) and it is depicted on the Boro-Budur temple complex in Java. The entire Avatamsaka cycle is preserved in Tibetan and also in several translations in the Chinese Canon.

It is in China that the Avatamsaka doctrine will receive its factual philosophical systematization, in which the acquired teachings of both Madhyamaka and Yogacara are integrated in to one "holistic" system. The foundation for this is laid by Tu-shun (557-640) and Chih-yen (602-668). The actual systematization belongs however to Fa-tsang (643-712). His works include: Chin-shih-tzu-chang (Essay on the Golden Lion); I-hai pai-men (One Hundred propositions on the Ocean of Thought); Hua-yen ching chih-kuei (Essential themes of the Avatamsaka Sutra). For the final touch-up Ch'eng-kuan (738-838) was also important.

The main ideas of Avatamsaka-thought are found in the Hua-yen ching I-240:

The One is the Many.

The Many is the One.

In the word the meaning is to be found.

In the meaning the word is to be understood.

Non-being is Being. Being is Non-being.

Formlessness is Form. Form is Formlessness.

Non-being is Being. Being is Formlessness.

Avatamsaka philosophy wants to provide an affirming answer to Nagarjuna's attitude of negation. It also manages to clarify some of the problems that had not or unsatisfactorily been answered within the Yogacara, e.g. the relationship between manas and alaya-vijnana (storehouse-consciousness). In this sense Hua-yen forms an organic whole of all essential elements of Mahayana Buddhism. In the Avatamsaka-and even more so in its Chinese form-the Hua-yen we will for the first time encounter a metaphysical approach, be it in a very subtle form. Up until then Buddhist philosophy had refused to venture along the path of metaphysics, e.g. by asking the question concerning the nature of the Absolute.

Hua-yen (maybe influence by Taoism?) dares to take the step to a "being outside of consciousness' (li = noumenon) and in doing so breaks through the limitations of consciousness, by which it became possible to conceive of a worldview.

Identity and Totality

In their true nature all things are identical.

Starting from a syllogistic structure

If A equals X

And B equals X

Than A equals B

we can exchange the terms A and B for 'dharma's' and X for sunyata (emptiness):

If dharma 1 = emptiness

And dharma 2 = emptiness

Than dharma 1 = dharma 2

Or, as Fa-tsang expressed it, exchanging the term dharma with the term "thing" or "phenomenon" (shih):

If shih 1 = k'ung (emptiness)

And shih 2 = k'ung

Than all things in their true nature, in their emptiness are equal to one another. Things only differ from one another through the relational context in which they find themselves.

In their unity "things" are identical. This identity leads towards a "totality" (the absolute, chen), the "suchness of beings" (Skt. Bhuta-tathata, Ch. Chen-ju). Seen from the point of view of the phenomenal it the "realm of phenonema" (dharmadhatu, fa-chieh). But seen from an Absolute point of view this is the "essence" or "suchness", the ultimate principle that lies at the basis of all beings, the "element of elements" (dharmata, fa-hsing). Soteriologically this absolute reality is the source of enlightenment, the "womb of the tathagatas (tathagata-garbha, ju-lai tsang); all beings therefore have Buddha-nature.

Bhutatathata, dharmadhatu, dharmata, tathagata-garbha are various aspects of the inexpressible absolute. Also alaya-vijnana is none other than such an aspect. To the Hua-yen, alaya-vijnana is the "Great Ocean Mirror" (ta hai yin), in which the countless drama's of the universe spontaneously and simultaneously reflects each other, in a harmonic play of mutual, multi-dimensional projections and interpenetrations.

R. Grousset (in Sur le Traces du Bouddha) describes this absolute as: "un absolu non plus supérieur aux phénomènes, mais entièrement inherent à eux...l'absolu en tant que processus même des choses." ("An Absolute not superior to phenomena, but entirely inherent in them...the Absolute as the process of things themselves.")

This leads us to a second remarkable point:

INTERPENETRATION

Not only are "things" in their true nature identical to each other or do they form a "totality", they are also present in one another. Each separate thing does not only reflect all other things but also reflects the Absolute in its totality. (cfr. Holographic model).

All things interpenetrate each other, contain each other:

All is in One-One is in All.

All things are present in Oneness,

Oneness is present in all things.

My ego-ness is present in the Absolute,

The Absolute is present in my ego-ness.

All beings are present in the Buddha,

The Buddha is present in all beings.

Nirvana is present in samsara,

Samsara is present in Nirvana.

The cosmos is present in each separate thing,

Each separate thing is present in the cosmos.

We have to be careful though not to lose sight of the 4th logical lemma!

In this context it is not inappropriate to quote Leibniz: "Infinitum continuum vel discretum proprie nec unum, nec totum, nec quantum est." In other words, we should not quantify this interpenetration.

An expression such as: "All is Buddha, Buddha is All" is wrong in the sense that from this one could conclude that all beings are Buddha, or that "I am a Buddha". This of course could never be the intention of the Hua-yen.

What we can conclude from this is that the totality of Buddhahood is present in each and every element of our personality (nama-rupa), i.e. the 5 skandha's (aggregates). As within a hologram the total picture is present within each part of that picture, so it is that within each part of our mind (and body...) enlightenment is present. In this way we partake in the Buddha-Body that manifests itself in the three (or more...) Buddha-Bodies.

But only an enlightened one sees this enlightenment.

The total interpenetration of things makes that also contradictions are present. However these do not exclude each other. This is the doctrine of "non-hindrance" or "all-embracing", also called the "total freedom of things in their true nature".

"Here we find that both time and space have lost their meaning and power as we understand and experience them. Here is not merely a realm-embracing-realm ad infinitum, but a total change-over, a thorough liberation from all obstructions. Here is a perfect melting and merging of all realms, the all-in-one and the one-in-all, the dissolving of being and non-being, the convergence of Voidness and existence, the "simultaneous abrupt arising" and the "perfect mutual solution". All these mysteries of Totality consist, however, in one basic principle; namely, all things of dependent-arising (pratitya-samutpada) are void....

To stress the "ego-less" aspect of this great mystery of sunyata, we have Hinayana Buddhism; to stress the void-aspect of this mystery, we have Madhyamaka Buddhism; to stress the non-clinging, non-abiding aspect we have Zen; and to stress the non-obstructing and all-embracing aspect, we have Hua-yen.

...we have found that the Totality and Non-obstruction of Buddhahood are expressed in these terms:

- That the universe can be infinitely vast or small depending on the scale of measurement, or the position from which a measurement is made.
- That the "larger" universes include the "smaller" ones as a solar system contains its planets, or a planet contains its atoms. This system of higher realms embracing the lower ones is pictured in a structure extending ad infinitum in both directions to the infinitely large or the

infinitely small. This is called in Hua-yen vocabulary the view of realms-embracing-realms.

- That a "small" universe, (such as an atom) not only contains the infinite "lesser" universes within itself, but also contains the infinite "larger" universes (such as the solar system), thus establishing the genuine Totality of Non-obstruction.
- That "time" has lost its meaning as merely a concept for measuring the flow of events in the past, present and future. It has now become an element of Totality which actualized the total interpenetration and containment of all events of past, present, and future in the eternal present.
- Upon the grand stage of the infinite Dharmadhatu, countless various dramas of religion are being enacted in numerous dimensions of space/time throughout eternity. (G.C. Chang, The Buddhist Teaching of Totality, 1971, p. 11-13)

Empress Wu Tse-T'ien (T'ang-dynasty, 684-705, first concubine of Emperor Kao-tsung) invited Fa-tsang to clarify to her the Hua-yen teachings of Totality and Interpenetration. The master adorned a hall of the palace with mirrors and in the center of the hall he placed a Buddha-image with a lamp beside it. The image reflected itself infinitely in all directions, the image was present everywhere. Then the master, standing in the center of the hall, held a small crystal ball in his hand. All of the mirror images where now captured in this one small ball.

Obviously these scenario is only a metaphor in which we should remind ourselves that it is only concerned with "images", that in fact there is neither a Buddha-image nor a lamp, that the mirrors only reflect their own emptiness to each other, that there is no-one looking into the mirror. And finally, that there "are" no mirrors!

In the Vows of the Bodhisattva Samantabhadra an image is projected of the "infinite" and the "interpenetration" of worlds.

All the innumerable separate is contained in the innumerable One. We have to remark here that things, although present in each other, are not necessarily identical. They are after all identical in their "true nature", not in their relative appearance.

THE TRUE SELF

Avatamsaka-thought is covered by the necessity to eliminate all forms of duality. So, e.g., the problem of self/non-self or the dichotomy of samsara/nirvana can be eradicated through the ascend into higher dimensions of the One Totality that is the "true nature of things".

The True Self (svabhava) hereby becomes identical with Enlightenment, Buddhahood (buddhata), Suchness (dharmata). The intellectual and emotional tensions associated with time/space fall away. Enlightenment is experienced as an "event" beyond any temporal/spatial context. Since traditionally samsara has no beginning ("it exists from the beginning of beginningless time"), while nirvana has no end ("it lasts until the end of endless time"), the transfer from the world of suffering to nirvana "happens" at the "moment of enlightenment" as long as samsara-and-nirvana are regarded as a "personal" event. Enlightenment "spans" both views and therefore has no beginning nor end.

With this Avatamsaka-thought also provided a solution to another Mahayana problem that had occupied Buddhist minds throughout several centuries: "Can Enlightenment still be realized by every being" (Ch. Shi-chüeh, J. shikaku: lit. "Entering upon Enlightenment")? Or, is Enlightenment already realized for all beings (Ch. Pen-chüeh, J. Hongaku: lit. "Original, Primal Enlightenment")? Also for this dilemma Avatamsaka will provide a solution: the tension between the "still to be realized" and the "already realized" Enlightenment is a purely dialectical one. Given that, from the perspective of Wisdom, Enlightenment is situated beyond any temporal/spatial context; from the perspective of Compassion, Enlightenment is to be realized in every moment by all beings. Indeed, time and history-as relative concepts-start anew in every moment (eka-ksana).

Since in Enlightenment Wisdom and Compassion are One, the difference between the two aspects of Enlightenment are solely epistemological and methodological, but in no way absolute.

PHENOMENON / NOUMENON

From Avatamsaka-thought in convergence with themes from the Lotus Sutra and Nirvana Sutra emerged the synchretistical view of the T'ien-t'ai school characterized by its strong mystical imprint. The metaphysical basis for this school was largely formed from Hua-yen philosophy. During the Sung Dynasty there arose a dispute within the T'ien-t'ai concerning the relationship between the relatively experienced (the phenomenal) and the all comprising Absolute (the noumenal).

The dispute started between two chief-disciples of the 11th T'ien-t'ai patriarch (Ch'ing-sun). One disciple, I-chi, later followed by Chih-li, proclaimed that the object of right meditation should be focused on the unenlightened within the mind and not on the pure and undfiled aspect of the mind, as was claimed by Chih-yen.

This disputatio, which started on the practical level of meditation, soon evolved into a dispute on the metaphysical level and is known as the shan-chia-shan-wai discussion (J. sange-sanrai). The "orthodox" T'ien-t'ai interpretation, which called itself "[The Teaching] on the Mountain", remained with the assertion that all phenomena (shih) are mutually and indifferently comprised within the absolute (li) with which they are identical. This is the shi-shi-wu-ai: phenomena are mutually unhindered and interfused. Contrary to this stands the doctrine of which it was said that it was too much "Avatamsaka" and therefore stranger to T'ien-t'ai; hence the name "Outside the Mountain". This teaching stated that phenomena are indirectly equal because they are with the all comprising Absolute. This than becomes: phenomena are not separated from the Absolute: (li-shih-wu-ai).

It is this kind of questions that have contributed to the need for extension of Buddhist thought in China (and later also in

Korea and Japan). Namely the necessity to overcome new historical situations. It is for example the broadness of the scope of thought within the T'ien-t'ai that provided the basis for later evolutions. The characteristic evolution of Japanese Buddhism during the Kamakura Era would have been inconceivable without the input of Avatamsaka through T'ien-t'ai. The fact that great reformers such as Eisai (Rinzai-zen), Honen (Jodo-shu), Shinran (Jodo-shinshu), Dogen (Soto-zen), Nichiren (Nichirenshu) all started their spiritual career within the Tendai (J. for T'ien-t'ai), is self-evident.

BUDDHIST LOGIC

Buddhism has from the beginning emphasized a logical structure. Examples of this can be found in the structure of the (midwifery) talks and discourses of the Buddha. This formulation, which is very often found back in the oldest texts, provides the 'key' to most 'typical Buddhist problems' towards their 'understanding' or their 'inconceivability' (e.g. the anatta-doctrine, the conception of sunyata, or the teaching of Totality within the Avatamsaka-teachings [see later]). What seems 'illogical' according to the binary logic (the so-called Aristotelian logic), becomes clear through the perspective of this tetralemma.

With its dissemination Buddhism unavoidably came into contact with other Indian spiritual currents. From this arose the necessity of having a set of polemic instruments at its disposal with which it could answer the argumentations of the formal-logically structured Hindu darsanas (especially Nyaya and Vaisesika).

Bibliography

Bell, Sir Charles: *Portrait of a Dalai Lama: The Life and Times of the Great Thirteenth,* Boston, Wisdom Publications, 1987.

Cook, Elizabeth: *Holy Places of the Buddha,* Berkeley, Dharma Publishing, 1994.

Dayal, Har: *The Bodhisattva Doctrine in Buddhist Sanskrit Literature,* London, Kegan Paul, 1932.

Eppsteiner, Fred: *The Path of Compassion: Writings on Socially Engaged Buddhism,* Berkeley, Parallax Press, 1988.

Gonda, Jan: *Vedic Literature: Samhitas and Brahmanas,* Wiesbaden, 1975.

Hakeda, Yoshito S.: *Kukai, Major Works,* New York, Columbia University Press, 1972.

Jones, Ken: *Beyond Optimism: A Buddhist Political Ecology,* Oxford, Jon Carpenter, 1993.

Keown, Damien: *The Nature of Buddhist Ethics,* New York, St. Martin's Press, 1992.

Lalwani. K.C.: *Kalpa Sutra of Badrabahu Svami,* Delhi, Motilal Banarsidass. 1979.

Mookerjee, Satkari: *Buddhist Philosophy of Universal Flux,* Delhi, Motilal Banarsidass, 1980.

Nyanatiloka, *A.: Guide through the Abhidhamma Pitaka,* Kandy, Buddhist Publication Society, 1971.

Powers, John: *Wisdom of Buddha: The Samdhinirmocana Sutra,* Berkeley, Dharma Publishing, 1994.

Sprung, Mervyn: *The Problem of Two Truths in Buddhism and Vedanta,* Boston, Reidel, 1973.

Thomas, E. J.: *The Life of the Buddha as Legend and History,* London, Routledge & Kegan Paul, 1927.

Wells, Kenneth E.: *Thai Buddhism, Its Rites and Activities,* Bangkok, Christian Bookstore, 1960.

Index

□□□